Field Methods in
the Study of Education

Field Methods in the Study of Education

Edited by
Robert G. Burgess

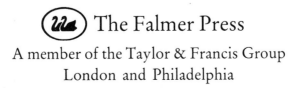 The Falmer Press

A member of the Taylor & Francis Group
London and Philadelphia

UK The Falmer Press, Falmer House, Barcombe, Lewes, East Sussex, BN8 5DL

USA The Falmer Press, Taylor & Francis Inc., 242 Cherry Street, Philadelphia, PA 19106-1906

First published 1985

Library of Congress Cataloging in Publication Data

Main entry under title:
Field methods in the study of education.

 Includes bibliographies and index.
 1. Education—Research—Addresses, essays, lectures.
2. Education—Field work—Addresses, essays, lectures.
3. Ethnology—Field work—Addresses, essays, lectures.
I. Burgess, Robert G.
LB1028.F43 1984 370′.7′8 84-13491
ISBN 1-85000-012-3
ISBN 1-85000-011-5 (pbk.)

Typeset in 11/13 Garamond by
Imago Publishing, Thame, Oxon

Printed in Great Britain by Taylor & Francis (Printers) Ltd, Basingstoke

Contents

Contents

Preface

A brief glance at the contents page of textbooks, collections of essays and sets of readings devoted to the conduct of social research in educational settings quickly reveals that quantitative approaches to social investigation no longer hold the dominant position in this field of study. Alongside discussions of questionnaires, formal interviews and survey methods can be found reviews of participant observation, informal or unstructured interviews and personal documents which are brought together under such terms as ethnographic methods, field methods or case study methods depending upon the theoretical perspective that is taken by the writer.

When methods of investigation are discussed and reviewed they are often presented in 'how to do it' books that provide 'cookbook' style recipes for applying research procedures to a variety of social circumstances. Such an approach omits key features of the research process. In particular, it fails to address theoretical issues and the way in which social theories shape the processes and procedures that are used to collect data. Secondly, it rarely presents the issues and problems associated with particular methods of investigation. Finally, it seldom takes account of the way in which particular methodologies can articulate with policy and practice; a topic that is especially relevant in a field of study such as education.

Accordingly, this set of essays does not merely present field methods as a set of techniques. Instead, the authors are concerned to deal with some of the issues and problems associated with the use of field methods in the study of education. As a consequence, discussions of methods are contextualized in analyses of theories and theorizing in education, relationships between theory, problem and method, the implications of particular methods for the research process, research procedures and research problems and, finally, the way in which particular methods may be used to contribute towards educational practice and educational policy. The contributors have all had extensive research experience in the study of education and have drawn upon their experiences to illustrate the different ways in which field methods can be developed, the theoretical approaches that can be used in field-based methodologies and the implications of this methodology for educational practice.

All the essays presented in this volume were specially commissioned to contribute to ongoing debates about the state and status of field methods in the study of education. The focus is upon issues and problems associated with this style of research when used in educational settings. It is, therefore, to be hoped that the material contained in these essays will help to advance the debate on the problems and procedures associated with using field-based methods in education as well as providing further insights for undergraduates, postgraduates and research workers who are attempting to understand the dynamics of the research process in educational settings.

Most of these essays were originally prepared for a two-day workshop on 'the ethnography of educational settings' held at Whitelands College, London in July 1982; the workshop focussed on methodological issues and problems in the study of educational settings. All the papers prepared for this workshop were pre-circulated so that most of the time in our workshop sessions could be devoted to discussion and debate which was tape-recorded. In the course of revising their papers for wider dissemination the authors have, therefore, had an opportunity to draw on this material. In addition to paper-givers, contributions were also made to discussions by Stephen Ball, Brian Davies, Tony Green, Jean Rudduck, Helen Simons and Barry Stierer who were all present at the workshop. Special mention should be made of the part played by Lawrence Stenhouse at this workshop. As at all workshops and conferences that he attended, Lawrence Stenhouse took an active part in the discussion by highlighting controversies, pinpointing problems and discussing strategies that were worthy of our attention. This was the last conference that he attended before his death in September 1982 but several papers are richer for his contributions that are now sadly missed at our educational gatherings. It is to be hoped that many readers will be stimulated by the essays in this volume to work on problems of using research methodology in educational settings — an area to which Lawrence Stenhouse made such a significant contribution.

The workshop at Whitelands College was made possible by a grant that I received from the University of Warwick Research and

Innovations Fund. I am, therefore, most grateful to members of the Research and Innovations Fund Sub-Committee who supported my proposal for work in this area of study. I would also like to thank all those who contributed papers, participated in workshop discussions and helped and encouraged me to edit the papers in a form that was suitable for publication. In this respect, I have been fortunate to work with a group of contributors who have been ready to offer help and advice on the shape of the final volume. Once more I am indebted to Hilary Burgess who has continued to provide support and constructive criticism throughout the project. Last, but by no means least, I have been fortunate to have a range of first-class secretarial assistance especially from Maureen Haynes who helped in the final stages of preparing this manuscript for publication. As always any errors or omissions are, of course, my own.

Robert Burgess
University of Warwick

Introduction

Robert G. Burgess

Social anthropologists and sociologists have devised a wide range of research methods that can be utilized in the study of culture. In the popular imagination sociological work is often equated with the use of social surveys, while social anthropologists deploy a set of more intensive methods of social investigation which are often referred to as 'ethnographic methods', 'fieldwork', 'case study methods', 'qualitative methods' or 'field methods'. However, this over-simplifies the situation as social anthropologists are as likely to use survey methods as sociologists are to use 'field methods'. Indeed, field methods have been used by sociologists in the course of studying elements of their own society.

In Britain it was Max Gluckman who argued that those methods that had been traditionally used in the study of small-scale societies could be used in the analysis of urban industrial society (cf. Gluckman, 1964; Frankenberg, 1982). This approach was developed in Gluckman's Department of Social Anthropology and Sociology in the University of Manchester where studies were conducted in a variety of social settings including rural localities (Frankenberg, 1957), factories (Lupton, 1963; Cunnison, 1966) and schools (Hargreaves, 1967; Lacey, 1970; Lambart, 1970). It was these school studies that were among the first intensive investigations of educational institutions in the United Kingdom.

While the 1960s were to witness the beginning of field studies in English schools, it was the 1970s that were to see growth and development in this area of study.[1] No longer did researchers confine themselves to selective secondary Schools but built on this tradition developed by the Manchester school of social anthropologists and sociologists in studying comprehensive schools (cf. Ball, 1981; Burgess, 1983). Furthermore, studies were no longer confined to secondary education as researchers worked in infant (King, 1978), junior (Sharp and Green, 1975) and middle schools (A. Hargreaves and Tickle, 1980) and also in higher education (Scott and Porter, 1983).[2] One of the major developments to occur alongside the study of schools was a series of investigations that took the classroom as their focus of study. In a recent review, Hargreaves (1980a) has identified the way in which not only sociologists but also psychologists and social psychologists discovered the classroom as an arena in which to focus their research activities. This work was characterized by a wide range of theoretical and methodological perspectives that Hargreaves has subdivided into three groups: first, systematic observational studies which emphasized quantification; secondly, ethnographic studies with their focus on participant observation and unstructured interviews; and finally, socio-linguistic studies.[3] Yet as Hargreaves indicates, such a categorization does not merely involve competing views as many workers engaged in these different areas of study are involved in debate and dialogue with each other (cf. McAleese and Hamilton, 1978).

Among the points of debate are the ways in which different theoretical and methodological positions can be utilized within intensive studies of educational institutions and educational phenomena. It is the wide range of positions that can be adopted in field-based studies of education that are represented within this volume. Among the contributors are those concerned with the development of sociology and the development of particular theoretical perspectives within the discipline alongside those who have a commitment to teachers and to the application of field-based methods and methodologies to the issues and problems surrounding educational practice and educational evaluation. In turn, some contributors have a greater interest in theory than in method or in the use of research findings rather than the methods of investigation themselves. Even among those whose central concern is with methods there is a wide range of different interests, with some focussing upon research problems rather than research procedures. Yet regardless of their different starting points and different emphases they are all united in a common concern for using field methods in the study of education and in turn focus upon various issues and problems involved in using field methods to study educational settings. But we might ask: what are field methods? What is the relationship between field methods and theoretical issues? What is the relationship between field methods and educational practice? All these questions concern various elements of the research process from the initial design of a project through to its publication and it is, therefore, to a brief review of the research process that we now turn.

The Research Process in Field Studies

A brief glance at many texts and readers devoted to methods of social investigation indicates that 'methods' are often equated with a set of techniques that researchers can use in the course of handling specific research problems (cf. Moser and Kalton, 1971; Bailey, 1978; Kidder, 1981). In contrast, field methods are not merely a set of techniques that can be applied to a social situation, for, as Freilich (1977) has indicated, there is a close relationship between *what* is done and *how* it is done. Accordingly, the field research process is as much concerned with the hopes, fears, frustrations and assumptions of the researcher as it is with mere techniques, for as Freilich argues:

> the fieldworker is not just a dogged follower of an artistic research design; he is not a puppet programmed to follow automatically a plan of research operations; he is not just the bearer of research tools; he is not just a 'reader' of questions found on questionnaires; and he is not just a dispenser of printed schedules. He is the *project*: his actions will make the field trip either a success or a failure. What he does in the field will tend either to attract or to repel information. He is the information absorber, the information analyzer, the information synthesizer and the information interpreter. (Freilich, 1977, p. 32)

As a consequence 'field method' is a somewhat ambiguous term that concerns not only techniques but also 'methodology' and 'research procedure'. The various elements involved might be defined as follows:

> *General methodology* concerns the systematic and logical study of the general principles guiding an investigation.
>
> *Research strategy or research procedure* refers to the way a particular investigation is designed and carried out.
>
> *Research technique* is a particular fact-finding manipulative operation that is used to yield social data.

It is these three distinct aspects of 'field method' that are brought together in the research process as they are *intertwined with each other* in the course of social investigation. Indeed, it is the way in which these various elements of the research process are concerned with one another that forms the basis of much of the discussion in the individual papers. Rarely are methodological issues discussed without specific illustration to field studies in education, nor are field techniques discussed by themselves. Accordingly, as Schatzman and Strauss indicate:

> Field method is not an exclusive method in the same sense, say, that experimentation is. Field method is more like an umbrella of activity beneath which any technique may be used for gaining the desired information, and for processes of thinking about this information. (Schatzman and Strauss, 1973, p. 14)

Accordingly, the researcher can blend together a wide range of methods to address the problem that is to be investigated. Indeed, the researcher can act pragmatically, having not been constrained to articulate either a specific problem or a specific technique in advance of the investigation.

While this open-ended approach may appear to hold many advantages, it does generate such questions as: how do you use field methods? how do you conduct field studies? When faced with these questions even acknowledged experts in the field of social anthropology appear to have some difficulty, as Evans-Pritchard reports:

> When I was a serious young student in London I thought I would try to get a few tips from experienced field workers before setting out for central Africa. I first sought advice from Westermarck. All I got from him was 'don't converse with an informant for more than twenty minutes because if you aren't bored by that time he will be'. Very good advice, even if somewhat inadequate. I sought instruction from Haddon, a man foremost in field research. He told me that it was really all quite simple; one should always behave as a gentleman. Also very good advice. My teacher Seligman told me to take ten grains of quinine every night and to keep off women. The famous Egyptologist, Sir Flinders Petrie just told me not to bother about drinking dirty water as one soon became immune to it. Finally, I asked Malinowski and was told not to be a bloody fool. (Evans-Pritchard, 1973, p. 1)

Similar accounts are also available concerning the North American anthropologist A.L. Kroeber: Agar (1981) reports that a graduate student who visited Kroeber to request advice on how to do fieldwork was told, 'Well I suggest you buy a notebook and a pencil.' It is accounts such as these that have led some researchers to conclude that 'all it [fieldwork] needs is (occasionally a suitable disguise, but always) just a notebook, a pencil and a lot of stamina and free time' (Ditton and Williams, 1981, p. 46). Such remarks might suggest to a research novice that there are no problems associated with the conduct of fieldwork; that it is simple, straightforward and unproblematic. On this basis it would appear that a researcher can pick up enough knowledge of fieldwork while a study is being conducted. However, the results of this approach are hazardous as the methodological learning of the previous generation of researchers is recapitulated at the same rate. In these circumstances it is assumed that the only way to learn how to do fieldwork is by going through the experience that has been followed by previous generations. As a consequence fieldwork is seen as an initiation rite whereby novices go through a period in the field in order to join the ranks of the experienced. However, as many writers have noted (Cohen and Naroll, 1973; Hargreaves, 1980b), the result is that much of the work is non-cumulative. There is also another problem associated with this approach. The emphasis is placed upon the acquisition of research technique with the result that the research process as such is overlooked. But we might ask: what constitutes the research process?

One account of the research process sees it as a number of steps or stages through which the researcher passes from the start (initial ideas) to the finish (the publication of a report) as shown in Figure 1.

Such an approach over-simplifies several aspects of the conduct of research. First, it reduces research to a set of technical operations which, it is argued, constitute the research process. Secondly, it assumes that each 'stage' is self-contained and leads to a subsequent stage. Thirdly, it overlooks the way in which data collection and data analysis actually occur as they are reduced to stages in the conduct of social research and there is no acknowledgement of the ways in which they are intertwined throughout the research process. Fourthly, it gives no indication of the importance of theorizing in the research process. Finally, no mention is made of the social, ethical and political problems that occur throughout the research process.

In recent years there has been a shift away from the notion of 'stages' in social research to a situation in which data collection, data analysis and theorizing are intimately related. For as Bechhofer

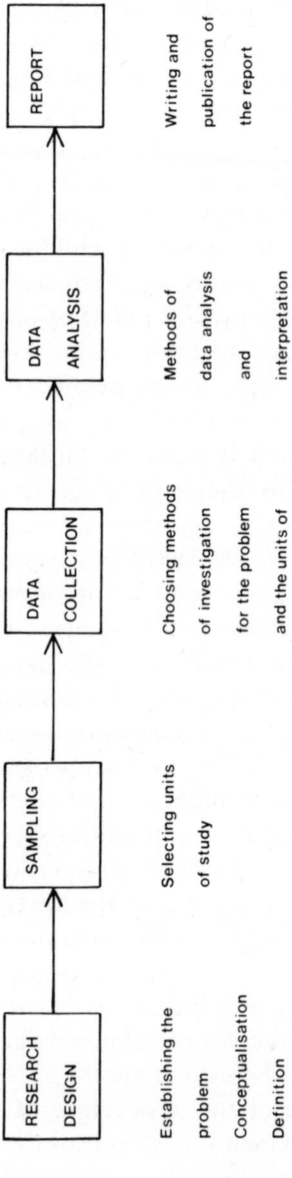
RESEARCH DESIGN
Establishing the problem
Conceptualisation
Definition
SAMPLING
Selecting units of study
DATA COLLECTION
Choosing methods of investigation for the problem and the units of study
DATA ANALYSIS
Methods of data analysis and interpretation
REPORT
Writing and publication of the report

Figure 1 An Ideal-Typical Research Process

remarks: 'The research process ... is not a clear-cut sequence of procedures following a neat pattern but a messy interaction between the conceptual and empirical world, deduction and induction occurring at the same time' (Bechhofer, 1974, p. 73). It is this statement that captures the research process for those engaged in fieldwork and the use of field methods.[4] However, it also highlights the fact that the research process deviates from the ideal-typical pattern, that research involves difficulties that the researcher has to come to terms with and, finally, that research has a theoretical or conceptual component that interacts with the technical aspects of social investigation.

A number of writers have presented these elements of the research process in sets of first-person accounts where they have discussed the ways in which they have conducted fieldwork in several settings including education (cf. Shipman, 1976; Burgess, 1984a).[5] Yet these accounts focus on analytic descriptions of social investigations rather than upon issues and problems in using field methods. It is, therefore, the purpose of this set of essays to examine some of the issues and problems that have been identified in field-based methods of social research, including the relationship between theory and method, the use of field methods, the problems (social, political and ethical) associated with field-based projects and the use of field methods in educational practice and educational policy-making. The essays, therefore, show an awareness that research does not follow a simple linear pattern but that the research process is such that theoretical issues will have implications for research practice and vice versa and that in turn questions surrounding educational practice and educational policy react back upon issues related to theory and method. As a consequence the papers in this volume have not been subdivided into sections as this would place an artificial straightjacket upon them which was never intended by the authors. Instead, the papers have been grouped together so that they may be related to each other in a variety of different ways which in part characterizes the research process. We now turn, therefore, to a discussion of the papers and the way in which they are organized in this book.

The Arrangement of the Papers

The papers in this volume are grouped together to reflect some of the major themes that arose at the workshop at which they were originally discussed. As Figure 2 illustrates, some of the papers contribute to more than one major theme. However, as readers will

Figure 2   Groups of Papers and Major Themes

Authors of papers	Theorizing and research	Gender, feminism and research	Some major themes Research problems	Research methods and research problems	Educational practice and policy
Edwards and Furlong	X				
Adelman	X				
Woods	X				
Davies	X	X			
Griffin	X	X	X	X	
Scott		X	X	X	
Wakeford		X	X		
Burgess			X	X	
Galton and Delamont			X	X	
Walker and Wiedel			X	X	X
Pollard				X	X
Elliott					X
Stenhouse					X
Shipman					X

discover, even this illustration of the way in which papers contribute to different themes leads to some over-simplification as many of the papers touch on most of the themes to a greater or lesser degree. In part, this depends on the style of writing that has been adopted:

> *An Autobiographical Approach* in which the researcher outlines the course of the research process and utilizes a first-person account to highlight particular aspects of the research process. In this volume the papers by Edwards and Furlong, Scott and Pollard follow this approach.

> *A Research Experience Approach* where the researcher uses research experience to discuss particular problems relating to field method that arise out of a research project. In this volume the papers by Woods, Davies, Griffin, Burgess, Galton and Delamont, Walker and Wiedel and Elliott adopt this style. In this respect, we are not provided with a discussion of all aspects of the research process but we are given access to certain aspects of the process in order to highlight particular research problems.

> *A Thematic Approach* in which the writer has taken a particular question or a particular method and illustrated the issue involved by making reference to work which he or she has conducted or work which has been conducted by others. In this volume the papers by Adelman, Wakeford, Stenhouse and Shipman take this approach.

However, regardless of the approach that has been taken, the central concern of all the writers has been to focus upon *issues* and *problems* that arise in the course of using field methods in the study of education. At this point it is usual for many editorial introductions to provide a brief summary of each paper. However, the authors are well able to speak for themselves and, therefore, the approach that is taken here intends to introduce readers to the key issues and questions that are posed in each paper and to relate them to each other and, where appropriate, to other literature on field methods and the study of educational settings.

Some Key Issues and Questions

The first group of papers deals with theoretical issues; these papers are placed at the beginning of the volume as it is often forgotten that the theoretical choices and assumptions that are made by a researcher influence other aspects of the research process.

We begin with a paper from Tony Edwards and John Furlong that provides a series of reflections on their book, *The Language of Teaching* (Edwards and Furlong, 1978), which reports on an investigation conducted in the Abraham Moss Centre. Their paper addresses the central question: what is the relationship between theory and method? In turn they focus on issues concerning the relationship between the research problem and theorizing and the way in which their own thinking and theorizing related to other theoretical perspectives deployed in sociological and educational studies. In particular, they address questions on the relationship between interactionism, theory generation and grounded theorizing. In short, their paper addresses the implications that theory has for the research process and raises questions about the relationship between the concerns of the researcher and the researched that are also taken up in the paper that follows by Clem Adelman.

The chapter by Adelman poses a question in the title and raises two central issues: first, the grounds on which the use of field methods makes claims to enhance an individual's understanding of the social world; secondly, the purpose of, and audience for, educational research. Adelman raises a number of theoretical questions that researchers need to come to terms with when conducting a study in an educational setting: whose conceptions should dominate the study? For whom does the researcher work? How does this influence the concepts and categories that are used in a study? In turn, Adelman goes on to raise questions about the theoretical perspective and the way in which the account that is generated might be negotiated by the researcher and the researched. In short, Adelman's paper complements the discussion provided by Edwards and Furlong about the use of different theoretical accounts in the study of educational settings.

Much has been written about the way in which different kinds of theorizing are possible in field studies. A now classic statement has come from Glaser and Strauss (1967) who distinguish between substantive and formal theory in the following terms:

> By substantive theory, we mean that developed for a substantive, or empirical, area of sociological inquiry, such as patient care, race relations, professional education, delinquency or research organizations. By formal theory, we mean that developed for a formal, or conceptual, area of sociological inquiry, such as stigma, deviant behavior, formal organiza-

tion, socialization, status congruency, authority and power, reward systems, or social mobility. (Glaser and Strauss, 1967, p. 32)

While the difference between formal and substantive theories is a useful distinction that can be deployed in the study of education, it should be noted that in practice there is often some interaction between different kinds of social theory. Indeed, as Peter Woods demonstrates through illustrative material from his own research and the research of other investigators, theory is not merely generated or developed as suggested by Glaser and Strauss, but can also be used by the researcher as a guide to data collection and analysis. Woods turns to some of the issues concerning the use of theory in relation to concepts and categories. In particular, he addresses a range of questions such as: how do field studies move towards theory? What are sensitizing concepts and how can they be used? How can concepts and categories be used to develop cumulative work in educational settings? In short, his paper deals with a set of issues that stress the importance of the researcher being engaged in theory construction rather than being nothing more than a research technician.

Subsequent papers would cast doubt on the idea that researchers are no more than technicians who utilize particular methods. Indeed, the next group of papers, that in some respects overlap with both theory and method, highlights the way in which a particular perspective influences the collection and analysis of data. In recent years much has been written on the influence of gender on research problems and processes and in particular the contribution of feminism to the development of research problems and research procedures (cf. Roberts, 1981; Stanley and Wise, 1983). The papers by Davies, Griffin, Scott and Wakeford all deal with the question of gender in as far as it influences the research process. In the essay by Lynn Davies we are introduced to five aspects of the research process where gender has some influence upon research procedure: identifying a target, adopting a methodology, the research relationship, the production of results and the implications of researching women. Her essay alerts both researchers and readers to the problem of generalization in social investigation and points to the hazards involved in making generalizations from specific groups of pupils to *all* pupils. She highlights the way in which male/female divisions can be used in projects and illustrates the way in which the concept of gender can be used to make familiar settings strange (cf. Delamont, 1981). She raises questions about gender and the status of the researcher and the influence that gender has not only upon data collection but also upon data analysis. She points to the importance of particular concepts and categories being used to collect basic sets of data in educational settings.

The paper by Lynn Davies also complements and engages with some of the remarks advanced by Christine Griffin. While the focus in Griffin's paper is upon the use of qualitative methods in a project devoted to young women and work, she also takes up questions about gender relations in the research process making reference to her project. In particular, she highlights the way in which the project was regarded as 'strange', while projects using all male groups are seldom regarded as problematic. In common with Lynn Davies' paper she addresses such questions as the influence of her personal position on the selection of a research problem and the collection and analysis of data. Some of the evidence presented in both papers indicates that there are sets of contradictions that have to be worked upon in the research process — a topic elaborated by Sue Scott in her account of the postgraduate education project.

Sue Scott's paper brings us closer to the research experience which she follows from the establishment of the project on which she worked with Mary Porter (cf. Porter, 1984) and John Wakeford. Her discussion looks at the way in which contradictions both of self and of methodology influence the collection and analysis of data. Her analysis builds further on the discussion by Davies and Griffin about the extent to which gender and feminism influence the research perspective and, in turn, areas that are included in or excluded from the project. Her paper takes up issues concerning the way in which interviews are designed and conducted and the importance of re-search relations for the conduct of interviews. Among the topics that Scott tackles is the extent to which research appointments may influence the subsequent reception of a project team and a study.

It is this theme that is taken up by John Wakeford whose paper focusses on the same project as considered by Sue Scott. These two papers, together with Porter (1984), also contribute to our knowledge of the politics of team-based research (cf. Bell, 1977; Platt, 1976). However, in this context Wakeford focusses upon some of the problems that face research directors who do not wish to reproduce the gender divisions and social divisions that exist within society in a research project. On this basis alone his paper complements Scott's analysis of the importance of gender on the postgraduate education project and in turn points to ethical and political problems that surround research sponsorship and research funding (cf. Mills, 1959; Stenhouse, 1984).

The paper by Wakeford also illustrates that research cannot merely be seen as the application of particular techniques of social investigation within particular social settings but that researchers have to be able to deal with sets of political problems that permeate the research process, influence research relationships and the way in which research is funded, sponsored, conducted, analyzed and reported. A similar perspective is taken by Burgess, who uses his own research experience to focus upon some of the ethical problems surrounding the use of field methods within a study of a comprehensive school. Again, the importance of flexibility in research design (cf. Schatzman and Strauss, 1973; Hammersley and Atkinson, 1983) is emphasized and the way in which researchers have to engage in a series of compromises throughout the research process (cf. Barnes, 1979).

These papers all provide a background to some of the subsequent papers on field methods as they cue the reader to recall that research methods are influenced by theoretical, political and ethical dimensions of the research process. Both the papers by Galton and Delamont and by Walker and Wiedel are based upon research conducted by research teams and therefore complement the work discussed by Scott and by Wakeford.

Although discussions of field methods focus very much upon observation and interview, many texts (cf. Denzin, 1970; Burgess, 1982; 1984a) advocate that researchers should use a variety of methods alongside each other — an approach commonly referred to as 'triangulation' where multiple methods may be used. Some writers have taken this further and discussed ways in which particular techniques can be integrated with each other in a particular project (cf. Sieber, 1973). It is to a discussion of the ways in which different styles of observation can be used that we turn to in the paper by Galton and Delamont, while the following chapter by Walker and Wiedel examines a similar theme by discussing the use of photography with interviews.

The work discussed by Maurice Galton and Sara Delamont is derived from their experience of working with a team of researchers on the ORACLE project that has been concerned with primary education and the transition from primary to secondary school. For many readers this project may be synonymous with a systematic style of observation. However, in focussing on the transition from primary to secondary school, ethnographic methods were used alongside systematic observation. In this paper, the researchers use their experience of the project to discuss the possibility of rapprochement between systematic and ethnographic styles of observation. Accordingly, their paper deals with these two styles of researching which have implications for the collection and analysis of data. This chapter, therefore, contributes to a discussion of how the principles of triangulation can be applied in practice. Furthermore, it links back to those papers that have focussed upon research problems and forward to the paper by Walker and Wiedel that also provides a discussion of research problems alongside a consideration of research method.

The project discussed by Rob Walker and Janine Wiedel broadens our traditional notion of what counts as a research method as they discuss the role of film making, video-recording and photography as techniques of social investigation with a view to considering the role of visual as well as literary materials in a research project. They address the question: how can photographs be used as data in a research project? They also consider the way in which photography and interviews can be used in a project which relates to earlier discussions of triangulation and the problems associated with the conduct of fieldwork. However, another important dimension to their project concerns the use of the investigation to the teacher in the classroom. A crucial feature of their chapter concerns the way in which a field-based project can have an action component that attempts to handle problems of educational practice — a topic that relates this paper to the last four chapters in this volume.

In recent years there has been considerable discussion about the role of the teacher in educational research and evaluation (cf. Stenhouse, 1975; Nixon, 1981; McCormick, 1982). Many of these accounts focus on the use of ethnographic or case study methods that can be used by teachers and by those engaged in action research projects. While Andrew Pollard's chapter falls distinctly within the ethnographic tradition and deals with problems and procedures of using particular approaches in school and classroom-based research, it also has another dimension as it illustrates the way in which a full-time teacher can handle a research role which is built on the teacher role. As such Pollard's work will help us to address the question: how can the teacher-researcher develop a research strategy in the school and classroom?

John Elliott's paper brings us back to a consideration of action research. However, in the course of his discussion he also illustrates how research notes, memoranda and documentary evidence can be used in a discussion of the methodology of a research project. The paper focusses on three key questions: who defines the focus of the research: teachers or the central project team? Who defines the pedagogical aims of the project: teachers or facilitators? What is the importance of an action project for teachers? — a key question in the process versus product debate. These questions are central to discussions of the way in which action research can be developed in relation to educational practice and are illustrated by Elliott in relation to his experience of the 'Teacher-Pupil Interaction and the Quality of Learning Project'.

The last two chapters continue to consider the role of intensive studies of schools and classrooms for educational practice and educational policy-making. Both papers by Stenhouse and by Shipman raise general issues. In particular Lawrence Stenhouse asks how the objectives of education and the study of education may be brought together through case study work. His paper suggests ways in which case studies can apply to educational practice. However, it is evident that this demands further attention by both researchers and practitioners if developments are to occur in this area of study.

Finally, Marten Shipman raises issues concerning the use of intensive case studies in educational policy-making. However, the style of his paper is such that it underlines the importance of some of the issues raised earlier in the volume, as well as pointing out that the research process does not merely involve the use of methods but also includes questions of report writing, dissemination and the use of evidence in policy-making. As with many of the other papers in the volume, he highlights the importance of relationships between teachers and researchers in the course of developing and using field-based methods in educational research.

The focus of all the papers included in this volume is, therefore, upon the principles processes, and procedures by which those individuals engaged in the use of field methods establish their problems and seek answers to their questions. The contributors, who have all had wide experience of educational research, represent a wide variety of disciplines, hold different disciplinary allegiances and give different kinds of emphasis to the ways in which they conduct educational studies using field-based methods. Nevertheless, their work raises a series of common issues and problems that recur in many of the papers, including:

1 the state and status of theory and theorizing in field projects;
2 the way in which the researcher's value position can influence the conduct of social inquiry;

3 the political dimensions of the research process and implications for the conduct of social research and the reporting of research evidence;

4 the importance of ethical issues and the ways in which they can be handled by the researcher;

5 the development of strategies and styles of investigation — the ways in which field-based methods can be extended, developed and used in conjunction with other approaches to social investigation;

6 the relationship between field-based methods and educational practice and policy-making.

These are some of the major issues raised in this collection of papers. Many of the authors have not only outlined the issues but also indicated the way they have handled them in the course of conducting research and highlighted the problematic areas that remain. It is, therefore, to be hoped that these papers will contribute not only to debates about the use of field methods in the study of education but also to discussions about the use of research methodology in the social sciences, as these are crucial areas in which the dialogue must continue.

Notes

1 Although developments in Britain date mainly from the 1960s and 1970s, there is much more American work, reviewed in Wilcox (1982) and Atkinson and Delamont (1980), which pre-dates British studies.

2 The references provided refer to work done by sociologists. There is also a vast range of work on schools that has been conducted by others. See, for example, the publications from the primary school project based at Leicester University whose methodology is discussed in the chapter by Galton and Delamont in this volume (cf. Galton *et al.*, 1980; Galton and Simon, 1980; Galton and Willcocks, 1983). Another base for detailed studies of schools in Britain has been the Centre for Applied Research in Education at the University of East Anglia. For case study work from this Centre see, for example, Stenhouse *et al.* (1982).

3 For a recent review of ethnographic classroom studies in Britain see Hammersley (1982).

4 For a similar view to that expressed by Bechhofer see Wax (1971), especially pp. 3–14.

5 The books by Shipman (1976) and Burgess (1984a) are the only two British collections entirely devoted to autobiographical accounts of educational studies, although Hammersley (1983) does contain two reflexive accounts. In addition, some papers written in this style by researchers

in the USA are included in Spindler (1982) and Popkewitz and Tabachnick (1981). For a review of some of the collections that include studies outside education see Burgess (1984a), pp. 1–13.

References

AGAR, M. (1981) *The Professional Stranger: An Informal Ethnography*, New York, Academic Press.

√ ATKINSON, P. and DELAMONT, S. (1980) 'The two traditions in educational ethnography: Sociology and anthropology compared', *British Journal of Sociology of Education*, 1, 2, pp. 139–52.

BAILEY, K. (1978) *Methods of Social Research*, New York, Free Press.

BALL, S.J. (1981) *Beachside Comprehensive: A Case Study of Secondary Schooling*, Cambridge, Cambridge University Press.

BARNES, J.A. (1979) *Who Should Know What?*, Harmondsworth, Penguin.

BECHHOFER, F. (1974) 'Current approaches to empirical research: Some central ideas', in REX, J. (Ed.) *Approaches to Sociology: An Introduction to Major Trends in British Sociology*, London, Routledge and Kegan Paul.

BELL, C. (1977) 'Reflections on the Banbury restudy', in BELL, C. and NEWBY, H. (Eds) *Doing Sociological Research*, London, Allen and Unwin.

BURGESS, R.G. (Ed.) (1982) *Field Research: A Sourcebook and Field Manual*, London, Allen and Unwin.

BURGESS, R.G. (1983) *Experiencing Comprehensive Education: A Study of Bishop McGregor School*, London, Methuen.

BURGESS, R.G. (Ed.) (1984a) *The Research Process in Educational Settings: Ten Case Studies*, Lewes, Falmer Press.

BURGESS, R.G. (1984b) *In the Field: An Introduction to Field Research*, London, Allen and Unwin.

COHEN, R. and NAROLL, R. (1973) 'Method in cultural anthropology', in NAROLL, R. and COHEN, R. (Eds) *A Handbook of Method in Cultural Anthropology*, New York, Columbia University Press.

CUNNISON, S. (1966) *Wages and Work Allocation*, London, Tavistock.

DELAMONT, S. (1981) 'All too familiar? A decade of classroom research', *Educational Analysis*, 3, 1, pp. 69–83.

DENZIN, N. (1970) *The Research Act*, Chicago, Aldine (2nd ed. published by McGraw Hill, 1978).

DITTON, J. and WILLIAMS, R. (1981) 'The fundable vs. the doable: Sweet gripes, sour grapes and the SSRC', *Background Papers 1*, University of Glasgow, Department of Sociology.

EDWARDS, A.D. and FURLONG, V.J. (1978) *The Language of Teaching*, London, Heinemann.

EVANS-PRITCHARD, E.E. (1973) 'Some reminiscences and reflections on fieldwork', *Journal of the Anthropological Society of Oxford*, 4, 1, pp. 1–12.

FRANKENBERG, R (1957) *Village on the Border*, London, Cohen and West.

Robert G. Burgess

FRANKENBERG, R. (Ed.) (1982) *Custom and Conflict in British Society*, Manchester, Manchester University Press.

FREILICH, M. (Ed.) (1977) *Marginal Natives at Work: Anthropologists in the Field*, (2nd ed.), New York, Wiley.

GALTON, M. and SIMON, B. (Eds) (1980) *Progress and Performance in the Primary Classroom*, London, Routledge and Kegan Paul.

GALTON, M. and WILLCOCKS, J. (1983) *Moving from the Primary Classroom*, London, Routledge and Kegan Paul.

GALTON, M. *et al.* (1980) *Inside the Primary Classroom*, London, Routledge and Kegan Paul.

GLASER, B. and STRAUSS, A.L. (1967) *The Discovery of Grounded Theory*, London, Weidenfeld and Nicholson.

GLUCKMAN, M. (Ed.) (1964) *Closed Systems and Open Minds: The Limits of Naivete in Social Anthropology*, Edinburgh, Oliver and Boyd.

√HAMMERSLEY, M. (1982) 'The sociology of classrooms', in HARTNETT, A. (Ed.) *The Social Sciences in Educational Studies*, London, Heinemann.

HAMMERSLEY, M. (Ed.) (1983) *The Ethnography of Schooling*, Driffield, Nafferton.

HAMMERSLEY, M. and ATKINSON, P. (1983) *Ethnography: Principles in Practice*, London, Tavistock.

HARGREAVES, A. and TICKLE, L. (Eds) (1980) *Middle Schools: Origins, Ideology and Practice*, London, Harper and Row.

HARGREAVES, D.H. (1967) *Social Relations in a Secondary School*, London, Routledge and Kegan Paul.

HARGREAVES, D.H (Ed.) (1980a) 'Classroom Studies', *Educational Analysis*, 2, 2, pp. 1–95.

HARGREAVES, D.H. (1980b) 'Classrooms, schools and juvenile delinquency', *Educational Analysis*, 2, 2, pp. 75–87.

KIDDER, L.H. (1981) *Research Methods in Social Relations*, (4th ed.) New York, Holt, Rinehart and Winston.

KING, R. (1978) *All Things Bright and Beautiful? A Sociological Study of Infants' Classrooms*, London, Wiley.

LACEY, C. (1970) *Hightown Grammar: The School as a Social System*, Manchester, Manchester University Press.

LAMBART, A. (1970) 'The sociology of an unstreamed urban grammar school for girls', unpublished MA thesis, University of Manchester.

LUPTON, T. (1963) *On the Shop Floor*, Oxford, Pergamon.

McALEESE, R. and HAMILTON, D. (Eds) (1978) *Understanding Classroom Life*, Slough, NFER.

McCORMICK, R. (Ed.) (1982) *Calling Education to Account*, London, Heinemann.

MILLS, C. Wright (1959) *The Sociological Imagination*, New York, Oxford University Press.

MOSER, C.A. and KALTON, G.K. (1971) *Survey Methods in Social Investigation* (2nd ed.), London, Heinemann.

NIXON, J. (Ed.) (1981) *A Teachers' Guide to Action Research*, London, Grant McIntyre.

PLATT, J. (1976) *Realities of Social Research*, London, Chatto and Windus for Sussex University Press.

POPKEWITZ, T.S. and TABACHNICK, B.R. (Eds) (1981) *The Study of Schooling: Field Based Methodologies in Educational Research and Evaluation*, New York, Praeger.

PORTER, M.A. (1984) 'The modification of method in researching postgraduate education', in BURGESS, R.G. (Ed.) *The Research Process in Educational Settings: Ten Case Studies*, Lewes, Falmer Press.

ROBERTS, H. (Ed.) (1981) *Doing Feminist Research*, London, Routledge and Kegan Paul.

SCHATZMAN, L. and STRAUSS, A.L. (1973) *Field Research: Strategies for a Natural Sociology*, Englewood Cliffs, N.J., Prentice Hall.

SCOTT, S. and PORTER, M. (1983) 'On the bottom rung: A discussion of women and women's work in sociology', *Womens Studies International Forum*, 6, 2, pp. 211–21.

SHARP, R. and GREEN, A. (1975) *Education and Social Control*, London, Routledge and Kegan Paul.

SHIPMAN, M. (Ed.) (1976) *The Organization and Impact of Social Research*, London, Routledge and Kegan Paul.

SIEBER, S.D. (1973) 'The integration of fieldwork and survey methods', *American Journal of Sociology*, 78, 6, pp. 1335–59 (reprinted in BURGESS, R.G. (Ed.) (1982) *Field Research: A Sourcebook and Field Manual*, London, Allen and Unwin).

SPINDLER, G. (Ed.) (1982) *Doing the Ethnography of Schooling: Educational Anthropology in Action*, New York, Holt, Rinehart and Winston.

STANLEY, L. and WISE, E. (1983) *Breaking Out: Feminist Consciousness and Feminist Research*, London, Routledge and Kegan Paul.

STENHOUSE, L. (1975) *An Introduction to Curriculum Research and Development*, London, Heinemann.

STENHOUSE, L. (1984) 'Library access, library use and user education in academic sixth forms: An autobiographical account', in BURGESS, R.G. (Ed.) *The Research Process in Educational Settings: Ten Case Studies*, Lewes, Falmer Press.

STENHOUSE, L. *et al.* (1982) *Teaching about Race Relations*, London, Routledge and Kegan Paul.

WAX, R. (1971) *Doing Fieldwork: Warnings and Advice*, Chicago, University of Chicago Press.

WILCOX, K. (1982) 'Ethnography as a methodology and its application to the study of schooling', in SPINDLER, G. (Ed.) *Doing the Ethnography of Schooling: Educational Anthropology in Action*, New York, Holt, Rinehart and Winston.

1 Reflections on the Language of Teaching

A.D. Edwards and V.J. Furlong

Whatever their methodological persuasion, it is always tempting for researchers to present their final report as 'the best possible interpretation of events, inferior versions having been discarded along the way' (Edwards and Furlong, 1978, p. 147). The appearance may then be given of an irresistably logical and systematic progression towards well-substantiated findings. But competent classroom research, like competent classroom interaction (Hammersley, 1981), is never a simple matter of knowing and following the right rules of procedure. There is a great deal of rule-governed creativity, and of responding to sudden problems and opportunities. Contributors to this book and to its companion volume (Burgess, 1984) have been encouraged to give less than usually tidied up versions of their work, and to admit some of the false starts, dead ends and changes in direction or scope.

They have also been asked to display some of the thinking which continued after their research had officially 'finished' and which is rarely reported at all. Such retrospection provides an opportunity to recognize lost opportunities — to admit the regrets which researchers often feel for the choices which they did not make and the ideas they had felt compelled to discard. This is what we begin by doing.

Theoretical Sampling and a Restricted View

The research we undertook during an entire school year at the Abraham Moss Centre in Manchester concentrated on teacher pupil interaction in one area of the curriculum (humanities) in the first two years of the comprehensive school. Given the general commitment of that school to resource-based learning and the unusually explicit justifications for it offered by its principal (Mitson, 1980), we regret now that we did not make a more extensive and comparative study in the five faculties which shared the Lower School curriculum. Such a study might have provided a useful demonstration of how differently a 'common' teaching policy can be realized in practice (see also Ball, 1981, pp. 163–237; Evans, 1982). As so often happens, however, considerable changes in theoretical or empirical interest occurred after the fieldwork began to run along its intended grooves, and those grooves then seemed too deep to climb out of.

We were initially drawn into an intensive study by a theoretical interest in how teachers' simultaneous management of classroom relationships and classroom meanings might best be described. At that time, we saw the research as being 'basic' rather than 'applied'. It was to be an attempt to develop ways of describing the 'language of teaching' which would build on our respective experiences of socio-linguistic and interactionist approaches to its recurrent patterns. We wanted to construct new methods of classroom analysis, not new matters of classroom fact. Even the choice of the Abraham Moss Centre as the school in which to work was not made directly because of its commitment to resource-based learning in mixed-ability groups. It was because we were theoretically oriented to classrooms which were out-of-the-ordinary. The obstinate familiarity of what is being observed has been a formidable difficulty in classroom research, leading too many observers to trade unreflectingly on what they already 'know'. We wanted examples of teaching sufficiently unlike what we had practised ourselves or witnessed elsewhere to make us regularly aware of having to work hard to understand what was going on.

The importance to the research of being allowed to work in Manchester's most obviously innovative school was therefore something to be heavily emphasized when negotiating access with the LEA and with the Principal. It was also indicated in the letter which we circulated to all staff at the school before the fieldwork began. Taken as a whole, that letter conveyed a self-conscious insistence that we were not going to do 'scientific' classroom research — that we had 'no experiments to carry out and no clearly defined hypotheses to test'. But while we agree with Ball (1984) that in ethnographic research what is to be important is a matter for discovery rather than the means of organizing the work from the outset, we did declare in general terms both what we were looking for and what we expected to find.

We begin by assuming that Abraham Moss teachers are trying to move away from traditional teacher-pupil relationships to establish new ways of working as well as new forms of curriculum content. What we hope to explore is how teachers use talk to define with their pupils what schoolwork is and what the learner's role is to be. (Edwards and Furlong, 1978, p. 75)

The further choice of a team of teachers from the Lower School was because of a particular interest, derived from our general orientation, in how new pupils were 'settled in' to ways of learning likely to be significantly different from those they had encountered before and so needing to be talked into existence more explicitly than was likely to be the case in more traditional classrooms. Theoretically, any department would have done provided that it was sufficiently 'different'. That it was a humanities team which we observed was largely because of a former MEd. student whom Edwards knew well. Not only had she just joined the team (as a new member of staff) but her husband was its coordinator. Her willing sponsorship and his active interest were invaluable. We also felt that the prospect of 'open' teaching would be enhanced in an area of the curriculum strongly associated with innovation.

Our choice of a research context was therefore achieved primarily through a process of theoretical sampling. We then had to live with the consequences of that decision. When classroom observation and recording began, we became increasingly intrigued by the procedures through which pupils' learning was organized, and particularly by the patterning of the instructional encounters between teachers and individual pupils. However, we also became aware of a considerable distance between what we were observing, and resource-based learning as it has been displayed in the mainly prescriptive literature about it and as we ourselves had expected to find it. By the time we had come to appreciate how useful detailed descriptions across the curriculum might be, we were tied in to prolonged sampling of a year's work in humanities. In a study unusually dependent on the continuing goodwill of teachers subjected to extensive observation, there may have been some reluctance to negotiate and maintain such close working relationships elsewhere in the Lower School. But the main constraint was our theoretical commitment to a detailed charting of teacher-pupil interaction as it developed sequentially through the school year.

The obvious narrowness in our work is its focus on teaching. What we could offer was an account of instructional encounters in which the teacher was a (and, as it happened, *the*) main participant.

Our preliminary review of evidence about the recurrent characteristics of classroom talk had indicated the predominance of highly directive styles of instruction, and the consequently limited communicative and semantic space left over for pupils. Yet the five teachers we observed at Abraham Moss did almost no class teaching. We were able to report something of the diversity of their encounters with individual pupils, the care with which they sought to diagnose and treat particular learning difficulties, and the extent to which they were aware of having had to learn some new skills. Our main conclusion, however, would have been much more persuasive if we had been able to record pupil-pupil talk. We argued that beneath some undoubtedly significant departures from traditional ways of transmitting knowledge in classrooms lay a continuing assumption that the pupil's task was to move as rapidly as possible towards the teacher's framework of meanings. A similar conclusion has been reached in more recent studies (for example, Mercer and Edwards, 1981; French, 1983). Yet we were not able to make recordings of pupil talk which, while shaped by the curriculum materials available, was free from that close, persistent and pervasive monitoring which the teacher normally provides.

We certainly observed and overheard such talk, noted the teachers' tolerance of 'working noise' and the consistency with which they marked it off from mere 'chatter', and reported what seemed to us to be generally high levels of 'busyness' in most of the lessons. That we did not record it was not a choice, but a necessary adaptation to the fact that financial support for the project was limited to the research associate's salary. Even the single radio-microphone used to record the teachers had to be borrowed from another department, and attempts to record small groups of pupils with more mundane equipment were abandoned because the background noise was too obtrusive. Barnes and Todd (1977; 1981) solved that problem by withdrawing groups of pupils into quiet rooms so as to demonstrate the quality of pupil talk possible if the teacher's authoritative direction were to be temporarily relaxed. We were mainly interested in analyzing what regularly happened in teacher-pupil encounters when the main burden of carrying information was 'delegated' to curriculum packages and the teachers were freed for other kinds of instructional intervention. Nevertheless, we missed (or were constrained into missing) opportunities to show something of the interpretive work 'by which pupils make meaning of meanings by talking through their interpretations ... in settings where their conversational partners participate on a more equal footing' (Walker, 1980, p. 331).

An 'Unprincipled' Analysis?

Our review of presumably relevant classroom research had certainly not provided us with ready-made routines for collecting and interpreting data. In any case, we were already convinced of the inseparability of theory and data, and so of the impossibility of any interpretation of classroom interaction founded on a period of 'pure' observation which would not in some way have foreshadowed it (Edwards and Furlong, 1978).

Our method was the conventional ethnographic approach of observing, recording, immersing ourselves in the transcripts until we felt able to discern some patterns in the interaction, and then checking those patterns through further listening and reflection. When the first recordings were made, we had only the most general ideas of what to look for, though we were certainly hoping that initial lessons with pupils new to the school, to humanities, and probably to resource-based learning, would expose the establishing of relationship rules and procedural rules with unusual clarity (Ball, 1980). Later recordings were made partly to examine what happened when many of these rules had become part of the 'background' of the interaction, partly to check on the range of teaching methods employed, and partly to include lessons which the teachers themselves expected to be relatively 'open'. Edwards deliberately delayed any observation to see what sense he could make of the transcripts alone, a procedure which reflected something of the ethnomethodological conviction that participants' perception of their situation will be made evident in the organization of their talk.

Our conclusion was that teachers and pupils organized their talk on the reciprocal assumptions of teacher-knowledge and pupil-ignorance (Edwards, 1980a). Certainly none of the instructional encounters which we recorded seemed to diverge from the basic pattern of a one-way movement towards the teacher's frame of reference. This was not what we had expected; it is what the data forced us to conclude. Yet the lack of any systematic categorizing of utterances or sequences leaves the analysis vulnerable to the charge admitted by Barnes and Todd — that evidence and interpretation are so run together that the reader, having nothing else to refer to than the extracts which illustrate the very interpretation being offered, is being implicitly invited to trust the honesty and sensitivity of the record. The weakness of that invitation is that the researchers may be substituting their own understanding for how the participants themselves 'heard' the talk as doing what it is described as doing (Walker, 1980).

It has to be admitted that our own sense of having been too unsystematic (in the ethnomethodological rather than Flanders sense) was reinforced by reading Michael Stubbs' criticism of how most classroom research has made 'unprincipled' use of isolated features of teacher-pupil talk as direct indicators of sociologically or pedagogically relevant categories (Stubbs, 1981; Edwards, 1981). A source of doubts more closely related to our own work than the linguistic high-mindedness advocated by Stubbs has been the application of conversational analysis to classroom settings (McHoul, 1978; Mehan, 1979; Payne and Cuff, 1982; French, 1983). Perhaps the nearest comparison with our own work is Mehan's, the studies being of similar duration and sharing the objective of revealing the structuring activities 'that assemble lessons as socially-organised events' (Mehan, 1979, p. 16). In the introduction to his research, Mehan approved of the 'sense of presence' which ethnographic methods had brought to the previously arid wastes of classroom research, but deplored a tendency to be anecdotal in displaying evidence and to choose the 'relevant' anecdotes without revealing the criteria used to select them. His criteria for what he calls a 'proper constitutive ethnography' are (1) that the data should be retrievable; (2) that their treatment should be comprehensive; (3) that analysis should focus entirely on interaction; (4) that there should be a convergence between the researcher's and the participants' perspectives. A rough reckoning suggests that we might just pass two of his tests. Our analysis certainly focusses on interaction, and to an extent which we now question (as the final section of this chapter will indicate). A considerable agreement with how their teaching was described, or at least an absence of strong disagreement, is implicit in the fact that the teachers and their location are named in the book. We will return to some of the implications of respondent validation. The retrievability of the data, however, is severely limited by the lack of any visual record of events and by the brevity of the field notes taken at the time. Finally, our analysis is certainly not 'exhaustive' in that we did not set out to construct a 'set of rules located in the interaction that describes the corpus of materials in their entirety' (Mehan, 1979, p. 33). Although we identified a similar 'social grammar' to his, rooted in the reciprocal assumptions of teacher-knowledge and pupil-ignorance, from which we recorded no significant departures, we failed to provide that comprehensive 'instancing' which Mehan claims to provide.

The criterion of a 'convergence of perspectives' raises some important issues which we want to consider in more detail. The five teachers were able to read early drafts of our account of their work, and were encouraged both to amend it in detail and to challenge it more broadly if they felt themselves misrepresented. That 'democratic' procedure is less reassuring than it may seem. Elsewhere in this book, Galton and Delamont note the power enjoyed by a writer over an 'associate' reader, especially where the reader may have neither the time nor (unless blatantly misrepresented) the motivation to rewrite the account. Indeed, the researchers' account may express such different concerns and priorities from those of the practitioners as not to invite a general challenge at all. Like some of the Beachside staff (Ball, 1984), the Abraham Moss teachers offered many corrections of factual detail — for example, about the extent to which they had modified the two curriculum packages (the 'Study of Man' and the Keele 'Integrated Studies Project') on which their teaching was based. But our main theme, that close teacher control over pupils' meanings had been maintained in different forms, was not questioned. We have wondered since what would have happened if there had been more divergence, and whether its absence reflects the extent to which an unconscious process of self-monitoring had filtered out from our account descriptions or judgments which might have caused unmanageable trouble.

We had felt committed from the outset to a collaborative relationship with the teachers we observed. Over the year, our appreciation of their high levels of skill was undoubtedly apparent to them. But the usual risks of writing an *unduly* appreciative account were increased by the necessity of naming the school, which was too distinctive to be disguised. Indeed, as we have said, it was because it was so out-of-the-ordinary that we had chosen to work there in the first place. Given the celebrity of the curriculum materials, the faculty could not have been hidden either. The freedom of critical manoeuvre obtainable by guaranteeing confidentiality was not ours to enjoy, and we were soon told explicitly that we would not be allowed to publish anything which might damage the school's reputation. That the book was 'cleared' after only minor revisions by the five teachers and the management team might be taken as evidence of the anodyne quality attributed by King (1984) to studies where confidentiality is not offered. Yet the book is often seen, for example by teachers using it on in-service courses, as being very critical of teaching strategies which retained an unintentionally strong didactic bias.

The humanities team themselves recognized that their practices were a long way from their intentions, and they found no revelations in our account of that divergence. While we ourselves were surprised at how closely the teachers' control over instructional encounters resembled that associated with more traditional forms of teaching, we were not claiming in that sense to be bringing 'news'. The conclusion was not that innovations are necessarily subverted in practice, only that our analysis might suggest to teachers ways of recognizing how and how far 'normal' strategies had been transformed in their own situation by drawing attention to certain generalizations which it may be possible to make about 'authoritative' teaching. That objective determined the style in which we tried to write the book. As mentioned earlier, our initial intentions had been more theoretical, and we then planned to report our work in conventional form. The change in focus confined overtly theoretical discussions to two chapters and some footnotes, and brought instead an emphasis on detailed description of classroom practices as a means of making more readily 'visible' what is often taken for granted as being what teaching essentially is. We would now accept Barnes' (1979) view that what we offered in the end was not a 'new language for talking about teaching' (as we might seem to promise in the first chapter of the book), but a heightened sense of how and how consistently teachers move pupils towards the teacher's frame of reference and keep them there.

Even at the time, however, we did not feel ourselves limited to the function of making the obvious more visible. Mehan's insistence on a convergence of view between researcher and researched recognizes the danger that researchers may impose their own frame of references on participants who are given no chance to talk back, or may use selected aspects of the situation they are studying to illustrate their own prior concerns. A similar view is taken by Adelman, elsewhere in this book, when he questions the integrity of ethnographic studies dominated by the 'immaculate conceptions' of the researcher. But is not respondent validation necessarily limited where the concerns of researcher and researched only partly overlap, and where the researcher may wish to do something other than simply confirm and be confirmed by professional commonsense? During the process of checking back with the Abraham Moss teachers, we were inevitably aware at times of some differences in perspective. Specifically, it was easier for us, as former teachers, to enter their professional frame of reference than it was for them to feel much interest in our attempts to explore and elaborate in a particular setting theories like Cicourel's (1973) about the assumptions underlying and reinforced by 'normal' talk.

One particular theoretical concern is only touched on at the end of the book. It had already become difficult for an interactionist study not to show some awareness of macro-structural constraints. In our case, the teachers themselves were well aware of organizational tensions between a collective commitment to more 'autonomous' pupil learning, credentialist pressures for examination success, and broader pressures to equip pupils with literacy and other skills needed to cope with their life beyond school. Two of the teachers were also aware of then current theories of how schooling functioned as a form of social control, especially in socially disadvantaged areas of the kind in which they worked. Yet our own analysis moved no 'further' from the interactions we observed and recorded than the catchment area of the school (Edwards, 1980c). In subsequent work, Edwards returned to an earlier interest in social class, language and learning, and re-examined conventional diagnoses of communicative disadvantage in relation to the communicative strategies which pupils are actually called upon to display (Edwards, 1980b; 1982). Furlong became actively engaged in research into pupil cultures, and into relationships between pupils' other social identities and the demands they face in schools (Bird *et al.*, 1981; Furlong, in press). The book itself, however, remained within self-imposed interactionist limits. It ended with our suggestion that an analysis grounded in close study of classroom interactions resembled Giddens' (1976) theoretical demonstration of the process of 'structuration'. It is with some second thoughts about this process that we will end.

Structuration

Throughout the study we had become increasingly concerned with the concept of authority, drawing a distinction between 'authority talk' and 'power talk'. Power talk was explicitly coercive, involving open threats and frequent imperatives. Authority talk, on the other hand, covered all those instances where the teacher avoided making control obvious by, for example, softening a command into the indirect form of a statement or request. It occurred most significantly and pervasively when the pupils routinely confirmed the teacher's control by accepting or appearing to work towards the teacher's frame of reference.

In our final chapter, we developed the concept of authority talk by suggesting that whenever knowledge was being transmitted, the talk through which transmission occurred only made sense as the 'working out of a power relationship'. The persistent recourse to the teacher's authority was the taken-for-granted foundation on which both teachers and pupils 'accomplished comprehensible talk and action'. Both sides used the structural relationship as a basis for expressing and analyzing meaning; they each relied on the notion of teacher authority as an essential feature in interpreting what the other meant. So, for example, persistent talking by a pupil became an act of defiance because pupil and teacher assumed an authority relationship. Without that assumption talking would have no meaning as a symbol of defiance. Tactically, the almost complete abandonment of class teaching at Abraham Moss had removed a normally extensive source of opportunities for pupils to recognize the teacher's authority by 'not talking when I'm talking' or to challenge it by talking 'out of turn' (Denscombe, 1980). What had *not* been transformed, however, was the teacher's right to define what was relevant, appropriate and correct during instructional encounters, whether (rarely) with a large group or an individual pupil. Only where the teacher conveys 'real' ignorance or uncertainty is the talk something other than authority talk. It was significant how rarely this occurred in the many lessons we observed.

Repeated analysis of our transcripts indicated that a sense of authority was constantly being utilized by teachers and pupils as a resource for making sense of each other's acts. In doing so, we suggested that they constantly reconstituted their relationship.

We only read Giddens' introductory discussion of 'the duality of structure' after we had completed our analysis, and it seemed to provide a 'more impressive-sounding' description of what we thought we had been doing all along. He had written that 'structuration as the reproduction of practices refers abstractly to the dynamic process whereby structures come into being ... social structures are both constituted *by* human agency and yet at the same time they are the very *medium* of this constitution' (Giddens, 1976, p. 121; see also Giddens, 1979, pp. 62–6). For Giddens, then, the idea of a structural relationship was inseparable from the process through which it was realized. An assumption of its existence was necessary for the very process of social interaction, while that assumption itself reconstituted the relationship. The parallels with our own work seemed close.

As already mentioned, the final chapter of our book reflects the then prevalent unease with any account of classroom interaction which remained embedded in the local context. We sought in the concept of 'structuration', as others have sought in 'coping strategies' (Hargreaves, 1978; Pollard, 1982) or 'frame' (Evans, 1982), a way of avoiding any separation of the 'structural' from the 'interactionist'. We felt that our analysis avoided the traditional distinction between macro- and micro- 'levels' of analysis by showing both the constitution of actors by society and the production and reproduction of society by actors. We now doubt that it does so much.

It is now apparent that in 1976 Giddens was hinting at something much broader and essentially much more interesting in this concept of structuration than we realized — though to be fair to ourselves the concept was not yet fully developed. Structuration is essentially an historical concept. Actors are seen as inserted into historically constructed situations and, while asserting that the production of society is brought about by the active constituting skills of its members, Giddens also suggests that they 'draw upon resources and depend upon conditions of which they are unaware or which they perceive only dimly' (Giddens, 1976, p. 157).

More recently Giddens has developed this further by distinguishing three different components of time, all of which should be involved in 'institutional studies' (Giddens, 1979, p. 110). The first is the temporality of immediate experience — the continuous flow of day-to-day life. This was something that we as ethnographers explicitly tried to capture in our description of classroom life. The second is the temporality of the life cycle of the organization; in our case, it was the Humanities Department at Abraham Moss Centre. This was something that we also attempted. By taking recordings of classroom language at selected points throughout a single year we were explicitly concerned with the sedimentation of meaning as classroom relationships developed. We were able to show how at the beginning of the year certain organizational and procedural knowledge was made explicit, only to become more implicit as the year progressed. We also demonstrated the cumulative nature of academic meanings, one topic in the curriculum building explicitly on the knowledge acquired in previous topics.

The third feature of temporality discussed by Giddens is the long-term sedimentation and development of social institutions. This was something that we did not address. We would now argue that the theoretical perspective we adopted did not make it possible to do so.

A number of ethnographers (Goodson, 1980; Woods, 1984) have recently been urging researchers to take seriously the personal biographies of their respondents. They argue the individuals' personal histories are of fundamental importance in understanding how they construct the world. This may indeed be true and it is something that we ourselves could have attempted with the group of teachers and pupils with whom we worked. Yet Giddens' notion of the long-term sedimentation of institutional life goes beyond personal history and for this reason fundamentally challenges much conventional widsom in educational ethnography.

To take the example of our own study, it is clear that the pupils were participating in a particular form of authority relationship which was pedagogically experimental and in which they were being given some slight control over the conditions of their learning. Yet it is equally clear that the pupils themselves were only dimly aware of how and why the conventional teacher-pupil relationship was being challenged, even though they were contributing routinely to the process of its reconstruction. A study which limited itself to re-searching pupils' consciousness would tell us comparatively little about that relationship. It would reveal only its surface form — its current realization.

What is true for the pupils is also true in part for the teachers. Their understanding of the educational process that they were daily involved in realizing was obviously fuller than their pupils, nevertheless we would argue that it was still ultimately bounded.

Resource-based learning as an educational ideology has its own history. Similar strands of thought can be traced back into the nineteenth century. Our group of teachers may or may not have been aware of this history. They were aware of some of the more explicit pronouncements of the headteacher elaborating and defending the school's educational ideology but they are likely to have been less clear on the complex way in which such an ideology became operationalized in the real world of schooling. In their transforma-tion from 'theoretical to practical forms of consciousness' (Giddens, 1979, p. 73) ideologies are subject to many changes. They may be subject to idiosyncratic interpretations — hence the need to take personal biographies seriously. They may also have to struggle with forces of equal strength. These forces might be quite explicitly enshrined in the law, such as the need for compulsory attendance (a notion that may at times fit uneasily with the objective of developing self-reliance and independence). Alternatively, the pressures may be more diffuse, such as parental concern over achievement in basic subjects such as English and mathematics. It is the way in which such conflicts are currently and historically have been resolved that underlies what is in effect 'realized' by teachers and pupils in their day-to-day interaction. Such compromises passed down through everyday practice are not always easily visible to either participants or researchers; their nature and consequences are something to be discovered.

It can therefore be argued that in our research, when we described the way in which teachers and pupils recreated their relationship through their day-to-day interaction, we were witnessing a process the implications of which not only they but also we were only partially aware of. We would however emphasize that this is not to discount teachers' and pupils' own reasons for their own actions. That would imply 'a derogation of the lay actor' (Giddens, 1979, p. 71). Rather it is to recognize that what an actor knows 'as a competent — but historically and spatially located — member of society "shades off" in contexts that stretch beyond those of his or her own day to day activity' (p. 73).

Although we very much applaud the way in which Giddens insists that the historical constitution of institutional relationships should be central to research, we do not as yet see in his work a clear methodology for achieving this. Certainly in his 'New Rules' his main methodological dictum of encouraging researchers to immerse themselves in a 'form of life' that can be comprehended as an 'ensemble of practices' is unlikely to take us very far. This is what we did, but at best that will only reveal the day-to-day life of the institution and some selected aspects of the life cycle. It will tell us nothing of the long-term sedimentation of social practice.

We would also argue that there are precious few clues to be found in any of the methodological textbooks on ethnography. These have almost universally been constructed within an interactionist framework (McCall and Simmons, 1969; Denzin, 1970; Atkinson, 1979).

Theoretically, interactionism's main concerns are with how actors make sense of their situation and with interpersonal relations as rooted and *comprehensible* in the spatial and temporal present. These distinctive features are clearly matched by two fundamental methodological axioms in participant observation work. The first is to describe the world as the participants see it, from which are derived notions of adequacy, reflexivity and so on. As is instanced in Mehan's work, the major criterion of external validity is still the ideal of presenting the researcher's account back to the researched. To be valid an account must have convergence with the experience of the researched. The second axiom is that qualitative evidence is more appropriate for theory generating than for theory testing; that is, 'the field itself' provides the resource for developing theory. It is from this axiom that the protocols of radical naivete, progressive focussing and the fetishism with grounded theory are derived. Having roughly followed both these axioms in our account of teaching, we are now more aware of their insufficiency. Despite some attempt to locate the teaching in its immediate social and organizational contexts, and a slight attempt in the final chapter to move 'out', we see the account as highly limited in scope. Given the methodological principles from which we worked, it was bound to be limited to the surface forms of structuration.

Methodologies are essentially theoretically informed techniques. Ethnography as conventionally portrayed is not a neutral technique but is one constructed to meet the canons of an interactionist theory. The implication of this is that in reconstructing fieldwork techniques the next steps are themselves theoretical. Only then can methodologies be constructed.

What is needed is a theory which identifies key 'sites' for research. One of the limitations of conventional participant observation texts is that the context for research is treated as theoretically unproblematic; almost any setting is considered valid for research. Yet the notion that institutional life is historically structured demands that research is not confined to a single 'site' such as a classroom. Other sites — historical and contemporary, economic and political — have a crucial significance for what is realized in that day-to-day classroom interaction that on the surface may seem so unproblematic.

References

ATKINSON, P. (1979) 'Research design in ethnography', in Open University Course DE 304 Block 3 *Research Design*, Milton Keynes, Open University Press.

BALL, S. (1980) 'Initial encounters in the classroom', in WOODS, P. (Ed.) *Pupil Strategies*, London, Croom Helm.

BALL, S. (1981) *Beachside Comprehensive*, London, Cambridge University Press.

BALL, S. (1984) 'Beachside reconsidered: Reflections on a methodological apprenticeship', in BURGESS, R.G. (Ed.) *The Research Process in Educational Settings: Ten Case Studies*, Lewes, Falmer Press.

BARNES, D. (1979) 'Communication and control', *English in Education*, 13, 3, pp, 66–9.

BARNES, D. and TODD, F. (1977) *Communication and Learning in Small Groups*, London, Routledge and Kegan Paul.

BARNES, D. and TODD, F. (1981) 'Talk in small learning groups: Analysis of strategies' in ADELMAN, C. (Ed.) *Uttering, Muttering*, London, Grant McIntyre.

BIRD, C. *et al.* (1981) *Disaffected Pupils*, Uxbridge, Brunel University Educational Studies Unit.

BURGESS, R.G. (Ed.) (1984) *The Research Process in Educational Settings: Ten Case Studies*, Lewes, Falmer Press.

CICOUREL, A. (1973) *Cognitive Sociology*, Harmondsworth, Penguin.

DENSCOMBE, M. (1980) 'Pupil strategies and the open classroom', in WOODS, P. (Ed.) *Pupil Strategies*, London, Croom Helm.

DENZIN, N.K. (1970) *The Research Act in Sociology*, London, Butterworth.

EDWARDS, A. (1980a) 'Patterns of power and authority in classroom talk', in WOODS, P. (Ed.) *Teacher Strategies*, London, Croom Helm.

EDWARDS, A. (1980b) 'Perspectives on classroom language', *Educational Analysis*, 2, 2, pp. 31–46.

EDWARDS, A. (1980c), 'Schooling and social change: Function, correspondence and cause', in BARTON, L. *et al.* (Eds) *Schooling, Ideology and Curriculum*, Lewes, Falmer Press.

EDWARDS, A. (1981) 'Analysing classroom talk', in FRENCH, P. and MACLURE, M. (Eds) *Adult-Child Conversation*, London, Croom Helm.

EDWARDS, A. (1982) 'Language difference and educational failure', *Language Arts*, 59, 5, pp. 513–19.

EDWARDS, A. and FURLONG, V.J. (1978) *The Language of Teaching*, London, Heinemann.

EVANS, J. (1982) *Teacher Strategies and Pupil Identities in Mixed-Ability Curricula: A Case Study*, unpublished PhD thesis, Chelsea College, University of London.

FRENCH, P. (1983) *Features of the Organisation of Teacher-Pupil Talk in the Classroom*, unpublished PhD thesis, University of Bristol.

FURLONG, V.J. (in press) *Pupil Culture: Ideological and Interactionist Approaches to Research*, Driffield, Nafferton Press.

GIDDENS, A. (1976) *New Rules of Sociological Method*, London, Hutchinson.

GIDDENS, A. (1979) *Central Problems in Social Theory*, London, Macmillan.

GOODSON, I. (1980) 'Life histories and the study of schooling', *Interchange*, 11, 4, pp. 62–76.

HAMMERSLEY, M. (1981) 'Putting competence into action: Some sociological notes on a model of classroom interaction', in FRENCH, P. and MACLURE, M. (Eds) *Adult-Child Conversation*, London, Croom Helm.

HARGREAVES, A. (1978) 'The significance of classroom coping strategies', in BARTON, L. and MEIGHAN, R. (Eds), *Sociological Interpretations of Schooling and Classrooms*, Driffield, Nafferton Books.

KING, R. (1984) 'The man in the wendy house: Research in infants' schools' in BURGESS, R.G. (Ed.) *The Research Process in Educational Settings: Ten Case Studies*, Lewes, Falmer Press.

McCALL, G.J. and SIMMONS, J.L. (Eds) (1969) *Issues in Participant Observation*, Reading, Mass., Addison-Wesley.

McHOUL, A. (1978) 'The organisation of turns at formal talk in the classroom', *Language in Society*, 7, pp. 183–213.

MEHAN, H. (1979) *Learning Lessons*, New York, Harvard University Press.

MERCER, N. and EDWARDS, D. (1981) 'Ground rules for mutual understanding: A social-psychological approach to classroom knowledge', in MERCER, N. (Ed.) *Language in School and Community*, London, Edward Arnold.

MITSON, R. (1980) 'Curriculum development and staff development at the Abraham Moss Centre', in EGGLESTON, J. (Ed.) *School-Based Curriculum Development in Britain*, London, Routledge and Kegan Paul.

PAYNE, G. and CUFF, E. (Eds) (1982) *Doing Teaching*, London, Batsford.

POLLARD, A. (1982) 'A model of classroom coping strategies', *British Journal of Sociology of Education*, 3, 1, pp. 19–38.

STUBBS, M. (1981) 'Scratching the surface: Linguistic data in educational research', in ADELMAN, C. (Ed.) *Uttering, Muttering*, London, Grant McIntyre.

WALKER, S. (1980) 'The Language of Teaching' (review) *British Journal of the Sociology of Education*, 1, 3, pp. 327–32.

WOODS, P. (1984) 'Teacher self and curriculum', in and GOODSON, I. and BALL, S. (Eds) *Defining the Curriculum: Histories and Ethnographies*, Lewes, Falmer Press.

2   Who Are You? Some Problems of Ethnographer Culture Shock

Clem Adelman

During the past five years Atkinson and Hammersley have thoroughly reviewed the literature on ethnographic fieldwork, drawing on such as Whyte (1955), Wolcott (1977; 1979), Erikson (1973), Smith (1980), Hymes (1976) and Burgess (1966) for their contributions to our understanding of the fieldwork experience in various settings. If there is anything of particular significance in our discussions, then it must be concerned with the nature of ethnographic fieldwork in *educational* settings, taking educational settings to be distinctive in their accommodation of concerns with curriculum, pedagogy and the particular forms of evaluation that are attendant on those first two concerns. If the study claims to be an ethnography, then it would include not only pupils and teachers, students and lecturers, consultants and housemen, but janitors, secretaries, teachers' aides and assistants, parents, governing bodies, administrators, careers counsellors, educational psychologists and so on. Wolcott's *'Teachers versus Technocrats'* is a fine example of the study of an educational setting by ethnographic means, although Wolcott does not claim that it is an ethnography.

Ethnographic methodologies are premised on the anthropological belief that all human beings share sufficient characteristics in common to begin to develop social relationships. Ethnographic researchers depend on being accepted by the community they wish to study. The ethnographic researcher tries to discover the range and variety of social and object relationships and the occasions of their manifestation and use, and the networks or relationships that are attendant on this shared knowledge. When teachers in schools ask the newly arrived ethnographer, 'Have you taught?' and 'Where do you work?', they are asking a stranger to give an account of his or her knowledge and practical experience of teaching and life in schools. Ethnographic studies within our own culture have to face difficulties of acceptance of the ethnographic researcher that arise from institutional status differences (higher education/school) and social class and regional antagonisms.

I see two major issues enmeshed here. One is concerned with the grounds upon which those using ethnographic methods make claims to enhance understanding of the social world; the other is concerned with the purpose of and the audience for educational research (the inevitable 'real-politik').

Participants observation is a, if not the, key *role* of ethnographic fieldwork. Through gaining entry and developing rapport, participant observation becomes possible. Reciprocity (Wax, 1952) and cultural responsiveness are the essential bases of participant observation, which may allow the researcher insight and greater understanding of the networks of meaning and the significance of social actions for those being studied. Yet the ethnographic researcher's aspirations to give accounts of the 'actors' ' emic are fraught with difficulties. The prolonged debate over the extent to which ethnographic research can provide accurate accounts of the emic flared up again in the anthropological literature after Goodenough's (1957) statement that the acid test of an ethnographer's claim to know the natives' rules of the culture would be whether the ethnographer could act in ways that would be acceptable within the culture of the natives. The debate settled around whether it was possible to know and to act out all the rules of 'natives' that would enable the ethnographic researcher to be acceptable as a competent member of the *ethos* (Harris, 1974; Keesing, 1973; Moerman, 1972).

This concern with 'folk' models versus analytic models had consanguine developments in ethnomethodology, cognitive psychology and sociolinguistics. I take it that a footnote in Garfinkel (1967), which lists the participants at a conference in California in 1954, marks the onset of these debates which, to a large extent, ended in the late 1970s. Agar (1982) suggests that the different problems emerging out of this debate have been claimed by the new academic collectivities of cognitive psychology, artificial intelligence and discourse analysis.

I became immersed in the issues raised by these debates and applied the techniques derived from ethno-semantics to derive and test an interrelated lexis that teachers on the Ford Teaching Project used to describe their pedagogy. During the same project, I also applied, I believe for the first time (Adelman, 1972), the recommendations that Cicourel, and others, had made to conduct triangulation in order to illustrate the intersubjective meanings of the actors in relation to the interpretations of the researcher. Two of these triangulations are discussed in Adelman (1981). Through eliciting the interpretations of the pupils, using audio-visual recorders as in common reference, it is possible in this second-order interpretation to resuscitate the moments in the communication which have led to misunderstandings. These misunderstandings often derive from a lack of sharing of a frame of reference common to pupil and teacher. In this sense I was trying to satisfy the requirements of the 'interpretive paradigm' and did, contrary to Karabel and Halsey's (1977) claim, 'consider as problematic the knowledge that is made available in such (classroom) interactions' (Young, 1971).

I do not think that it is possible to penetrate and provide full, accurate accounts of the 'social construction of reality', whether ethnocience methods are used or not. Whatever the depth of detail and cross-checking for accuracy one makes with individuals, educational settings comprise to a greater or lesser extent diversity and heterogeneity of 'reality constructions'. How to deal fairly with this diversity and heterogeneity has been a major concern of some researchers who use ethnographic methods.

But having tried to represent the meaningfulness of 'actors' involved in educational settings and having questioned my own interpretations and values, I had reason to worry whether this was sufficient to be applicable for the purposes of the improvement of educational practice. The opportunity to test the applicability of these ethnographically derived notions was available during the Ford Teaching Project as the teachers were able to develop ways of monitoring and theorizing about their own practice. About one-third of the teachers were able to sustain monitoring of particular issues within their own classrooms, draw upon the language of description and to theorize about their own attempts to change aspects of their practice. Indeed, such attempts to enter the networks and meaning of the others are 'time consuming and expensive' (Delamont, 1978). Does participant observation have integrity if only the researcher's immaculate conceptions dominate the pages of the report or thesis?

What is the purpose and who is the audience for ethnographic study, are the crucial questions. In short, on whose behalf is the ethnographer working? These concerns would not affect the methods — participant observation, interview, and so on — but could well affect the topics covered, the right of those reported to negotiate, to comment critically on accuracy, coverage and fairness of draft reports. These rights of 'subjects' to comment on and criticize the reports of enquiries run counter to the view that it is this 'perspective of sociologists as outsiders reflecting upon the categories of insiders which provides our unique contribution ... the categories employed by the native are important but as data, not as theoretical or analytical tools' (Deutscher, 1969).

I would argue that 'actor' or 'native' categories, considered in isolation from other categories and in isolation from their context of use, are liable to be interpreted as 'mere' descriptors used by that culture. But if the ethnographic researcher takes the trouble and care to theorize through trying to interrelate many 'native' categories, taking into account their context of use, then what emerges may be nearer to 'native' theory of his or her culture than to mainly academic theory. Which of these two epistemological paths to follow depends on whether the researcher's priority is to enhance others' understanding of the culture so that they could in part fulfil, at least through their imagination, Goodenough's (*op. cit.*) dictum, as Douglas (1973) illustrates so well.

The other priority of this dichotomy is to contribute to the literature of the academic community. Few studies attempt, or manage, to meet both aspirations.

Even symbolic interactionists would not accept 'actors' ' criticisms and comments as grounds for modifying their constructions of reality. For instance, Denzin (1978) wrote: 'Many sociologists now call for a more active involvement in the world of social problems. Such a stance, I contend, demands a reconception of the sociologist's role — a reconception that I reject. It demands a more active involvement in the political as opposed to the scientific aspects of sociology. It calls for a professional as opposed to a scientific conception of sociology as an enterprise. In my judgment the efforts of applied sociologists to treat social problems have been relatively fruitless. Neither a betterment of social conditions nor the improvement of sociological perspectives has been forthcoming. The proper perspective — and this, of course, is a value commitment on my part — is a dedication to sociology for its own sake.' Coleman (1979) offers a contrary view in admitting to the naivety of social science in its own relations to the society in which it is located.

> The rapid growth of social policy research and its increasing importance for social policy have begun in recent years to push social scientists and social philosophers toward what both the classical and the modern theorists have neglected: the development of a theory of purposive or directed social change. One major aspect of such theory, at the more

macrosociological level, must be, in effect, political theory: the way in which diverse interested parties not all sufficiently well organised to initiate research, can nevertheless obtain feedback to inform their decisions and thus their politically relevant actions. Another aspect must concern the relation between authority and research-generated information. Under what conditions does that information strengthen authority, and under what conditions does it strengthen opposing interests? In addition to these political or macrosociological questions, there is a microsociological theory of social policy research to be developed as well. How does the position of the investigator affect the initiation and utilization of the research? How do the differences between the world of the discipline and the world of action affect the execution of the research? How does the social structure within which the policy decision is to be made, (e.g. centralised decision versus dispersed decision) affect the utilisation of the research?

It can be expected, as the quality of social policy research expands and as its impact on social policy increases, that such theory, nearly absent in sociology until now, will develop with some rapidity. And because of its intimate relation to political theory, it is likely to have impact on the way social policy research is institutionalised in society.

The view that Denzin expresses, that social science should stay away from the political, is particularly naive when the educational institutions and programmes that embody change and innovation inevitably entangle the ethnographic researcher in their webs of affiliation. But the willingness to engage in participant observation in the institutions of one's own culture is fraught with the real-politik of possible choices between co-option and independence, maintaining or breaking confidentiality and whether data is jointly owned by the researcher and the 'actors' (as if the ethnographic researcher were not an 'actor'). Amongst the researchers who have confronted these issues are social policy analysts, Rein (1976) and Wildavsky (1972; 1979), social anthropologists, Barnes (1979), psychologists, Bruner (1980) and Smith (1980), and educational evaluators, McDonald (1977; 1980; 1981; 1982) and House (1973; 1980).

These researchers, who work in the dark and difficult region between 'what is' and the decision-makers' 'what ought to be' have faced and written about in methodological and theorized terms confidentiality, the ownership of data, the notion of the nature of independent research, the rights of the subjects to judgments that involve the attributes of fairness, coverage and accuracy. Related to all these has been the development of procedures and principles for negotiation of data with the various interested parties. Becker's (1970) retort, 'how would you study a corrupt police department using these methods?', has partly been demonstrated by Graef's documentary film, *Police* (1982). In the attempt to apply these principles and procedures, an extensive literature has become available to sociologists and anthropologists who study educational settings but they seem not to have taken this literature into account in their work. What has been acceptable within this 'corpus' has been the work that most closely feeds the paradigms of anthropological and sociological work. For me, a major criterion of whether this work is educational would be whether it tries to illuminate educational practices and provide information for the wide range of people who would make practical decisions which would lead to adjustment or change and, hopefully, improvement. I would take the side of Schensul (1980) and, like him, might be accused of being atheoretical. But whose theory? I would contend that the majority of ethnographic researchers who have worked in educational settings have done so as sociologists, endeavouring to test a priori hypothetical constructs in particular cases rather than engage in negotiation with the subjects to arrive at ways of dealing with 'conflicting accounts'. For all the literature on social change and the construction of reality, most sociologists avoid such entanglements with the 'actors'. This contrasts markedly with the work of Schensul (1980), Peattie (1958), Smith (1980), Wolcott (1977), McDonald (1977, 1980, 1981, 1982), and Simons (1980).

Most UK sociological studies of educational settings using ethnographic methods have been conducted in circumstances of continuity and stability. Of course, there are discrepant points of view and interpretations within these settings but they are not fraught with the problems of innovation, threat of closure and demand for evaluation. In short, there may be the everyday institutional politics for the 'actors' and the ethnographic researcher to contend with, but these do not represent instabilities. Not only have most of the studies been of continuity where, through recurrences and regularities and patterns, the normative may be adduced over the 18 months–8 years of such studies, but the ethnographers concerned have, for the most part, studied only one set of 'actors' and so are able only to make comparisons with each other's accounts or other literature.

Fieldwork, whatever the circumstances, is time and energy consuming. Those whose purpose is primarily to complete academic degrees avoid disorder, relatively inflexible deadlines for reports and the hassles of negotiating with a wide range of audiences. When I hear accounts of ethnographic studies of educational settings, I want to know how the looking, asking, recording, reflecting, comparing and reporting have been carried out. I am not particularly concerned with the a priori theoretical firmament to which the study might contribute, but I am concerned about the ways in which ethnographers treat their informants, the institutions and, by reciprocity, the way in which the informants act as ethnographers. As Hymes (1976) puts it, 'ethnography is a way of discovering what is the case, an essential way, and social programmes [concerned with education for the purposes of this paper] that ignore it are blind; but ethnography that ignores values and goals is sterile.'

The cultural immersion that participant observers write and speak about can develop only if the researcher is accepted by the communities as a 'competent member'. I have already referred to this competence as being a knowledge of and action which complies with 'rules of the culture', and have also mentioned that this is inadequate. However, it raises a dilemma for the participant observer; to test their knowledge of others' culture, they have to try to act as a 'member'. Stoddart (1974), Keiser (1970) and others have given accounts of how these attempts have badly misfired, even though 'rapport' has been established. There are problems 'even' with entry to schools, particularly now that the context includes closures, redundancy, demands for public accountability and a well-founded suspicion of the educational researcher.

The presentation of self by aspiring ethnographers to members of the community that they wish to study may lead to access and to the development of rapport. However, the many instances of rejection of researchers (using this as a generic term to cover ethnographers, action researchers, curriculum developers) are rarely reported. Where the university researcher requests permission of the Chief Education Officer to study schools in a county, and gains permission, the schools have to (at least) tolerate the presence of the researcher. Acceptance — the beginning of participant observation — may develop if this essential precondition of ethnography is fulfilled through cultural reciprocity, itself dependent on the personal qualities of the ethnographic researcher.

But the real social identity of the ethnographic researcher has to be known to people with whom that researcher has engaged in the collaboration. Deception — pretending to be in another role — is one cause of the 'dissonance' that participant observers frequently report.

Such 'dissonance' is difficult to sustain over time. Gans (1968) gives an example of the ethnographic researcher succumbing to the temptation to declare whose side one is on.

> The participant observer is also driven toward involvement by participating in situations in which his values are being questioned or attacked. As Mrs Bohannon explains, one cannot really shed one's own values even in an African tribe and an action based on opposing values evokes, at the minimum, an internal reaction in the field worker. When one studies people in one's own country, this happens more often. I had no trouble remaining uninvolved in local zoning disputes in Levittown, but when people talked disparagingly about racial integration or when they resorted to anti-intellectualism, I became involved, and the urge to argue became strong. Sometimes, this urge can lead to open involvement. When I first came to Levittown, its government was still run by old residents who were all conservative Republicans (the township in which Levittown was built had never elected a Democrat in its almost 200 years of existence), and, although I was not aware of it, listening to their attacks on liberal and radical ideas had evidently upset me considerably. After three months of field work among them, I ran into four men who were about to form a Democratic club, and, as an independent who often votes for Democrats, I was so pleased that I impulsively said so, and even offered to do what I could to help. Ten minutes later, the possible consequences of my remarks suddenly dawned on me; if people found out I was a Democrat, my future chance of obtaining data from Republicans was nil. I rushed back to the club founders, withdrew my offer, and made them promise never to mention what I had said to them. (As far as I could tell, they never did, and my own political position remained a secret in Levittown.) Most often, one can keep one's cool enough to offer foolishly to participate, but the urge to argue remains, and must be suppressed constantly, except when it is used as an interviewing method.

I can attest to this temptation and to the alienation that long-term participant observation produces in the ethnographic researcher (Adelman, 1980). Fletcher, having a strong sense of the inadequacies of distanced fieldwork in fulfilling the sociological tradition, decided to engage in collaborative research from the beginning of the

Sutton-in-Ashfield five-year study (Fletcher and Adelman, 1981). Having gained entry and succumbed, maybe more than once, to the temptations that Gans (1968) illustrates, there is still the question of the extent to which the ethnographic researcher has adequately 'penetrated' the 'actor's' world to provide an account of their cultural knowledge, and their semantic nets.

When ethnographic researchers take it for granted that probationary teachers as part of the community of a school are reliable informants, as with Sharp and Green (1975), or when as with *The Glasgow Gang Observed* (Patrick, 1973) the participant observer tells us of how he displayed revulsion at some of the gang's activities, the protestations of insight through participant observation ring hollow. As a human being, my sympathies are not with the tale told by the ethnographer but with the community that is being misrepresented by those who are in privileged positions with greater access to the means of publishing. Such participant observation is inspired more by *Cooling out the Mark* than by *Street Corner Society*.

Erikson (1973) maintains that the ethnographer 'must not suppress a *sense* of outrage whilst in the field', but stay and take advantage of one's rage, using it as a barometer to engage high salience. Those aspects of culture which are simply intolerable are probably the key to the difference between that culture and one's own. The method is not that of 'objectivity' but of 'disciplined subjectivity'.

I cannot find justification for deceit — what some people call 'passing' (Ditton, 1977; Patrick, 1973). Where is the reflexive sense in this sort of work? Bulmer's (1982) collection contains extensive discussion of the ethics of covert participant observation. Let me be excused a moral outcry here. To the fair comment that sociologists and, I would say, ethnographic researchers have gone to the easy game of studying the poor and the powerless rather than the rich and the powerful, the covert participant observers have, for the most part, added to that infamy by deceit to further their own personal ends. Bulmer (*op. cit.*) quotes Erikson (1967) on the consequences.

> Research of this sort is liable to damage the reputation of sociology in the larger society and close off promising areas of research for future investigators.... We are increasingly reaching audiences whose confidence we cannot afford to jeopardise, and we have every right to be afraid that such people may close their doors to sociological research if they learn to become too suspicious of our methods and

intentions.... Any research tactic which attracts unfavour-
able notice may help to diminish the general climate of trust
toward sociology in the community as a whole. (Erikson,
1967, p. 369)

A story about the PhD student, quoted in Spindler (1970), encapsu-
lates some of the inadequacies and pitfalls of 'passing'. The student
had gained access and was passing as a member of a street gang. Data
collection augured well for an early completion of the thesis. The
participant observer was present at a meeting of the gang when it was
making plans to conduct a large-scale robbery. The participant
observer became alarmed when he realized the plan was sure to fail
and some of his subjects would surely be arrested thus causing
disruption to his study. His anxiety prompted him to suggest an
alternative plan which turned out to be successful. On reassembling
to take stock of spoils, the gang decided unanimously to hand over
the leadership to the PhD student. At this point the student had to
decide whether such further collaboration was within the traditions
of ethnography. He sought his superior's advice and, sad to tell, was
unable to complete the fieldwork for his thesis.

The maintenance of reciprocity is a form of barter, there being,
at least initially, no common currency. The 'actor' gives what the
ethnographic researcher has not. The ethnographic researcher ack-
nowledges the trade and will, in the course of participant observation,
help out when requested or even, as with Lacey (1970), Hargreaves
(1967) and Ball (1981), present an offering by teaching classes within
the school. The answers to the questions, 'Who are you?' and 'What
are you doing here?' become more complicated, as Gans (1968)
illustrates when immediate local issues are present in the setting.
However, it is when there is some threat to continuity, to status, to
cherished plans, that those two questions become red hot. For
instance, in a study of bilingual schooling in Boston, one of the
teachers with strong pressure-group and political connections outside
the school, asked to see the researcher's notes. This request was
willingly complied with in accordance with the principle that the data
belong jointly to the researchers and the people cited in the report.
The teacher received a written report that evening, and the morning
after expressed her concern that this seemed to misrepresent her
purpose and pedagogy. 'Such reports would play into the hands of
the antagonists should they ever become public', she said. Like the
rest of the members of the school, she knew that one of our research
colleagues was interviewing both protagonists and antagonists, politi-

cians and administrators in the state and that the study would eventually be made public. She wanted to know who our colleague had been interviewing, who were the others on the schedule and, with understandable concern for the future of the school, alerted other teachers within the school to be suspect of our presence there. We had professed that we were to study the classrooms, the curriculum and the organization of the school and its links with the community. We had answered the questions 'Who are you?' and 'What are you doing here?' adequately for the initial entry, but our connection with the external colleague and the boundaries he was exploring raised those same questions again, but this time not from the inside but vice versa.

In summary, there are three points I wish to emphasize. First, I have suggested that ethnographic methods embody an ethic. The integrity of ethnographic methods is put under severe strain when research is conducted in a politicized context. Secondly, I have indicated that researchers from diverse backgrounds, such as anthropology (Schensul, Peattie, Wolcott), cognitive psychology (Bruner), learning theory (Smith), sociology (Fletcher) and curriculum and policy evaluation (McDonald, Simons), share similar views about the ownership of data and negotiation. Thirdly, I have argued that the majority of studies of educational settings in Great Britain have not been for the purpose of contributing to an enhanced understanding of educational practice but to fit the abstractions of academia, particularly those of symbolic interactionist and functionalist sociology. Attempts to develop an ethic and methodology for systematic enquiry that allows participation or even collaboration with the 'natives' have yet to appeal to those who can make do with analytic knowledge alone. Negotiation with significant others outside academia sharpens the sense of contradiction between the ideal and the actual.

References

ADELMAN, C. (1972) *Recordings and Interpretations*, Ford Teaching Project, CARE, University of East Anglia, mimeo.
ADELMAN, C. (1980) 'Some dilemmas of institutional evaluation and their relationship to preconditions and procedures', *Studies in Educational Evaluation*, Vol. 6, pp. 165–83.
ADELMAN, C. (Ed.) (1981) *Uttering, Muttering*, London, Grant McIntyre.
AGAR, M.H. (1982) 'Whatever happened to cognitive anthropology: A partial review', *Human Organisation*, 41, 1, pp. 82–6.

Clem Adelman

BALL, S. (1981) *Beachside Comprehensive: A Case Study of Secondary Schooling*, Cambridge, Cambridge University Press.

BARNES, J.A. (1979) *Who Should Know What? Social Science, Privacy and Ethics*, Harmondsworth, Penguin.

BECKER, H.S. (1970) *Sociological Work: Method and Substance*, Chicago, Aldine.

BRUNER, J. (1980) *Under Five in Britain*, London, Grant McIntyre.

BULMER, M. (Ed.) (1982) *Social Research Ethics*, London, Macmillan Press.

BURGESS, E. (1966) 'Discussion', in SHAW, C. *The Jack Roller*, Chicago, University of Chicago Press.

COLEMAN, J. (1979) 'Sociological analysis and social policy', in BOTTOMORE, T. and NISBET, R. (Eds) *A History of Sociological Analysis*, London, Heinemann.

DELAMONT, S. (1978) 'Sociology and the classroom', in BARTON, L. and MEIGHAN, R. (Eds) *Sociological Interpretations of Schooling and Classrooms: A Re-appraisal*, Driffield, Nafferton Books.

DENZIN, N.K. (1978) *The Research Act. A Theoretical Introduction to Sociological Methods*, (2nd ed), New York, McGraw Hill.

DEUTSCHER, I. (1969) 'Language methodology and the sociologist', *Sociological Focus*, 3, 1, .

DITTON, J. (1977) *Part-Time Crime: An Ethnography of Fiddling and Pilferage*, London, Macmillan.

DOUGLAS, M. (1973) *Rules and Meanings*, Harmondsworth, Penguin.

ERIKSON, F. (1973) 'What makes school ethnography "ethnographic"?' *Council on Anthropology and Education Newsletter*, 4, 2, .

ERIKSON, K.T. (1967) 'A comment on disguised observation in sociology', *Social Problems*, Vol. 14, pp. 366–73.

FLETCHER, C. and ADELMAN, C. (1981) 'Collaboration as a research process', *Journal of Community Education*, Vol. 1, pp. 15–24.

GANS, H.J. (1968) 'The participant-observer as a human being: Observations on the personal aspects of fieldwork', in BECKER, H.S. *et al.* (Eds) *Institutions and the Person*, Chicago, Aldine.

GARFINKEL, H. (1967) *Studies in Ethnomethodology*, Englewood Cliffs, N.J., Prentice-Hall.

GOODENOUGH, W.H. (1957) 'Cultural anthropology and linguistics', Georgetown University Monograph Series on Language and Linguistics No. 9, in GERUN, P. (Ed.) Washington, reprinted in HYMES, D. (Ed.) *Language in Culture and Society*, New York, Harper and Row.

HARGREAVES, D.H. (1967) *Social Relations in a Secondary School*, London, Routledge and Kegan Paul.

HARRIS, M. (1974) 'Why a perfect knowledge of all the rules one must know to act like a native cannot lead to the knowledge of how natives act', *Journal of Anthropological Research*, Vol. 30, pp. 242–51.

HOUSE, E. (1973) *School Evaluation: The Politics and Process*, California, McCutchan Publishing.

HOUSE, E.R. (1980) *Evaluating with Validity*, Beverley Hills, Calif., Sage.

HYMES, D. (1976) *Ethnographic Monitoring*, prepared for the symposium 'Language Development in Bilingual Setting' (March 19–21), sponsored by the Multi-lingual/Multicultural Materials Development Center, California State Polytechnic University, Pamona, California.

KARABEL, J. and HALSEY, A.H. (Eds) (1977) *Power and Ideology in Education*, New York, Oxford University Press.

KEESING, R.M. (1973) 'Paradigms lost: The new ethnography and the new linguistics', *South Western Journal of Anthropology*,

KEISER, R.L. (1970) 'Fieldwork among the vice lords of Chicago', in SPINDLER, G. (Ed.) *Being an Anthropologist*, New York, Holt, Rinehart and Winston.

LACEY, C. (1970) *Hightown Grammar: The School as a Social System*, Manchester, Manchester University Press.

McDONALD, B. (1977) 'The portrayal of persons as evaluation data', in NORRIS, N. (Ed.) *Theory in Practice*, CARE Occasional Publication No. 4, University of East Anglia.

McDONALD, B. (1980) 'Letters from a headmaster', in SIMONS, H. (Ed.), *Towards a Science of the Singular*, CARE Occasional Publication No. 10, University of East Anglia.

McDONALD, B. (1981) *Mandarins and Lemons — Executive Investment in Program Evaluation*, paper presented to the American Educational Research Association, Los Angeles, April, in a symposium entitled 'Case Study in Policy Evaluation: Paradoxes of Popularity'.

McDONALD, B. and SANGER, J. (1982) *Just for the Record? Notes towards a Theory of Interviewing in Evaluation*, paper presented to the Annual Meeting of the American Educational Research Association (19–23 March), New York, in a symposium entitled 'Evaluation Methodology'.

MOERMAN, M. (1972) 'Analysis of Lue conversation: Providing accounts, finding breaches and taking sides', in SUDNOW, D. (Ed.) *Studies in Social Interaction*, New York, Free Press.

PATRICK, J. (1973) *A Glasgow Gang Observed*, London, Eyre Methuen.

PEATTIE, L.R. (1958) 'Interventions and applied science in anthropology', *Human Organization*, Vol. 17, pp. 4–8.

REIN, M. (1976) *Social Science and Public Policy*, Harmondsworth, Penguin.

SCHENSUL, S.L. (1980) 'Anthropological fieldwork and sociopolitical change', *Social Problems*, 27, 3, pp. 309–19.

SHARP, R. and GREEN, A. (1975) *Education and Social Control: A Study in Progressive Primary Education*, London, Routledge and Kegan Paul.

SIMONS, H. (Ed.) (1980) *Towards a Science of the Singular*, CARE Occasional Publication No. 10, University of East Anglia.

SMITH, L. (1980) 'Some not so random thoughts on doing fieldwork: The interplay of values', in SIMONS, H. (Ed.) *Towards a Science of the Singular*, CARE Occasional Publication No. 10, University of East Anglia.

SPINDLER, G.D. (Ed.) (1970) *Being an Anthropologist*, New York, Holt, Rinehart and Winston.

STODDART, K. (1974) 'Pinched: Notes on the ethnographer's location of argot', in TURNER, R. (Ed.) *Ethnomethodology*, Harmondsworth, Penguin.

WAX, R.H. (1952) 'Field methods and techniques: Reciprosity as a field technique, *Human Organization*, Vol. II, Fall. pp. 34–41.

WHYTE, W.F. (1955) *Street Corner Society*, (2nd ed.), Chicago, University of Chicago Press.

WHYTE, W.F. and HAMILTON, E. (1975) *Action Research for Management*, Illinois, Irwin Dorsey.

WILDAVSKY, A. (1972) 'The self-evaluating organisation', *Public Administration Review*, September/October.

WILDAVSKY, A. (1979) *Speaking Truth to Power: The Art and Craft of Policy Analysis*, Boston, Mass., Little, Brown and Co.

WOLCOTT, H.F. (1977) *Teachers versus Technocrats: An Educational Innovation in Anthropological Perspective*, Center for Educational Policy and Management, University of Oregon.

WOLCOTT, H.F. (1979) *Mirrors, Models and Monitors: Educator Adaptions of the Ethnographic Innovation*, University of Oregon.

YOUNG, M.F.D. (Ed.) (1971) *Knowledge and Control: New Directions for the Sociology of Education*, London, Macmillan.

3 Ethnography and Theory Construction in Educational Research

Peter Woods

There is now quite a large literature on data analysis in ethnography within which the views of Glaser and Strauss (1967) have been very influential. The main emphasis is on discovery rather than testing of theory, but analysis is sequential — it is both guided by and guides data collection. Categories and their properties are noted and 'saturated'. Concepts emerge from the field, are checked and re-checked against further data, compared with other material, strengthened or perhaps re-formulated. Models of systems are built up in the process of research, and gradually a theory comes into being with its distinctive characteristic of explanation and prediction linking the revealed concepts into an integrated framework, the operationalization of which has been demonstrated. Its plausibility may be strengthened by further case studies in the same area, though it may be continuously refined since it must accommodate all data, and not simply answer to a 'majority of cases'. Later the level of abstraction might be raised by this 'substantive' theory becoming 'formal' theory, as case studies from other substantive areas are compared and examined for common elements.

However, this general formula is not without difficulties (particularly in the development of formal from substantive theory), and I would contend that the drift of ethnographic studies in education in Britain over the last decade has actually gone against the realization of its promise in the area of theory. I am not alone in this, and others have given their diagnosis and offered remedies. A. Hargreaves (1980) has called for a greater synthesis of approaches, Hammersley (1980) for teamwork, Delamont (1981) for more comparative work, D. Hargreaves (1981) for a more conscious application to existing theory. I do not disagree with any of these suggestions, but I wish to add to some of the points they raise and to make a different point of emphasis. Theory does not simply 'emerge' or 'come into being'.

Though it has been argued that it is grounded in the facts of the situation, it is not immediately *revealed*. However detailed and perspicacious the observations, at some stage there must be a 'leap of the imagination' (Ford, 1975) as the researcher conceptualizes from raw field notes. This, just as much as later stages of theorizing, requires certain attitudes and qualities of creativity. I want to suggest that creative powers may have been subdued by developments in the area of data analysis, and that they are due for revitalizing. I should make clear that while I speak of a community, I am taking myself and my own work as my main example. It is, I believe, not untypical. I want first to offer my diagnosis, and then to make some suggestions about how theory might be developed. In a peculiar way, some of the methodological recommendations of the classic ethnographers run against the creative grain, and I want also to examine how this has come about.

Theoretical Limitations of Ethnography

Grounded theorizing poses considerable inherent difficulties. It is perhaps no coincidence that some of the more ambitious theoretical formulations (in the sense of coordinating concepts and linking conceptual spheres, particularly between micro- and macro-areas), like those of Sharp and Green (1975), Willis (1977), and Anyon (1981), have been constructed either before or after the researchers have left the field; nor is it any surprise that these have met with considerable criticism from mainstream ethnographers for 'distance' between theory and data, so that from the point of view of 'grounding' this kind of theory is, in fact, considered weak (D. Hargreaves, 1978; Hammersley, 1977; A. Hargreaves, 1982). The fact is that while much in ethnography has had a liberating effect, other aspects have imposed a certain restrictiveness. This, I would argue, is due to three related factors:

1 the nature of ethnography;
2 trends in educational research;
3 the desire to make ethnography a more rigorous scientific study.

The Nature of Ethnography

Ethnography by definition is descriptive. In anthropology it means, literally, 'a picture of the way of life of some interacting human group' (Wolcott, 1975, p. 112). In sociological ethnography in particular great attention is often devoted to the intricate detail of the picture, and the ethnographer, like the artist, works with great care at capturing both the general and essential characteristics, and the myriad finer points which underpin them. The artist, however, has more freedom of interpretation. Faithfulness to a culture as it is found is one of the guiding principles of ethnography, and immersion in the culture under study the general strategy towards this end. However, while it may aid descriptive finesse, it may also block theory construction. As Sjoberg and Nett (1968, p. 72) argue, 'a researcher must often be able to remove himself intellectually and emotionally from the immediate social situation, to step back and examine his activities in broader perspective.' But immersion and retraction do not go well together. A typical fear of the sceptics of ethnography, therefore, is that they 'might be left with endless description and a sequence of plausible stories' (Eldridge, 1980, p. 131). They might also be quite unrelated to each other, for it was feared that as the common criticism of the Chicago school goes, they 'so stressed the uniqueness of their subjects' worlds, they could not articulate the linkages and interdependencies of these groups and the larger social system' (Brown, 1977, p. 63).

There is the oft-quoted Howard Becker remark to a student who asked his opinion of how to choose a theoretical framework: 'What do you want to worry about that for you just go out there and do it' (Atkinson, 1977, p. 32), often taken (incorrectly) to imply a devaluing of theory. The student might also have been given Denzin's warning that 'if sociologists forget that the major goal of their discipline is the development of theory, a process of goal displacement can occur such that operational definitions and empirical observations become ends in themselves' (1978, p. 58). The problem becomes not how we can explain what is happening, but how we can describe what is happening. The researcher's inventive powers are thus directed towards representation.

Another trend which has tended to militate against theory has been the extent of concentration on the construction of meaning of interactants. It was felt that sociologists were running much too free with their second-order constructs, while the views of people in the real world on their own actions and thoughts were being disregarded. But a concomitant of 'bringing people back in', a highly laudable aim, was to crowd out analysis with a torrent of first-order constructs. As Eldridge (1980, p. 130) argues, 'Having brought people back in, perhaps the sociologist, a privileged observer, commentator *and* theorist should be brought back in as well.' Moreover it tends to become a representation of a culture as a snapshot, a picture frozen in time. This immediately compromises the main aim and offends, for interactionists, the basic principle of 'process and flux'. However conscious of past and future the ethnographer may be, consideration of those must always be of a different order to that of the present period of data collection. The fact is, however, that few ethnographic studies (my own included) have taken past and future into consideration to any extent. We have looked at situations as we have found them, and have become so 'immersed' that we have spent much of our time documenting and classifying. The problems of the moment consume much of our time, effort and ingenuity. We hear frequent references to 'muddling through'. Indeed, this is the preferred mode. Wolcott (1975, p. 113), for example, thinks ethnography best served when the researcher feels free to 'muddle about' in the field setting. Our attention is drawn to the precariousness of the situation (Burgess, 1984), to the enormous logistic demands (rushing off to the loo to make field notes) and to severe ethical questions. These problems are always present for any ethnographer. The development of a more sophisticated methodology provides comfort but does little to remove them. Ethnography, too, is a highly personal affair. A community of ethnographers is a community of individuals, far more so than any other group of researchers within sociology. This is, in part, a product of the belief that all situations are unique, and that consequently, in a sense, the research worker makes a unique study with individualized adaptable methodology. In part, it is a product of the unavoidable conditions of research work, which involve individuals investing a great deal of time in a single organization. The ethnographer, as his/her own major research tool, emerges imprinted in part with the peculiarities of his/her own private negotiation with one particular organization.

Apart from being inherently an individualized approach, the history of the current ethnographic trend in Britain has not yet allowed for much collective appraisal. Ethnographic studies have mostly been produced by individuals persuaded by the interpretive approaches that were coming back into favour in the early 1970s. Research followed from the conceptual persuasion, and we struggled through as best we could. There were no coordinated efforts (apart from the Manchester-based studies of the 1960s — D. Hargreaves, 1967; Lacey, 1970; Lambart, 1976). What we have, therefore, is a number of localized case studies, with their own points of reference, which here and there happen to touch on common concerns, but which for the main part are heavily introspective. This is not peculiar to educational ethnography (Payne *et al.*, 1981, p. 114). Though this may have been unavoidable to date, in the long run it is not conducive to the generation of theory.

Trends in Educational Research

The requirements of *educational* research have also put a premium on description. Early sociologists of education in Britain in the 1950s and early 1960s showed an almost exclusive concern with input/ output factors, and used quantitative survey techniques. Since the 1970s the 'black box' (Lacey, 1976) of the school has been opened up, and ethnographers have been celebrating the find ever since. There have been so many fascinating areas to investigate. Armed at last with an appropriate method, we have sailed into the innermost recesses of the school to try to uncover its secrets. We might characterize ethnographic work in schools over the last decade as a 'charting' or 'mapping' of areas of social life within the school. This has been an essential task, and I do not wish to underrate it. We can justly claim that our understanding of school life and of institutions in general has improved, that we have demonstrated a more adequate 'sociology of the school' than has heretofore appeared, and that much of what has been produced has been of practical value to the teacher (Woods, 1983). Not everybody would agree with this. McNamara (1980), for example, has accused ethnographers who have been working in schools of being 'arrogant outsiders', unappreciative of the problems faced by teachers in their work. And it certainly appears that ethnographic research as yet has made little impact on teacher action, school structure or curriculum. But it has also made little impact on sociological theory, and from that side of the fence it has been argued that educational ethnography has produced a picture that is 'all too familiar' (Delamont, 1981). There is a danger, therefore, that educational ethnography might fall between two stools: practice and policy on the one hand, and sociological theory on the other.

I prefer to regard what has been done so far as phase 1 of the overall enterprise. There has been some theoretical development, notably in the areas of teacher socialization, culture and strategies, but overall the conceptual level has remained close to the data. In a sense, the data have outrun the theory — in some cases categories have continued to be discovered and few have reached saturation point, while in others categories have 'flooded over' (e.g., negotiation

— which I discuss later) (the reverse of work, for example, at the CCCS, where theory tends to outrun data — see Cohen, 1981).

My claim, therefore, is that ethnographers have, for the most part, been riveted to a descriptive approach, because on the one hand of their attention to fine-grained detail, and on the other of the size and complexity of the substantive area confronting them, and the pressures to 'cover' the ground of a new area. There have been easy riches for the picking, and armchair theorizing has been left to other approaches which value empirical work less highly.

Methodological Rigour

Academic study always generates a methodological commentary running alongside it, and the ethnography of the last ten years has been no exception. Not surprisingly, in view of the objectives rehearsed above, attention has focussed largely on the primary tasks — the delicacies of gaining access, the intricacies of data collection, the niceties of the ethics involved, and the root question of validity, the essence of the ethnographic achievement. So ethnographers have addressed the question of validity with almost phobic zeal, rehearsing various forms of naturalism, techniques of observing, taking notes, employing informants, triangulating and presenting. I do not wish to disparage this work; on the contrary, I believe the methodology has been considerably refined during the ethnographic surge in recent years. My point, rather, is that it understandably perhaps has followed the contours of the work that has been done, and that has been data collection. The generation and formulation of theory has been a lesser concern.

I should make clear again that I am speaking in general terms of a movement within sociology. Some ethnographers have been more theoretically minded than others, and certainly there exists within the corpus of studies that we now have considerable theoretical purchase. I shall discuss in the next section how I am trying to get to grips with some of this in my current projects.

Towards Theory

There are various things that we can do to encourage theoretical sensitivity. In addition to what others have put forward, I would suggest that we need to give careful thought to:

1 selection of topics for study;
2 greater openness; and
3 how to improve our powers of theoretical insight.

This last, in particular, is given scant treatment in methodological texts. We probably regard it as God-given quality — you either have it or you do not, but even if this were true, its emergence and use would depend on other factors such as resources and context. These, then, merit consideration.

Selection of Topics for Study

The emphasis hitherto has been on 'grounded' theory. Taking Glaser and Strauss' (1967) recommendations to heart in the midst of what appeared to be a great deal of 'ungrounded' theory, ethnographers have in effect started again with each study, comparing results with other studies *after* their own data collection and preliminary analysis. We might question this need for perpetual grounding. We might assume that a number of other studies already meet this requirement, constituting a body of knowledge about the educational process and system, and, in some instances, making conceptual and theoretical advances. In an important sense, therefore, we are no longer going into institutions 'for the first time' to uncover heretofore unsuspected pieces of material detail. The opportunity is there for cumulative/developmental work which will advance theoretical formulation. This possibility is in fact recognized by Glaser (1978, p. 45), though he stresses the continual importance of checking the emergent fit of the theory against his own data. Some of this can be done outside the field. Indeed, I would argue that we have reached a stage where we could do with less fieldwork and rather more armchair reflection. We must beware of simply 'adding on to', 'illustrating' or 'replicating' existing theory (D. Hargreaves, 1981). But there is a need to move towards 'sensitizing' as opposed to 'descriptive' concepts (Blumer, 1954; Bulmer, 1979). It is also useful to 'develop' or 'fill in' existing theory (Hammersley, 1979), and it is possible to begin to formulate it. I want to suggest some ways in which this might be done, specifically within the area of educational ethnography.

1 From Descriptive to Sensitizing Categories Descriptive categories are those organized around common features as they are first observed or represented. Sensitizing categories are more generalized, concentrating on common characteristics among a range of descriptive categories, which at first sight appear to have nothing in common, but which are revealed by comparison with other sensitizing categories. It is in this sense that the concepts behind the categories have careers (Denzin, 1978; see also Glaser and Strauss, 1967; Glaser, 1978; Becker, 1958). There are stepping stones to theory, and there are certain areas where we can make use of them. One example is in the area of pupil perspectives of school. There is now a considerable amount of data on these. Ethnographers interested in discovering how pupils represent the reality of school have found that they do not like teachers 'who are a load of rubbish', all straitlaced, putting them down, not knowing who they are (Marsh *et al.*, 1978); that they are opposed to excessive routine, regulation and restriction (Woods, 1979); that they like teachers who can 'have a laugh' with them, who are 'fair', reasonable and understanding, but who can also 'teach' and 'control' (Nash, 1976; Gannaway, 1976; Delamont, 1976). Several of these seem to have a common quality — the individual's concern with what they experience as dehumanizing institutionalization. It would appear that teachers also experience this in some form (Woods, 1979). We might hypothesize that some conflictual elements at least between teacher and pupil are rooted in the institution, and slant a future enquiry accordingly. Such an enquiry would immediately engage in 'theoretical sampling' (Glaser and Strauss, 1967), exploring aspects of teacher and pupil role and school structure through teacher and pupil perspectives. Since such research is sectional rather than holistic, there might also be afforded the luxury of a comparative study with two or more schools with contrasting structures.

This, then, is one example of a 'phase 2' project, that is, one using existing ethnographic studies as a launching pad, more theoretically conscious in the early stages, and engaging in theoretical sampling, hypothesis formation and testing. There is not the same need to 'muddle through', though it is important to stress that the existing theory is not accepted until the data are re-grounded in the new research situation. Continual adjustment would be necessary to accommodate any new deviant cases (Lindesmith, 1947). It is possible, of course, that new categories may be discovered, and the existing ones unverified. That, then, simply adds to the baseline descriptive categorization. With more and more studies of this nature, however, this will happen less and less.

Another example of this kind of development is in the area of teacher and pupil cultures. In the former, David Hargreaves (1980) has already done a kind of ideal-typical analysis, distinguishing three main themes in teacher occupational culture — competence, status and relationships. This area is replete with theoretical possibilities, for as Hargreaves says, '. . . the teachers' culture is a significant but inadequately formulated "intervening variable" between the macro and micro levels of sociological analysis, which we are currently seeking to articulate. . . . Between the experiential teacher dilemmas and the structural contradictions lies the mediating culture of teachers' (1980, p. 126). It is an area worth examining for that reason, but there are other directions theoretical developments might take. We might discover, for example, that pupil cultures are also distinguished by their emphasis on these same three elements. They may be 'differentiated' and 'polarized' (Hargreaves, 1967; Lacey, 1970) in other ways, but it does seem likely that pupils of all social classes, genders, ages, races, nationalities, and so on are concerned with competence, whether it be in school work, meeting the norms of the peer group, or being a 'proper' person (*ibid.*; Willis, 1977; Woods, 1983); relationships (Davies, 1980; Measor and Woods, 1983; Willis, 1977; Woods, 1979; Meyenn, 1980); and status (Hargreaves, 1967; Measor and Woods, 1983; Bryan, 1980).

We must not, of course, commit the error of 'post hoc' analysis, that is impose categories on the data. But one does not, in fact, have to search the literature very deeply to recognize their significance — they do, then, in a sense, 'emerge'. Further ethnographic work might 'fill in' some gaps in the data — with different kinds and ages of pupils, with different schools, and so on. But in another direction, interesting possibilities would appear to be opened up in the area of formal theory (Glaser and Strauss, 1967). For the substantive categories of teacher competence, status and relationships appear to have formal properties by this comparison with pupils. They have a wider applicability than the particular circumstances of the teacher role and job. They have to do, it would seem, with human association in society, particularly in adapting to institutional life.

This reflection might then lead us to examine different substantive areas that consider similar kinds of relationships, such as those that appear in Becker *et al.* (1968). We might speculate that these concerns are the product of the individual's struggle for identity in the modern world, and that their form and emphasis will vary depending on a number of elements, such as economic and political factors determining resources and policy, institutional structure, environment, and so on. This in turn both suggests further areas for enquiry, and the potential usefulness of other theoretical traditions, in this case identity theory. In this way, there is dialectical interplay between theory and data collection, precipitated by the initial theoretical cast of the study.

2 Cumulative Studies In some areas there has been cumulative work which illustrates the promise in maintaining the dialectic between theory and data collection. One of these areas is that of 'social' (Lacey, 1977), 'coping' (A. Hargreaves, 1978), or 'survival' (Woods, 1979) strategies. It is interesting that these three approaches to essentially the same phenomenon were all made, in the first instance, independently of and unknown to the others. In my study, I documented and categorized teacher 'survival' strategies, a particular form of 'social ' or 'coping strategy' at one end of a continuum governed by resources and policy. Hargreaves was interested in developing the theoretical base behind the notion of 'coping' as it was acted out at the intersection of micro-interaction and macro-structures; while Lacey was concerned to fill out a balanced model which allowed for consideration of personal redefinition of situations as well as situational redefinition of persons.

How did the notion of 'strategy' emerge from the data? For me, it resolved certain paradoxes and inconsistencies in my observations — the humanity of teachers and pupils while apart, their inhumanity together; how teacher accounts differed from my observations; certain peculiarities in teacher styles (such as a teacher going through the motions of teaching a manifestly totally inattentive class); the heavy emphasis throughout the school day on time-filling, routines and ritual; the extraordinary importance of what seemed to me petty items (such as aspects of school uniform, the loss of a 'free period'); and conversations with teachers which at times revealed the gulf between private aspirations and public possibilities. Through all of this, I came to realize, ran a strategical thread. It seemed enough, in the first instance, to stitch the various discontinuous elements together with this common theme.

This I regard as a fairly typical phase 1 ethnographic study. Lacey rooted his theoretical argument within the Chicago school discussion of perspectives and cultures (Becker *et al.*, 1961), and it could therefore be regarded as a refinement of some of that work. I later drew on this when reconsidering some data I had acquired on two teachers in a previous study (Woods, 1981). I was thus able to provide further documentation of the model as it might apply to more experienced teachers (Lacey was concerned with students and

noviciates), and some extension of it through the further consideration of two individuals (thus maintaining the 'grounded' nature of the
emerging theory). I also in this study developed some of my own
previous work on commitment.

A further example of what might be regarded as 'phase 2' work
was then provided by Pollard (1982), who, in considering the
Hargreaves' analysis of coping, found it stronger on the macro end of
the dimension than the micro. As Lacey had done, Pollard found an
imbalance in existing work, and sought to strengthen the weaker area.
He did this by developing my work on teacher survival, through the
notions of 'self' and 'interests-at-hand' (the latter well-documented in
his own ethnographic work — see Pollard, 1979; 1980). Thus where
Hargreaves tended to approach coping from the macro side, from the
point of view of what had to be coped with, Pollard concentrated on
the subjective meaning of coping, and emphasized the importance of
teacher biography, while attempting to pull all relevant factors
together in a theoretical model.

This now makes a useful springboard for further empirical and
theoretical work. One feature of all this work is the extent of its
grounding in the data. There has even been confirmation and
extension of the 'survival strategy' data base (Stebbins, 1981). Now
some aspects of the Pollard model, derived by what we might call
'logical integration', demand investigation. One such aspect is
'teacher biography'. We have little knowledge of how teachers' early
experiences affect their careers and strategies. But if we are to
investigate this area, we shall need to go beyond ethnography (I
discuss this shortly).

In this development we can identify some distinctive guidelines
for consolidating and stimulating theoretical research. These are in
the first instance the initial theoretical *emergence* of the concept
'strategy', from ethnographic data, and the *description* and 'saturation' of the various types. This led to the production of the concept
'strategy' and its theoretical refinement. That this should occur
contemporaneously in three independent studies was itself a *test* and
confirmation of the concept, as well as an indication of the influence
of the general approach — in this case symbolic interaction — leading
people in the same direction. Also in evidence is a desire for *balance*
and fair play in approaches and conclusions, and a drive for *integration*
of various, and often apparently disparate, elements into a coherent
framework. These last two indicate an interest in *scope* of the theory
to cover a wide range of situations. Once the various studies begin to
face each other openly, instead of going their own separate ways, then

Peter Woods

cumulation begins to occur. This of course is not a neat task of simply adding bits of theory together. Like the basic approach that guides it, the theory itself that is produced is a continuous *process*. *Critical* testing goes on and further questions of balance arise continually. For example, the Pollard model may prove too complex to be of any theoretical use. We may, for instance, discover too many factors operating on teacher biography to hold all of them separate in any meaningful way. But that remains to be seen. Behind it all is the desire to *explain* teacher behaviour, and to *predict* the possibilities given certain factors. What differential weight must we give to resources, policy, 'institutional bias', personal commitment and identity and so on, in what teachers do? What combination of factors is likely to put teachers 'at risk' of failure? To what degree can personal drive compensate for structural impediment? These are some of the questions to which research may be able to offer answers.

This kind of cumulative work proceeds from an initial identification of the concept to an elaboration of theory around it. Another kind is to work from some existing, already well-formulated theory. This may happen comparatively frequently within a discipline area like the sociology of education, concerned with the practical application of theoretical work. But this application is never a simple matching of theory against data. Rather, the theory provides guidelines for interpreting the data. Characteristically, the theory helps so far, but no further, at which point one must refine or develop the theory. This is happening in our current study of the transfer of pupils from middle to upper school (Measor and Woods, forthcoming). For this, Glaser's and Strauss' theory of status passage (1971) is clearly relevant. We can easily identify several of the properties in their analysis, and by their relative strength and distribution gain some idea of the character of pupil transfer as a status passage. But our study of the phenomenon provides, we feel, further theoretical insights. In particular, the phases of these passages appear to have been inadequately specified (Van Gennep, 1960; Turner, 1969; Musgrove and Middleton, 1981); and the whole area of identity transformation or development in the process underwritten, as a result of previous concentration on social aspects. We may, therefore, be able to develop the formal aspects of this theory, taking into account not only material unearthed in our own study, but also related findings from recent studies of status passages in different substantive areas (Hart, 1976; Ditton, 1977; Oakley, 1980). Once we have identified these lacunae in the existing formal theory, they

62

become a major focus of study, and we indulge in 'theoretical sampling' (Glaser and Strauss, 1967).

In this example, we begin with the desire to improve our understanding of a particular educational phenomenon, which we believed to be of increasing *relevance* (owing to the growing compartmentalization of the pupil career). Initial data collection *mapped* the contours of the experience primarily from the pupil's perspective, and '*rediscovered*' the relevance of several of the properties contained in the *existing formal theory* on the subject. It also identified certain undeveloped areas of the theory, and attention then turned to *refining* some elements (in the area of phases) and *generating* other strands to the theory (in the area of identity transformation), these theoretical concerns now *guiding* later collection of data. It would be inappropriate to have assumed that this one substantive instance necessarily affected the formal theory greatly, but here we were able to take into consideration several other recent individual ('phase 1') studies in other substantive spheres, and thus to demonstrate that these new elements had *formal* properties.

3 Corrective Studies David Hargreaves has noted the proliferation of theories in the sociology of education, and the degree to which most are 'notable for one feature: their extremely weak link to supportive empirical evidence' (1981, p. 9). He also notes the 'atheoretical nature of so much empirical work in the sociology of education' (*ibid*). We have bread, but no meat in our sandwich. Theoretically-based ethnography has much to contribute here.

Ethnography can contribute to certain theoretical areas as a corrective. Here, research may not be designed to test any existing theory, but material is discovered that raises questions about it, and corrects certain aspects of it, without entirely invalidating it. Rather, it acts as a 'synthesizer'. A useful illustration is within the field of pupil cultures. Work here reflects developments within both sociology and education, and reminds us that the *historical* element has to be taken into account in the construction of theory. In the 1960s Hargreaves (1967) and Lacey (1970) posited their differentiation/polarization model of two pupil subcultures, one pro- and one anti-school. These were linked to social class, but fostered by the school streaming structure. Differential norms and values were generated, to which individuals gravitated. This subcultural model was too restrictive for my own Lowfield study, which revealed a wider variety of responses, which underwent change along temporal and situational dimensions. I had recourse to an adaptational model as reworked by Wakeford (1969) on a Mertonian basis, and extended this in accordance with my data. This model rests on adaptations to official goals and means. All inmates are required to make a response to these, even if it is to reject both, but it assumes a priority which may actually misrepresent many pupils — and teachers. This was picked up by interactionists working closer to the fine detail of the lived moment. Furlong (1976), strongly criticizing Hargreaves for not taking pupil knowledge into account, developed his notion of 'interaction set', a more amorphous and transient grouping than a subculture, in and out of which pupils shaded; and Hammersley and Turner (1980) considered the pupil's adjustment to school primarily in terms of his or her own interests, revealing the problematic nature of 'conformist' or 'deviant' labels. Whether pupils conform, they argue, depends on whether the school has the resources to meet their interests.

I would argue that this represents a cumulative sequence, though not all the contributors to it might agree, and though the studies involved are pitched at different levels of generality and abstraction. It is distinguished again by the search for *balance*, and this particular series of studies does exhibit a certain roundedness. Theoretical purchase is immediately gained by selection of an *appropriate* area where there is a body of non-ethnographic theory available, in an area where ethnography can make a signal contribution. The ethnographic studies were undertaken first in a spirit of challenge and *critique*, focussing first on the deficiencies of previous theories in directing data collection toward their repair. This, in turn, created a new imbalance, which itself found one kind of rectification in the *synthesis* offered by Ball (1981), where he shows that the major bi-polar cultures still exist, but that a range of adaptations exists within them.

We can secure theoretical primacy, then, by how we select topics for study. I have suggested that we have sufficient baseline studies for others now to build on, and that there should be both cumulative and corrective work. For this, we shall also need a new emphasis in our methodology. We shall need to give rather more attention to data analysis and theoretical construction; and we shall need to consider how we might cultivate appropriate attitudes towards it. Two of these at least, I feel, have become somewhat lost along the way. They are 'openness' and 'creativity', and neither has had much consideration in the ethnographic methodological texts.

Openness

Ethnographers need to be more aware of and open to other substantive studies both in their own area and in others, to other theoretical approaches and to other methodologies. There is limited usefulness in replicating studies, and continually 'rediscovering' the same things. There are signs of this 'one-dimensional' approach, for example, in the areas of 'negotiation' and 'deviance' (I include some of my own work in this, I hasten to add — I am as 'one-dimensional' as the next ethnographer).

In the area of deviance, we find, for example, 'deviance-insulative' and 'deviance-provocative' teachers (Hargreaves *et al*, 1975), 'judgmental', 'explanatory/understanding', and 'fraternal' teachers (Grace, 1978), 'coercive' and 'incorporative' teachers (Reynolds and Sullivan, 1979). In negotiation, we have various metaphorical representations of forms of agreement as 'truce' (Reynolds, 1976), 'aided colonization' (Woods, 1979), 'negotiation' (Martin, 1976; Delamont, 1976; Woods, 1978; Ball, 1980; Turner, 1982; 1983), 'working consensus' (Hargreaves, 1972; Pollard, 1979), and 'avoidance of provocation' (Stebbins, 1970; A. Hargreaves, 1979; D. Hargreaves *et al*., 1975; Bird *et al*., 1981). The subject demands the kind of cumulative phase 2 work, spoken of earlier, which takes a bird's eye view of these various studies, each for the most part contained within its own separate case study, and which seeks to formalize the elements and properties of negotiation. If this were done in this particular instance, we might be forced to consider issues of 'power', for example, which some outsiders claim interactionists are unable to handle. Negotiation of course is all about power, but it is rarely abstracted to any extent from the base-line description.

Further to this, the proliferation of studies in this area at phase 1 level causes one to wonder whether more cannot be done at source. We have our conferences and seminars, and other exchanges. But might we not consider the advantages of building such interaction structurally into our research? Mutual research projects, shared research personnel, multi-site ethnography, research teams, are all ways of spanning the divides and overcoming the basically insulating effects of the method once it is under way. By advancing on some kind of team basis, we can economize on the basic steps of data collection, identification and saturation of categories and their properties and so forth, and more quickly arrive at the stage of sharper definition of concepts.

Peter Woods

Such associations can be as loose or as tight as the people concerned wish to make them. Team research can pose problems, and indeed prove to be more counter-productive than productive, more 'draining' than 'stimulating' (Glaser, 1978, p. 139; see also Payne *et al.*, 1981 on ethnographic 'teams'). Team work may pose special problems within ethnography, for, as noted, not only is the nature of the research extremely personal, but also for that very reason it may attract strongly individualistic people. But this can, and should, be allowed for. There could be a range of alliances. At one extreme, we might have a fairly loose-knit organization where individuals or groups planned their work collectively, perhaps on different, but related, aspects of the same substantive or theoretical area, and where regular meetings, where data were pooled and ideas advanced, were built into the design of the research. At a more local level, the virtues of collaboration have been attested by, for example, Glaser (1978, p. 29).

> ... *when it works*, its energizing potential is fantastic, each stimulates the other's thinking usually faster than a solo approach, each keeps the other on his toes and each can spell the other during periods of depression, decompression and laying fallow. A project can be done better and faster and finished more easily, since good collaboration takes over the solution of each other's problems during research such as 'can't write' or 'can't finish', 'can't interview such and such', 'can't face a certain aspect of the research' and so forth. One can conceptualize while the other talks data, thus working two levels at once with maximum energy. They can continually sensitize each other to the theory in the data....

Lynda Measor and I have had a taste of this during our research on pupil transfer (Measor and Woods, 1983; and forthcoming). Lynda did all the fieldwork, for a period of about eighteen months. During that time we met regularly and discussed the progress of the research, and it is fair to say, I think, that it 'evolved' between us. Several papers were produced, Lynda preparing the first draft, I the second, and both of us the third. The final report is being prepared in the same way. We have, of course, by this time worked out our underlying theory by a process of dialogue and testing. But organizing the basic data around this theory is a huge task, let alone raising the conceptual level to dominance. Sharing the work certainly eases this task. Lynda has first crack at data organization. I then edit this and suggest possible concepts and/or new categories and their properties. Lynda then tells me which of these are sufficiently grounded in her data or are otherwise appropriate, and we develop them together. She also tells me which important points I have 'edited' out of her account, and we ensure they are written back in more strongly. The eventual product will be, I feel, stronger than if either of us had worked on it alone. It is, after all, a form of triangulation from source, rather than in the objects of the solitary researcher's attention.

In short, the collaboration aids in these distinct respects: 1 *refining* the categorization and conceptualization; 2 as a check on *validity*, testing the strengths of data for conclusions drawn, and the strength of theory for the available data; 3 providing a broader basis for *comparative* work, since the total range of experiences and knowledge is increased enormously. This also can work for greater *balance* in outlook. In our case, for example, it helped to have both a female and male outlook. It is a useful corrective to *hidden biases*; 4 accomplishing *distance* from the data. This is not always easy for the fieldworker who has been intent on *immersion*. But it also permits the fieldworker to indulge in that, not to the extent of 'going native', but at least to indulge in *participant* observation, which is hardly practised in current ethnographies; 5 *pacing* the work — allowing time to draw breath and recover after the totally exhausting work of data collection and initial analysis, without the sense of loss of impetus; 6 *generating ideas*, which are often sparked off in discussion.

As well as openness to others that might allow for more coordinated work, we might be more open to other areas of substantive content. A. Hargreaves (1980) and Hammersley (1980) have both argued for more 'macro' concern on the interactionist ethnographer's part. But there is also another world within the individual, beyond the surface meanings. For example, symbolic interactionists have been drawn to focus on the world of subjective meanings, and have ignored the emotions and the subconscious. We shall obtain a very partial view of school life if we continue to do so. But we must, perforce, move into other theoretical areas if we are to consider them. Lynda Measor and I have attempted to do this, in our current research on pupil transfer, where we uncovered a corporate body of pupil myths on the subject (Measor and Woods, 1983). To move towards an understanding of these, we drew on structuralist and functionalist approaches, and a Freudian analysis of the unconscious. However, this took place within an interactionist framework, and we tried, in the interpretation of the fantasy world of myth, to remain faithful to the pupil life world as it was revealed to us by observation and interview. A condition of this kind of approach, we feel, is that data and analysis should be kept separate in presentation. In other words, the analysis should not obtrude on the data to the extent that it prevents other interpretations (see also Ball, 1965; A. Hargreaves, 1980).

Openness to other substantive and theoretical areas will also require openness to other methodologies. Questionnaires and surveys have their uses in ethnography, a fact not always realized since Cicourel's (1964) attack against them (see, for example, Ball, 1981; Woods, 1979; Reynolds, 1976; Payne *et al.*, 1981). They can provide useful objective information, and also act as a partial test of theories generated locally. The problem of grounding such data might be met partly by design of the questionnaire, so that indicators of least typicality are omitted, partly by sampling where detailed studies have already been conducted in related areas, and partly by selective deeper study of the population surveyed.

However, there are methodologies that complement ethnography more precisely, and which can assist in generating theory. One of these is the life history method, popular among the Chicago school in the 1930s and now promising to undergo a revival (Faraday and Plummer, 1979; Goodson and Walker, 1979; Goodson, 1980; Bertaux, 1981; Plummer, 1983). It is, in a way, a natural progression. As Goodson (1980, p. 74) has argued,

> Life history investigations set against the background of evolutionary patterns of schooling and teaching should provide an antidote to the depersonalized, ahistorical accounts to which we have become accustomed. Through the life history, we gain insights into individuals coming to terms with imperatives in the social structure. . . . From the collection of life histories, we discern what is general within a range of individual studies; links are thereby made with macro theories but from a base that is clearly grounded within personal biography.

This is not to say that the life history method is all promise and no problems. It has been criticized for its apparently atheoretical and unscientific nature. Of all techniques, it was the one that seemed most likely to produce the descriptive, journalistic, individualized account. But as Faraday and Plummer (1979) have argued, the selection of any research technique depends upon the general goals of the research. It would appear, for example, to be well-suited to the exploration of the biographical arm of the coping strategies model discussed earlier. For it combines the various elements of the model within the life history, yet retains the traditional interactionist emphasis on subjective meanings, process, flux and ambiguity, and 'totality' (*ibid*). In such an instance, it begins with a firm base within theory, and might lead to a reformulation of it. Its chief theoretical contribution is likely to be exploratory, generating sensitizing concepts in new areas. While it will not provide general theories about social structures, it might illuminate those structures and the individual's relationship with them in a revealing way. As Faraday and Plummer comment, 'When one conducts a life history interview the findings become alive in terms of historical processes and structural constraints' (*ibid*., p. 780). But they themselves prefer what they term 'ad hoc fumbling around' to generating theory in the streamlined way advocated by Glaser and Strauss, which they found too limiting. This was because their major concern was exploring a whole substantive area hitherto neglected in research. The technique is at its best, they conclude, 'when it is being used in an exploratory fashion for generating many concepts, hunches and ideas, both at the local and situational level and on a historical structural level, and *within* the same field, and in *relationship* to other fields' (*ibid*., p. 785). The theoretical interest is preserved by 'systematic thematic analysis', whereby the sociologist blends the individual's own account with themes derived from theory (see also Glaser, 1978).

However, 'hunches' and 'ideas' do not appear in a vacuum. They may be stimulated by certain cues, and some research techniques might throw up such cues more than others. But there is another element — the most important instrument in ethnographic research upon which recognition of cue, formulation of idea, analysis of data and construction of theory depends — and that, of course, is the researcher. We can refine our methods as much as we like, but in the last resort, research — and particularly theory construction — will be as good as the people doing it. Its quality will depend not on the slavish adherence to technique, but in the free exercise of the creative mind.

Creativity

There is some good advice in the literature on the cultivation of the power of insight, although discussion on this subject is often consigned to an appendix or otherwise very limited. For example, in Glaser's book specifically on *Theoretical Sensitivity* (1978) there are only two pages on 'creativity'.

The most comprehensive statement on the matter is still that of C. Wright Mills (1959). He urges total personal involvement, the cultivation of intellectual craftsmanship, the keeping of a 'reflective' journal. He also draws a useful contrast:

> The sociological imagination . . . in considerable part consists of the capacity to shift from one perspective to another, and in the process to build up an adequate view of a total society and of its components. It is this imagination, of course, that sets off the social scientist from the mere technician. Adequate technicians can be trained in a few years. The sociological imagination can also be cultivated; certainly it seldom occurs without a great deal of often routine work. Yet there is an unexpected quality about it, perhaps because its essence is the combination of ideas that no one expected were combinable . . . . There is a playfulness of mind back of such combining as well as a truly fierce drive to make sense of the world, which the technician as such usually lacks. Perhaps he is too well trained, too precisely trained. Since one can be *trained* only in what is already known, training sometimes incapacitates one from learning new ways; it makes one rebel against what is bound to be at first loose and even sloppy. But you must cling to vague images and notions, if they are yours, and you must work them out. For it is in such forms that original ideas, if any, almost always first appear. (pp. 232–33)

Are we in danger, in our concentration on certain aspects of method, of becoming ethnographic technicians, and of foreclosing on the possibilities of original thought? Again, the issue would appear to be one of balance. Most agree that the ideal-typical circumstance in which ideas emerge is a mixture of, on the one hand, dedication to the task, scrupulous attention to detail and method, and knowledge, and, on the other, the ability to 'let go' of the hold of this rigorous application, to rise above it as it were and to 'play' with it, experimenting with new combinations and patterns (*ibid*; Denzin, 1978; Glaser and Strauss, 1967; Becker, 1970; Glaser, 1978; Weber, 1946). Certainly some of what I consider my better ideas, such as they are, come to me when I am actually relaxing from the task — walking the dog, gardening, driving to work, listening to music. I have to make an immediate note of these, or they may vanish as quickly and mysteriously as they appeared, or some 'brilliant' ideas might be driven out by even more 'brilliant' ideas! Needless to say, many 'brilliant' ideas turn out to be not so brilliant when considered at length later! But a great number have to be rehearsed for a few of them to stick.

However, ideas never appear in a vacuum. The problem with all its ramifications has already been analyzed and *keyed* into the mind. The mind, too, has been '*programmed*' with all the relevant materials to come up with a solution — other studies on the subject, certain theoretical formulations, a social scientific orientation which *disciplines* the production of ideas at the same time as they are stimulated, a host of past experiences, certain initial experimental attempts at putting things together. The mind is also *energized* in the sense that the problem nags and worries, there are, perhaps, curious anomalies in one's data, or they differ substantially from other studies in the same area, or one may feel intuitively, without being able to resolve it, that there is a relationship among certain, apparently disparate, elements, or some thoughts may have been 'pigeon-holed' for future reference during the data collection.

The achieving of this kind of psychological state has attracted some attention to specific techniques (see, for example, Denzin, 1978, pp. 68–74). We are advised to search for *negative* evidence (Becker *et al.*, 1961), to develop drive, curiosity, reflective consciousness and to 'de-stabilize' concepts (Sjoberg and Nett, 1968), to cultivate insights from personal experience (Glaser and Strauss, 1967). I wish to make a more general point to do with our overall orientation towards our subjects of study. A distinction is sometimes made between scientific and novellistic ethnography. As social scientists, we would want to identify with the former, and have been concerned to improve the scientific rigour of our work. In an influential article, Becker (1958) argued that qualitative research should become more a 'scientific' and less an 'artistic' kind of endeavour. This was highly appropriate at the time, but ethnography now stands to lose by such a separation. For theory can be aided by an artistic frame of mind. Popper observes that theories are 'the result of an almost poetic intuition . . .' (1963, p. 192). Brown argues that 'the choice for sociology is not between scientific rigour as against poetic insight . . . [but] between more or less fruitful metaphors, and between using metaphors or being their victims' (1977, p. 90). Brown advises cultivating 'aesthetic distance' for promoting 'perceptual and compositional activity' (*ibid*; p. 53) and for sociologists to bracket their own world along with everything else. Twenty years ago Nisbet (1962) wrote an essay on 'Sociology As an Art Form', in which he argued that 'the science of sociology makes its most significant intellectual advances under the spur of stimuli and through processes that it largely shares with art; that whatever the differences between science and art, it is what they have in common that matters most in discovery and creativeness' (p. 544). He refers to 'processes of intuition, impressionism, iconic imagination ... objectification' (p. 545). His thesis is that art and science became divided in the nineteenth century, and they succumbed to myths, the one that it involved 'genius or inspiration' and was concerned with beauty, the other, rigorously controlled method and objective truth. But, Nisbet argues, both are concerned primarily with *reality*, and with understanding. Both depend upon detachment. But it is the artist, or the artist in the scientist, who provides the 'leap of imagination'. He quotes from Rabinowitch:

> The artist is the most sensitive individual in society. His feeling for change, his apprehension of new things to come, is likely to be more acute than of the slower-moving, rational, scientific thinker. It is in the artistic production of a period, rather than in its thinking, that one should search for shadows cast in advance by coming events ... the revelation, in the framework of artistic production, of the mental attitudes which only later will become apparent in other fields of human endeavour. (quoted in Nisbet, p. 549)

And from Morse, that

> discovery in mathematics is not a matter of logic. It is rather the result of mysterious powers which no one understands, and in which the unconscious recognition of beauty must play an important part. Out of an infinity of designs a mathematician chooses one pattern for beauty's sake, and pulls it down to earth, no one knows how. Afterward the logic of words and of forms sets the pattern right. Only then can one tell someone else. The first pattern remains in 'the shadows of the mind'. (quoted in Nisbet, p. 550)

Likewise with sociology, argues Nisbet, ideas like Durkheim's theory of 'suicide' were derived not from data processing or logic, but from a creative blend more typical of the artist. There is also a strong aesthetic element in Simmel's work, and it is in that that Nisbet feels his creativity resides.

The message is a simple one: that science and art rely on the same kind of creative imagination; and that where art is defined out of science, the latter loses a great deal of its creative stimulation. There is a real danger, I feel, that as we go on constructing the ethnographic methodological edifice, it might take us over, and we might become slaves to technique.

We might learn too, from studies on humour. Humour shares with art the same kind of creativity, the ability to see the familiar from a new perspective. It is what allowed Willis' (1977) 'lads' occasionally to 'penetrate' their conditions of existence. It is what Mary Douglas meant when she referred to the humourist as a 'minor mystic ... one of those people who pass beyond the bounds of reason and society and give glimpses of a truth which escapes through the mesh of structured concepts' (1966, p. 373).

Koestler (1964) argues that the humourist must have some originality — 'the ability to break away from the stereotyped routines of thought' (p. 93) and gains inspiration in the same way as the artist, by a kind of 'thinking aside', or by stumbling on it, or by intuition, in other words through unconscious processes. It involves 'creative stress, intellectual exercise, a feat of mental acrobatics ...' (p. 95).

Vallance (1980) is alive to this in her consideration of some areas of education. She makes a distinction between 'solemn' and 'serious' studies. The former seem to be 'self-conscious', 'a little pretentious', 'try hard to be taken seriously' and are 'on the defensive'. She thinks the social sciences in general are suffering from solemnity by comparison with the physical sciences, which are 'secure and serious'. She suggests the distinction might be applied to the kind of problems selected for study, the methods used in research, and the practices implemented in schools. I wonder how our ethnographies would stand up to such a scrutiny? Vallance recommends that we try to cultivate 'the art of finding the humorous by identifying the solemn' (p. 188), of seeing things 'from the reverse'. Humour will aid reflection, creativity and the production of theory. I do not refer, of course, to the forms of humour that are frivolous or that are conflictual, but to the purer forms of incongruity humour. Nor am I suggesting that we make a joke out of all that we do. Rather, that as part of the art of cultivating aesthetic distance, of creative thinking, of coordinating the unconnectable and of detecting the 'solemn', we could perhaps benefit from occasionally casting a humorous eye about us. (For one example of this technique see Julienne Ford (1975) *Paradigms and Fairy Tales*.)

I am not arguing that we should not have a rigorous methodology with due attention to matters of validity, access, ethics, data collection, and so on, nor that we should not have tested and recognized techniques and routines, rather that, as part of that methodology, we should give more attention to the cultivation of mental states conducive to the production of theory rather than the collection of data. The former require discipline, discovery and method, the latter liberation, creativity and imagination. In some ways, they tend to work against each other, and where we put more emphasis on one, the other will suffer. The first decade of ethnographic revival has inevitably been concerned mainly with exploration, establishment, credibility. The next phase, I submit, must focus on the frames of mind, the circumstances, the resources that promote the creativity and originality that go into theory construction. Only then, I feel, will ethnography achieve its full potential.

Acknowledgement

I am grateful to Martyn Hammersley for his observations on an earlier draft of this paper.

References

ANYON, J. (1981) 'Social class and school knowledge', *Curriculum Inquiry*, 11, 1, pp. 3–42.

ATKINSON, J.M. (1977) 'Coroners and the categorization of deaths as suicides' in BELL, C. and NEWBY, H. (Eds) *Doing Sociological Research*, London, Allen and Unwin.

ATKINSON, P. and DELAMONT, S. (1977) 'Mock-ups and cock-ups: The stage-management of guided discovery instruction', in WOODS, P. and HAMMERSLEY, M. (Eds) *School Experience*, London, Croom Helm.

BALL, D. (1965) 'Sarcasm as sociation: The rhetoric of interaction', *Canadian Review of Sociology and Anthropology*, 2, 3.

BALL, S. (1980) 'Initial encounters in the classroom and the process of establishment' in WOODS, P. (Ed.) *Pupil Strategies*, London, Croom Helm.

BALL, S. (1981) *Beachside Comprehensive: A Case Study of Secondary Schooling*, Cambridge, Cambridge University Press.

BECKER, H.S. (1958) 'Problems of inference and proof in participant observation', *American Sociological Review*, 23, 6, pp. 652–60.

BECKER, H.S. (1970) *Sociological Work*, Chicago, Aldine.

BECKER, H.S. *et al.* (1961) *Boys in White*, Chicago, University of Chicago Press.

BECKER, H.S. *et al.* (Eds) (1968) *Institutions and the Person*, Chicago, Aldine.

BERTAUX, D. (Ed) (1981) *Biography and Society: The Life History Approach in the Social Sciences*, Beverley Hills, Calif., Sage.

BIRDS, C. *et al.* (1981) *Disaffected Pupils*, Educational Studies Unit, Brunel University.

BLUMER, H. (1954) 'What is wrong with social theory?', *American Sociological Review*, Vol. 19, pp. 3–10.

BLUMER, H. (1976) 'Sociological implications of the thought of G.H. Mead', in COSIN, B. *et al.* (Eds) *School and Society*, London, Routledge and Kegan Paul.

BROWN, R.H. (1977) *A Poetic for Sociology*, Cambridge, Cambridge University Press.

BRYAN, K. (1980) 'Pupil perceptions of transfer between middle and high schools', in HARGREAVES, A. and TICKLE, L. (Eds) *Middle Schools*, London, Harper and Row.

BULMER, M. (1979) 'Concepts in the analysis of qualitative data', *Sociological Review*, 27, 4, pp. 651–77.

BURGESS, R.G. (1984) 'Autobiographical accounts and research experience', in BURGESS, R.G. (Ed.) *The Research Process in Educational Settings: Ten Case Studies*, Lewes, Falmer Press.

CICOUREL, A.V. (1964) *Method and Measurement in Sociology*, New York, Free Press.

COHEN, S. (1981) *Folk Devils and Moral Panics*, (2nd ed.) London, Martin Robertson.

DAVIES, B. (1980) 'Friends and fights: A study of children's views on social interaction in childhood', unpublished paper, University of New England, Armidale.

DELAMONT, S. (1976) *Interaction in the Classroom*, London, Methuen.

DELAMONT, S. (1981) 'All too familiar? A decade of classroom research', *Educational Analysis*, 3, 1, pp. 69–83.

DENZIN, N.K. (1978) *The Research Act*, New York, McGraw-Hill.

DITTON, J. (1977) *Part-Time Crime: An Ethnography of Fiddling and Pilferage*, London, Macmillan.

DOUGLAS, M. (1966) *Purity and Danger*, London, Routledge and Kegan Paul.

ELDRIDGE, J. (1980) *Recent British Sociology*, London, Macmillan.

FARADAY, A. and PLUMMER, K. (1979) 'Doing life histories', *Sociological Review*, 27, 4, pp. 773–98.

FORD, J. (1975) *Paradigms and Fairy Tales*, London, Routledge and Kegan Paul.

FURLONG, J. (1976) 'Interaction sets in the classroom', in HAMMERSLEY, M. and WOODS, P. (Eds) *The Process of Schooling*, London, Routledge and Kegan Paul.

GANNAWAY, H. (1976) 'Making sense of school', in STUBBS, M. and DELAMONT, S. (Eds) *Explorations in Classroom Observation*, London, Wiley.

GLASER, B. (1978) *Theoretical Sensitivity: Advances in the Methodology of Grounded Theory*, Mill Valley, Calif., The Sociology Press.

GLASER, B.G. and STRAUSS, A.L. (1967) *The Discovery of Grounded Theory*, London, Weidenfeld and Nicolson.

GLASER, B.G. and STRAUSS, A.L. (1971) *Status Passage*, Chicago, Aldine.

GOODSON, I. (1980) 'Life histories and the study of schooling', *Interchange*,

11, 4.

GOODSON, I. and WALKER, R. (1979) 'Putting life into ethnography', paper presented at SSRC Ethnography of Schooling Conference, 10–12 September, St Hilda's College, Oxford.

GRACE, G. (1978) *Teachers, Ideology and Control*, London, Routledge and Kegan Paul.

HAMMERSLEY, M. (1977) 'Teacher perspectives', Unit 9 of Course E202, *Schooling and Society*, Milton Keynes, Open University Press.

HAMMERSLEY, M. (1979) 'Analyzing ethnographic data', Block 6, Part I of DE 304, *Research Methods in Education and the Social Sciences*, Milton Keynes, Open University Press.

HAMMERSLEY, M. (1980) 'On interactionist empiricism', in WOODS, P. (Ed.) *Pupil Strategies*, London, Croom Helm.

HAMMERSLEY, M. and TURNER, G. (1980) 'Conformist pupils?', in WOODS, P. (Ed.) *Pupil Strategies*, London, Croom Helm.

HARGREAVES, A. (1978) 'Towards a theory of classroom coping strategies', in BARTON, L. and MEIGHAN, R. (Eds) *Sociological Interpretations of Schooling and Classrooms*, Driffield, Nafferton.

HARGREAVES, A. (1979) 'Strategies, decisions and control: Interaction in a middle school classroom', in EGGLESTON, J. (Ed.) *Teacher Decision-Making in the Classroom*, London, Routledge and Kegan Paul.

HARGREAVES, A. (1980) 'Synthesis and the study of strategies: A project for the sociological imagination', in WOODS, P. (Ed.) *Pupil Strategies*, London, Croom Helm.

HARGREAVES, A. (1982) 'Resistance and relative autonomy theories: Problems of distortion and incoherence in recent Marxist analyses of education', *British Journal of Sociology of Education*, 3, 2, pp. 107–26.

HARGREAVES, D.H. (1967) *Social Relations in a Secondary School*, London, Routledge and Kegan Paul.

HARGREAVES, D.H. (1972) *Interpersonal Relations and Education*, London, Routledge and Kegan Paul.

HARGREAVES, D.H. (1978) 'Whatever happened to symbolic interactionism?' in BARTON, L. and MEIGHAN, R. (Eds) *Sociological Interpretations of Schooling and Classrooms: a Reappraisal*, Driffield, Nafferton.

HARGREAVES, D.H. (1980) 'The occupational culture of teachers, in WOODS, P. (Ed.) *Teacher Strategies*, London, Croom Helm.

HARGREAVES, D.H. (1981) 'Schooling for delinquency', in BARTON, L. and WALKER, S. (Eds) *Schools, Teachers and Teaching*, Lewes, Falmer Press.

HARGREAVES, D.H. et al. (1975) *Deviance in Classrooms*, London, Routledge and Kegan Paul.

HART, N. (1976) *When Marriage Ends: A Study in Status Passage*, London, Tavistock.

KOESTLER, A. (1964) *The Act of Creation*, New York, Macmillan.

LACEY, C. (1970) *Hightown Grammar*, Manchester, Manchester University Press.

LACEY, C. (1976) 'Problems of sociological fieldwork: A review of the methodology of Hightown Grammar', in HAMMERSLEY, M. and WOODS, P. (Eds) *The Process of Schooling*, London, Routledge and Kegan Paul.

LACEY, C. (1977) *The Socialization of Teachers*, London, Methuen.

LAMBART, A.M. (1976) 'The sisterhood', in HAMMERSLEY, M. and WOODS, P. (Eds) *The Process of Schooling*, London, Routledge and Kegan Paul.

LINDESMITH, A.R. (1947) *Opiate Addiction*, Bloomington, Ind., Principia Press.

McNAMARA, D. (1980) 'The outsider's arrogance: The failure of participant observers to understand classroom events', *British Educational Research Journal*, 6, 2, pp. 113–25.

MARSH, P. *et al.* (1978) *The Rules of Disorder*, London, Routledge and Kegan Paul.

MARTIN, W.B.W. (1976) *The Negotiated Order of the School*, Toronto, Macmillan.

MEAD, G.H. (1934) *Mind, Self and Society*, ed. by C.W. MORRIS, Chicago, University of Chicago Press.

MEASOR, L. and WOODS, P. (1983) 'The interpretation of pupil myths', in HAMMERSLEY, M. (Ed.) *The Ethnography of Schooling*, Driffield, Nafferton.

MEASOR, L. and WOODS, P. (1984) *Changing Schools: Pupil Perspectives on Transfer to a Comprehensive*, Milton Keynes, Open University Press.

MEYENN, R. (1980) 'School girls' peer groups', in WOODS, P. (Ed.) (1980) *Pupil Strategies*, London, Croom Helm.

MILLS, C.W. (1959) *The Sociological Imagination*, New York, Oxford University Press.

MUSGROVE, F. and MIDDLETON, R. (1981) 'Rites of passage and the meaning of age in three contrasted social groups', *British Journal of Sociology*, 32, 1, March.

NASH, R. (1976) 'Pupils' expectations of their teachers', in STUBBS, M. and DELAMONT, S. (Eds) *Explorations in Classroom Observation*, London, Wiley.

NISBET, R. (1962) 'Sociology as an art form', *Pacific Sociological Review*, Autumn.

OAKLEY, A. (1974) *The Sociology of Housework*, London, Martin Robertson.

OAKLEY, A. (1980) *Women Confined: Towards a Sociology of Childbirth*, London, Martin Robertson.

PAYNE, G. *et al.* (1981) *Sociology and Social Research*, London, Routledge and Kegan Paul.

PLUMMER, K. (1983) *Documents of Life*, London, Allen and Unwin.

POLLARD, A. (1979) 'Negotiating deviance and "getting done" in primary school classrooms', in BARTON, L. and MEIGHAN, R. (Eds) *Schools, Pupils and Deviance*, Driffield, Nafferton.

POLLARD, A. (1980) 'Teacher interests and changing situations of survival threat in primary school classrooms', in WOODS, P. (Ed.) *Teacher Strategies*, London, Croom Helm.

POLLARD, A. (1982) 'A model of coping strategies', *British Journal of Sociology of Education*, 3, 1, pp. 19–37.

POPPER, K. (1963) *Conjectures and Refutations: The Growth of Scientific Knowledge*, London, Routledge and Kegan Paul.

REYNOLDS, D. (1976) 'When teachers and pupils refuse a truce', in MUN-

GHAM, G. and PEARSON, G. (Eds) *Working Class Youth Culture*, London, Routledge and Kegan Paul.

REYNOLDS, D. and SULLIVAN, M. (1979) 'Bringing schools back in', in BARTON, L. and MEIGHAN, R. (Eds) *Schools, Pupils and Deviance*, Driffield, Nafferton.

RILEY, J. (1979) 'I wonder what it's like to write a unit?', *Teaching at a Distance*, No. 14, Spring.

SHARP, R. and GREEN, A. (1975) *Education and Social Control*, London, Routledge and Kegan Paul.

SJOBERG, G. and NETT, R. (1968) *A Methodology for Social Research*, New York, Harper and Row.

STEBBINS, R. (1970) 'The meaning of disorderly behaviour: Teacher definitions of a classroom situation', *Sociology of Education*, Vol. 44, pp. 217–36.

STEBBINS, R. (1981) 'Classroom ethnography and the definition of the situation', in BARTON, L. and WALKER, S. (Eds) *Schools, Teachers and Teaching*, Lewes, Falmer Press.

TURNER, G. (1982) *'Conformist' Pupils in the Secondary School*, PhD thesis, Open University.

TURNER, G. (1983) *The Social World of the Comprehensive School*, London, Croom Helm.

TURNER, V.W. (1969) *The Ritual Process*, London, Routledge and Kegan Paul.

VALLANCE, E. (1980) 'A deadpan look at humour in curriculum discourse', *Curriculum Inquiry*, 10, 2.

VAN GENNEP, A. (1960) *The Rites of Passage*, London, Routledge and Kegan Paul.

WAKEFORD, J. (1969) *The Cloistered Elite: A Sociological Analysis of the English Public Boarding School*, London, Macmillan.

WEBER, M. (1946) *From Max Weber: Essays in Sociology*, Ed. by GERTH, H.H. and MILLS, C.W., New York, Oxford University Press.

WERTHMAN, C. (1963) 'Delinquents in schools: A test for the legitimacy of authority', *Berkeley Journal of Sociology*, 8, 1, pp. 39–60.

WILLIS, P. (1977) *Learning to Labour*, Farnborough, Saxon House.

WOLCOTT, H. (1975) 'Criteria for an ethnographic approach to research in schools', *Human Organization*, 34, 2, pp. 111–27.

WOODS, P. (1978) 'Negotiating the demands of schoolwork', *Journal of Curriculum Studies*, 10, 4, pp. 309–27.

WOODS, P. (1979) *The Divided School*, London, Routledge and Kegan Paul.

WOODS, P. (1981) 'Strategies, commitment and identity: Making and breaking the teacher role', in BARTON, L. and WALKER, S. (Eds) *Schools, Teachers and Teaching*, Lewes, Falmer Press.

WOODS, P. (1983) *Sociology and the School*, London, Routledge and Kegan Paul.

4   Ethnography and Status: Focussing on Gender in Educational Research

Lynn Davies

This chapter attempts to isolate and discuss those issues in ethnographic research which may be specifically pertinent to gender.[1] This task is approached in a somewhat exploratory way, because, ironically, although my own research[2] was about girls, and I complained about lack of awareness of the female in the subject area, I rarely addressed directly any problems of gender in the initial research *methodology*. Thus some of what follows is retrospective; although in the true traditions of grounded theory, many issues arose during and from the research.

Immediately vast hurdles loom up when isolating 'gender'. Ethnography is by definition about the small-scale, and it is at the small (shallow?) end that we start. If we raise questions about large social categories like gender, then presumably we ought really to be constantly aware of other broad categories such as social class, race, age or religion: an impossible task. But if I outline some of the concerns which seem relevant to gender, we can see whether they also provide a framework for bearing in mind those other social divisions. Hence I see five main areas of interest, and will use them as examples. They appear at the different stages of the research process: the identification of a research 'target'; the adoption of a methodology; the actual research relationship; the production of results; and finally the long-term implications of ethnographic research on women in particular.

Identifying a 'Target'

Here the paradoxes start to emerge. If one attempts to rectify the invisibility of women in sociological endeavour by embarking on small-scale research about them (or highlighting sex differences in mixed groups), then one is assuming that sex membership is possibly the crucial variable in explaining behaviour. If one finds 'this group does things differently', then is this attributable to the fact that its members are female, or is it a product of that localized setting in which the group operates? With regard to educational contexts, for example, one finds that many of the traditional female scripts of helplessness, withdrawal, apathy and so on orchestrate well with pupil scripts in general — that is, they are the reaction of oppressed groups with little institutionalized power. How then can one say with conviction that this is a 'female' reaction as opposed to a 'pupil' reaction?

Now there *are* some instances where I think the researcher would have been wise to pay attention to the fact that his (sic) subjects were girls. Furlong's (1976) critique of polarization theory, and his very necessary replacement of 'subcultures' with 'interaction sets' strangely fails to relate the flexibility he found amongst pupils to the point that these particular pupils were all *girls*. It may still be likely that boys are constrained by subcultural norms in a way that girls are not. Similarly, Woods (1976) notes in 'Having a laugh: An antidote to schooling' that 'pupils' distinguished between what he termed 'natural' laughter and 'institutionalized' laughter: for there were different behaviours associated with 'acting silly' at school, and managing to have a good laugh while 'acting your age' outside school. His supporting quotations come in fact from a group of girls; and one thing that emerged from my own research was the possibility that girls might be more adaptive to context than boys — that is, they were more likely to behave significantly differently outside school, in an adult world, than inside school when treated as children. They did not necessarily translate a female culture *directly* into a school response in the way that Willis (1977) sees that boys translate male working-class responses: it was merely one of a set of alternatives. My conclusion was that 'correspondence theory', the claim that school replicates the work-place, may, in spite of the boys' outward themes of toughness and independence, be more salient for males than for females.

If, then, there are occasions when a researcher should be specifically aware that the subjects are female, there should not be temporary amnesia either when the subjects are all boys. There are too many instances of a research account initially outlining the (all male) sample, but subsequently positing conclusions about 'kids', 'pupils' or 'working-class youth', instead of *continuously* bearing in mind the partial nature of the original sample (e.g. Corrigan, 1979).

One tends not to find a female researcher studying females doing this: she is usually consciously aware of the intention to study female youth rather than 'youth'. Presumably the assumption still persists that a study of male youths will enable generalizations about all young people; or the implication is that girls are somehow outside 'youth'. Either stance is dangerous and arrogant.

Where then I see ethnography as particularly useful in gender issues is in the *refinement* of broad conceptual frameworks. I found, for example, that both 'sex-typing' and 'the culture of femininity' were inadequate to explain girls' reaction to their school or to their community environment. Much theoretical literature portrays girls as 'sex-typed' or 'socialized' into female roles. But it does not take much observation of the girls 'in action' to discover that 'the female sex role' is only one of a range of possible scripts in the repertoire for coping with school. The girls could be aggressive (both verbally and physically), confrontational, lazy, loud, untidy — all the attributes traditionally associated with boys. They had not 'internalized' a passive, docile stance. McRobbie (1978), in her use of the 'culture of femininity', does attempt to demonstrate the more *creative* appropriation girls may have of experienced aspects of their structural position; but I did not find this culture as all-pervasive as with McRobbie's study. It was perhaps to be drawn on if necessary or appropriate; but it was not a dominating force. Some of the girls were openly 'tomboys' or 'scruffs'; most were more unpredictable than would be implied by the notion of their being part of an agreed culture. I do not claim that McRobbie was 'wrong'; merely that we need a *bank* of ethnographic accounts to demonstrate how flexible people are in response to, *and to exert influence over*, particular settings.

Ethnographers tend to play 'hunt the culture', or at least 'hunt the subculture': for one goes in with the notion that there is going to be something identifiably distinct to discover and then portray. I was no exception to this in my target for research of 'deviant girls': I wanted the fearless exposé, the female equivalent to the Glasgow gangs, the Smash Street kids. The lack of any identifiable subculture among the group of girls I was studying was initially a disappointment, but then became a source of fascination; and led, I hope, to a more delicate, albeit tentative depiction (Davies, 1980).

Perhaps one of the major benefits of ethnography is therefore initially not so much to uncover what things *are*, but to suggest what they are *not*; and this 'corrective' function, which Woods in this volume also documents, is particularly true of aspects of gender.

Lynn Davies

First, small-scale study of girls reminds us of the obvious, but strangely oft-forgotten, fact that groupings of girls do not exhibit all the same features as groupings of boys, and we should be wary of any generalizations about 'youth' or 'youth culture'; secondly, such study demonstrates that these differences may not be a question of *degree*, but of faults in substantive theory. It is not, as has been posited, that girls do not form subcultures 'as much' as do boys, but that the notion of 'subculture' is itself an over-simplistic and over-used device. Using simple translations of male paradigms (e.g. machismo will find its opposite in the culture of femininity) is both hazardous and unthinking; for by assuming the necessary existence of mirror images it downgrades women to shadows, and ignores their complexities. It also gives tacit assent to the 'rightness' of male-oriented conceptualization and theory. I am not even sure, for example, about Chris Griffin's choice of the terms 'cultural break-down' or 'cultural fragmentation' to describe the individuality of women (chapter 5): while the aim is, rightly, to demonstrate the diversity of friendships among girls, the way they continually break and reform in line with current male friends, the unintentional implication of such phrases is that strong adherence to the group is the norm and that women are deviant. What I would argue, therefore, is that ethnography about women (or ethnography that aims to admit sex differences) contains the usual elements of discovery and appreciation, but may at this stage have value not so much to further generalizations about 'the female', but to cut swathes through generalizations about 'mankind'.

Adopting a Methodology

In social science research in general, debates about non-sexist and feminist methodologies, and whether there is a distinction between them, have already been generated (Roberts, 1978; 1981). The very language, theories, models and ways of 'doing rationality' are recognized as inextricably bound up with the dominant male culture of the university environment. In searching for a non-sexist methodology, one would think at first sight, however, that ethnography would raise few objections. Women have traditionally been more involved in qualitative rather than quantitative research — it is a Well Known Fact that they are not good at counting — and indeed 'soft' data seem more in line with feminist researchers' insistence on the recognition of personal experience in sociological study. Paradoxically, however, the desire to prove qualitative research to be as 'scholarly' as the numbers game sometimes results in long earnest discussions of bias elimination, of the 'correct' techniques of interviewing to avoid contamination, or, when in real doubt, in a falling back on a highly technical reiteration of the rigours of grounded theory. I think it has taken women researchers to point up the myths of 'hygienic' research: the case is made that not only should one insist on reflexivity about personal bias and intrusion, but one should see these as positive aspects of the research. Oakley (1981), for example, convincingly argues against the notion that interviewing can be a one-way procedure, with the interviewer withholding her own views and resisting friendship or involvement. In her discussion of the sorts of questions women 'asked back', and of the quality of the research which emerged from the reciprocity and intimacy of her own research relationships, Oakley strongly resists the attitude which relegates interviewees to a narrow objectified function as 'data'. I sometimes feel that the term 'qualitative' implies a depth and a long-term caring which is simply not there. As a male sociologist has pointed out:

> Thus, while there may be something sexist in the use of the actual terms 'hard' and 'soft' data we cannot assume that the use of 'softer' methods is in some way less sexist than the use of techniques which might be labelled 'hard'. Qualitative methodology and ethnography after all has its own brand of machismo with its image of the male sociologist bringing back news from the fringes of society, the lower depths, the mean streets, areas traditionally 'off limits' to women investigators. (Morgan, 1981)

The combination of 'what counts as science' and 'what counts as newsworthy' may mean that ethnography is as masculinist in its orientation as any positivist approach.

A side issue, but a symptomatic one, is the intellectual and sexual division of labour within the research process itself. Wakeford in this volume described his difficulty as a male director with female research assistants in attempting *not* to reproduce in the research process itself the general social and familial subordination of women. Such dilemmas occur even 'further down' the research hierarchy. Ethnography usually generates tape-recording, which in turn re-quires transcribing — a possibly alienating and boring task if one is not involved in the topic. Hence Roberts and Barrett decided early on in their investigation of women and their doctors not to have tapes transcribed by an audio-typist, although their own labours were neither 'fun' nor solved the larger problem of hierarchies within research (Roberts, 1981). At one level the dilemma is similar to the career wife who agonizes over exploiting another woman to do her less rewarding domestic tasks; but it goes deeper than that. On the one hand (as has been pointed out to me), to worry about secretaries' possible boredom may merely reflect my own intellectually arrogant stance, which unwittingly demonstrates that I despise and look down on 'their sort of work'; but on the other hand, I do feel such concerns evince basic questions which should be tackled from the outset about control and about involvement by *everyone* concerned. While the ideal of non-hierarchical research is probably unattainable, and divisions of labour inevitable, at least these should be brought to the surface and people's need for recognition acknowledged. The active involvement of secretarial staff in the planning discussions about aims, procedures and timings, plus some real consultation about the sorts of decision-making they could undertake throughout, would be just a start. It is not only good managerial practice, but could aid in insights about the research itself. Otherwise, although purporting to open up certain social worlds, research may have a hidden curriculum which leaves unquestioned many other social worlds — especially those 'hidden from history' like (female) office workers. I am suggesting that ethnography, in the social relations of its production, should not merely confirm existing assumptions about work and sex roles.

The Research Relationship

As with relationships between 'researchers', some forethought on relationships between researchers and researched is clearly advisable. The ethnographer is a sort of tea strainer, who may exhibit much decisiveness about the interpretation of the tea leaves, but who has less impact on the amount and blend of the brew that is poured onto her/him. There are two major concerns here: one is the perceived status of the researcher as denoted by her clients; and the other is the nature and past experience of the strainer which is sieving the results. How far the ethnographer decides to 'go native' results from a mixture of theoretical appropriateness and practical expedience. With regard to the latter, one's age and social class are immediate constraints; gender may also be a constraint in the investigation of single-sex groupings. I would hold that in educational research which includes pupils, 'going native' is a fraud because of the age/outsider factor; we have to examine whether being the same sex as one's subjects is advantageous or not. Brake (1980), in claiming that 'girls make a detailed study of femininity', adds in parenthesis 'the only group likely to accurately see through a transvestite's performance are pubescent girls. Any male trying to pass in street drag dreads meeting them.' The example is tantalizingly left there, but the point is made: a female would be in a better position to assess real female performances, and presumably then be more likely to be party to 'true' action. One does save time: we see Andrew Pollard in Chapter 11 being forced to use female members of staff to interpret other females' 'manoeuvrings'.

Yet it is not all gain. On the one hand, being the same sex may aid in familiarity and confidences — for example, to me the girls would throw in explanations of acts relating to periods, or delay in them, with little self-consciousness; on the other hand, however, I might have lost out on the 'cultural stranger' role which is able to explore seemingly 'commonsense' explanations of the world, and which benefits from seeing unremarkable events as phenomena to be unpacked. As the anthropologist Kluckhohn once commented, 'It would hardly be fish who discovered the existence of water' (quoted in Wolcott, 1975). A focus on gender itself is, of course, a way of 'making the familiar strange' for male or female observers of classrooms, as Delamont (1981) has pointed out. She cites the spotlighting of sex role differentiation as one way of overcoming the assumption of researchers (who have all themselves gone through school) that everything in classrooms is 'natural'.

There may also therefore be benefits in cross-sex ethnography. I noticed in Meyenn's account of his research on middle school girls that he was aware of the curiosity of his position, for he ironically begins, 'It is not at all odd for a man to be interested in young girls, even in groups.' Yet he may have learned something from his 'interest', because of the surprises it holds: 'There was ... considerable internal fighting ... with the girls "breaking friends" with surprising (to me, at least) frequency and usually within a short time making friends again.' He could frame 'obvious' questions with impunity:

Josephine: Modern clothes in it — we've all got modern clothes.
BM: What does that mean? I'm very ignorant. What does it mean ... modern clothes?

> *Josephine*: Knee length and high shoes and things like that.
> *BM*: So, you have to wear these, what do you call them, wedges?
> *Josephine*: You don't have to wear them, but....
> *Sylvia*: All of us have got them.

Meyenn later remarks on the wearing of different shoes in summer and winter (as a woman I would have taken this for granted) and is able to note the cultural norms and pressures behind this (Meyenn, 1980). Hence there are swings and roundabouts in same-sex/cross-sex ethnography in terms of the availability of information. All one can ask is that researchers are aware of where they win and where they lose.

A different aspect, however, is that of status, particularly, for example, in a hierarchical institution such as a mixed comprehensive school. I might want to argue that men have greater status and therefore their requests for access or interviews would be accorded greater consideration. Would teachers be more willing to give of their time? There is now evidence that teachers (of both sexes) tend to prefer boys for classroom interaction, giving reasons of responsiveness, acceptance of discipline, enthusiasm and so on (Fuller, 1979; Davies, 1973; 1980): what we do not know is whether teachers and heads also prefer males for research interaction. There may be the counter-argument that women, because of their traditional invisibility, blend in with the wallpaper more, and are able to eavesdrop on conversations with greater insidiousness; that, similarly, because teachers may care less about the approbation of a woman than they do of a man (with regard to academic matters at least), they may choose their responses, or their classroom 'front', less carefully, and that a woman researcher benefits from eliciting a more 'honest' approach. Even with the pupils the same may apply: as I taped the girls' conversations, they would enquire:

> *Julie*: Do you ever play this back to your husband?
> *LD*: Why?
> *Julie*: Just wondered. Case he wondered, who's this girl carrying on.
> *Debbie*: Does he ever talk about some of we? Like does he say, who's that?

The irony was that, although it was in my interests as objective listener that they did not care what I thought of them, their concern about what my husband thought confirmed my own mere intermediary status.

Conversational practices are a linked issue here. It is now well documented that in mixed-sex exchanges, men dominate the talk, not only in the amount of time each participant has, but in the direction the talk takes (Spender, 1980a). Spender cites a study showing that up to 98 per cent of interruptions in mixed-sex conversations were made by men. Women learn from an early age to be more accommodating in talk, to be more polite, to listen more, to make more supportive and encouraging remarks. This 'facilitating' role may mean that women are more adept at interviewing techniques; but it may lead to problems. Sue Scott in this volume (Chapter 6) highlights the lack of information on doing feminist research on men, particularly powerful men; in interviews she found many of them more in control of the data than she was. Any 'training' of ethnographers should include recognition of the effects of 'normal' conversational rights between males and females.

There are then a variety of gender combinations in ethnographic research: a man researching males, a woman females; a woman researching males, a man females; either researching mixed groups, or a mixed team researching males, females or mixed groups. The question has been raised of whether it is possible to conceive of ethnography *upwards* in class society; similarly, blacks researching whites is more a source of humour than acclaim, such as the classic 'Source of the Mersey' expedition spoof, where black 'researchers' asked astonished Liverpool dwellers about their matrilineal and patrilineal descent patterns. Women researching 'men' as a group may also meet with some surprise, and, I suspect, some patronage. It would be impossible to state with certainty, however, the specific effect of gender on any research relationship; all one can ask for again is that it might at least be borne in mind in planning and execution.

The Production of Results

Easier to pinpoint is perhaps the influence of one's own gender and sexual constructs on the interpretation and presentation of data, once collected. Willis (1977) might be taken as an example of this. In his study of working-class 'kids', he portrays the girls as giggling sex objects, peripheral to the lads' culture and initiatives: 'The girls respond with giggles and talk amongst themselves.' Note that whereas the lads laugh, the girls 'giggle'; the lads' negotiative styles are interesting phenomena to be analyzed, but the girls' negotiations are dismissed in one line as 'contortions and strange rituals'. Whether Willis' depiction of the girls' 'domination' has validity, or is merely a reflection of his own masculine concerns coinciding with those of the lads, I leave open; certainly the girls he mentions seem to bear little resemblance to my own group, who could be openly sexual, would size up the boys in the disco, could refer to them in just as objectified terms: 'He's been passed around, that chap has, you know.' And yet Willis' claims become even more outrageous later on: 'The ability to take the initiative, to make others laugh, to do unexpected or amusing things, to naturally take the active complement to the appreciative passive, these are all profoundly masculine attributes of the culture. . . .' If it is masculine to want to make others laugh, heaven help women comics, let alone all the girls in school we know who effectively use humour for both entertainment and as a demonstration of power (see Davies, 1983).

In linguistic terms, just as I am by now sensitized to choices such as 'giggling' and 'passive', I am also interested in the need to deepen claims about the male world. Here is Willis once more: 'Despite the increasing numbers of women employed, the most fundamental ethos of the factory is still profoundly masculine.' Not content with the tautology of 'most fundamental', there comes his favourite 'profoundly masculine'. What, I wonder, is shallowly masculine? Have I any chance of becoming profoundly feminine? Yet Willis is not alone in this. Robins and Cohen (1978), talking of girls' fighting crews, conclude: '*Needless to say*, this aggro did nothing to alter the girls' *fundamental* one-down position in the local youth culture — as in other areas of their lives' (my italics). And this was after one lad was so badly beaten up by one of the girls he had to be taken to hospital. I enjoyed Brake, too: '. . . the sexist jokes and shouts that girls and women have to put up with daily is an indication of the *complex* desire and hatred of that desire that men have for women' (Brake, 1980; my italics). The validity of all these statements I will leave for empirical research. I am merely interested in the seemingly necessary (defensive?) use of 'profound', 'fundamental', 'complex' in order to support arguments about the importance of the masculine world. (It is perhaps in the same way that whenever anyone has doubts about their model, they refer to it as substantive theory.) The use of the passive tense is another clue to lack of evidence: 'Women are judged, then, not on their occupational status but on their femininity', concludes Brake. But judged *by whom*? By all? By men? By women? Male observers may fall into the trap of assuming that male perceptions of the world necessarily will include female perceptions (and one might want to look here at Dale Spender on the nonsense of how 'he' and 'his' were deemed to include 'she' and 'her' by male grammarians in the last century).

Adjectives, then, and grammar may be clues to latent sexism; finally, in this language section we might turn to the use of metaphor. Here we need go no further than Frankenberg's wonderful demolition job on Young and Willmott's *The Symmetrical Family*:

> Young and Willmott's first reference to the role of women in society comes on page 6.
>
> '(Towns in the metropolitan area) also had many commuters. Waiting for them when they returned at night from London were lines of cars stretching away from the stations, many with wives and dogs in the front seats. If he was not met by his wife a husband would walk down the line until he found a woman or a dog whom he recognized as a neighbour.'
>
> Willmott and Young have always recognized the vital role of dogs in middle-class culture.... They return to the identification six pages later. 'One wife was just about to say "working-class", her mouth half-open, when her husband, a printer, stopped it with a look and then said, "what a dumb wife I've got". She changed in mid-sentence and answered "middle-class", whereupon he nodded, as if to a performing dog, to tell her, yes, that was the right answer.' (Frankenberg, 1976)

The refreshing thing about Frankenberg is his analysis of his own past sexism: 'I also failed to see the irony of my statement: "Glyn people are strongly egalitarian in outlook. Among themselves they consider every *man* is every bit as good as the next" (new italics)'.

If I were to go through past publications of my own I am sure I would find similar examples of unconscious sexism, for I am not claiming that men have copyright over sexist language. Women writers and researchers may be just as prone to linguistic usages which confirm the very picture they are trying to deny. I have just failed to find any examples.

Researching Women

After discussion of the parameters of research, and the access to and writing up of data, I want to move back to the broader question of 'researching women'. In spite of my doubts about a totally male-dominated world, a totally oppressed female populace, there is the dilemma of colluding in the notion of women as a minority group if we do identify them as research targets. We seem to be able to talk about 'the woman question' as we cannot talk about 'the man question'. Wolcott comments:

> Like other humans, ethnographers sometimes fail to maintain their objectivity. They seem particularly susceptible to evoking sympathy for certain groups they study — e.g. ethnically different pupils and the poor — than for other groups — e.g. white, middle-class teachers, administrators or bureaucratic functionaries. (Wolcott, 1975)

I might add 'women' to his list of sympathy-evoking groups being studied. Why was I, for example, interested in girls' deviance, and should there be some introspection about my own background to provide honest answers to motivation? A salutary reminder came from a mental hospital administrator:

> Someone rang up, said they were keen to visit our establishment. Very keen to know about the sexual problems of our men. So I said that I would be very happy to see them because I was particularly interested in the sexual problems of special educators. (Varnier, 1971)

We have to be concerned about the results of the research, and about our subjects, whatever noble aims we have personally about the improvement of theory advocated earlier. Ethical questions are raised frequently throughout this collection. Burgess in Chapter 8 feared that the school might use his material merely to 'control' pupils. I, too, had the dilemma that if subsequent to my research the school was better able to 'handle' difficult girls, had I contributed to their oppression rather than politicized their resistance? If research on the other hand makes no appreciable difference to school policy, are there ethical questions both about the invasion of privacy and about yet again demonstrating girls as unimportant in school decision-making? Research on girls specifically may single them out and relegate them in a way research on boys does not, the latter (as noted earlier) often implying that 'boys' are synonymous with 'pupils'.

Hence there are admitted ambivalences in my stance. On the one hand, I am arguing for constant recognition of gender when studying single-sex groups; on the other hand, I am aware that this presents particular problems for the study of women. Unlike all-male studies (still a 'normal' sample, as affirmed by the latest mobility surveys) all-female studies may have 'freak' value. It is as if one were investigating two-toed sloths, or meths drinkers; homing in on an all-female group seems to confirm its strange, researchable, outsider status. The inquiry can end up providing the token chapter on females in a general collection on deviance, or on pupil perception (see Davies, 1978; 1979.)! There is a discernible quandary. I do think that females may present significantly different responses from males in particular contexts; yet highlighting such differences, given the *existing* status of women, may merely endorse their marginal/peripheral contribution to 'society'. Nor do I think the answer is more studies of women executives, headmistresses or other high-powered ladies: they are even more freaky, with their lack of maternal instinct, of passivity, of British Home Stores underwear. What we need, in fact, is a plethora of studies on 'ordinary' girls and women, yet which do not treat them in isolation *but include their effects on men*. Willis speaks of lads 'partially creating' identities for the girls; nowhere is it suggested that girls may 'partially create' identities for the lads. The *reciprocal* impact of the sexes needs to be remembered if ethnography is going to restore the notion of efficacy and power to females instead of always demoting them to the status of an 'oppressed' group.

Yet the question of the dubious benefits of publicity and intervention has deeper implications. Various strands come together when I think about this. There was the elderly lady living in a deprived area who said wryly, 'The one thing I have come to dread is being *worked amongst*.' There is the realization in Third World projects that it must be women themselves who collect data about their 'position', and define their 'needs'. International data collated by men classify work, for example, always in terms of wage labour — hence the large majority of women are not seen to 'work', in spite of their predominance in agricultural as well as domestic sectors. Aid funds and projects have thus been aimed almost entirely at men, on the western, male assumption that it is they who are the breadwinners, they who should be taught to use agricultural machinery and techniques. Many women's traditional roles have been destroyed in this process. And in this country those attempting to rehabilitate slum housing estates have long realized the importance of giving responsibility to tenants with regard to decision-making committees as well as to the eventual monitoring of the estate. They must define as well as solve the 'problems'. An interesting description from a female project worker was of her work as 'block-building':

> You take each particular problem, one at a time, and try to solve it. You can't do it all at once. You can't expect it to stay done once you've done it. It's like tidying your sitting room, something you have to keep on and on doing. You don't give up because it gets untidy again. (*The Guardian*, 19 February 1982)

I suspect this may be particularly a female way of doing things — to suspect the grand master plan, the master theory, the definitive research, and see more value in (as the American feminists call it) 'white-anting' — or chipping away at the edges. Certainly women who *have* determined their own projects in the Third World have rejected the large-scale agricultural schemes in favour of village cooperatives, or small-scale self-help schemes.[3] They have realized the need for education, not in terms of formal schooling for technology or general literacy, but to learn about accounting, about bank loans and credit schemes, and about how to assert themselves, communicate and persuade of ideas. In this, and in wanting to collect their own data about 'needs', they have seriously questioned the whole pattern and distribution of educational development aid to date.

Where all this leads when I reflect on research about education and women is the fear that we may not be able to leave ethnography at the anthropological level. A test for the so-called adequacy of an ethnographic account is supposed to be 'whether a person reading it could subsequently behave appropriately as a member of the society or social group about which he [sic] has been reading' (Wolcott, 1975); but the question is, with regard to low status groups, would anyone *want* to? Is it enough for ethnography to be accurate portrayal, a sort of art form? And should we retain the 'expertise', the authorship of the data for ourselves? It would be a daunting enough task to make the report comprehensible to the people it is about; better still might be for they themselves to collaborate in compiling it. We might then avoid the extremes of impermeable prose and the evident temptation to impress and be impressed by unintelligibility. This phenomenon has been tested by having academics rate the 'competence' of passages from journals, whereupon it was found that obfuscatory English received higher ratings for 'competence' than the identical meanings couched in simpler versions (Armstrong, quoted in *The Times*, 9 June 1980). The readability of work to structurally powerless groups should be a prime concern. In her studies of housework and childbirth, Oakley's resolution of the problem was to produce one book for the lay reader and one for the sociologist; but this may still imply an us-and-them dichotomy. Just as I would like to see some ethnography depicting 'ordinary' women and girls as influential, I would also like them to see for themselves their own power; not only that, but to see an influence from the publication of descriptive accounts and reports.

It is, then, a question of motives. Interestingly, of course, ethnography is not free from what Morgan terms 'academic machismo':

> The arenas of the practice of academic rationality — the seminars, the conferences, the exchanges in scholarly journals — are also arenas for the competitive display of masculine skills ... the symbolic leaders or academic folk heroes are sharp, quick on the draw, masters of the deadly put down.... (Morgan, 1981)

Even if one managed to do and write ethnography in a non-sexist way, the dissemination of 'results' — and results there must be — may be subject to competitive one-upmanship rather than being the cooperative enterprise which some feminist academics are attempting to pursue (as in Spender, 1980b). Whether this particular collection does coalesce to constitute a corporate venture or remains an uneasy juxtaposition of individual aspirations, I will leave the reader to decide.

But what would collaborative ethnography look like? It clearly aims at new sets of relationships and new outcomes. Minimizing the hierarchies and possessiveness *within* research 'workers' has already been mentioned; then comes the avoidance of competition and point-scoring *between* different research projects; but most importantly there is the insistence on the ideal of real collaboration between researchers and their 'subjects'. While this appears quite feasible with adult respondents — Elliott in Chapter 12 highlights the benefits of 'collaborative reflection' between the teachers in his research whereby they defined their own 'problems' — the contribution of lower status or younger groups needs some imaginative leaps. Pollard in Chapter 11 describes how he incorporated middle school children as his 'interviewing team', with highly profitable consequences for all parties. Not only did he get 'better' information, but the children's self-confidence grew, and they themselves learned much about the research process. Many ethical problems of rights and access to the data could be solved by turning 'subjects' into 'producers' of data. While I had a good relationship with the girls in my study, and they were gratified to be 'consulted' on their views, I regret now not having the grace to let them actively influence the shape of the research. They could have, as in Pollard, 'interviewed' each other; they could have 'observed' in classrooms; they could have 'saturated' their own categories, aided in 'grounding' the theory; and they could have had more hand in writing the final accounts than simply being relegated to representative quotations. Many researchers will confirm the typical disappointment my girls expressed when 'assured' their names would not appear in any published material; but did the girls not have the right to decide questions of anonymity? Is the stress on anonymity not at least partially the result of the (masculinist) academic urges towards scientific objectivity? Delamont's disputes with her colleagues over names versus 'Pupil 312' reflect just such concerns (see Galton and Delamont in this volume, Chapter 9). Yet even more important than simply producing a readable narrative is the need to humanize one's respondents. I feel a sense of waste now: while highlighting the general lower status of females in a school setting. I did nothing to promote these specific girls. They cannot, as I can, look at a book and say, 'I wrote that' or 'that was my idea'; they cannot even see their names in print and say 'that's me'. If ethnography is so technical or so mysterious that it cannot be shared out among all concerned, is it worth doing? Feminists have been leading the field in working towards the elimination of hierarchical attitudes and rituals, of closed shops, of competitiveness in academic and political life; in 'studying' already less powerful groups like pupils or (some) females, a feminist ethnography might point the way to a truly participative, mutually productive and status-raising process.

Summary

Concerns about ethnography and gender manifest themselves at various levels. First, in educational research we need to be cognisant of when the fact of being male or female (black or white, high or low ability) is of more significance than being a 'pupil' or 'teacher', and when not. Pupils of course share many commonalities with respect to their basic power position in any institution (as do teachers), but I would ask that an ethnographer always state whether research is in a single-sex or mixed school (it is amazing how often this is left out in the final accessible accounts), as well as delineating the social class, 'ability' and organizational features of the school. This way the importance that gender may have (in *combination* with streaming practices) is always kept in mind, even if the proliferation of female studies that I am asking for does not materialize.

Secondly, there is ethnography's function of acting as a critique of generalized theories about the social world. We need to counter the notion that 'working-class youth' can be satisfactorily explained by boys' accounts and perspectives; we need to resist the insistence that the work-place is predominantly (profoundly?) masculine (and that therefore by implication school is also because it acts as a preparation for that world of work).

Thirdly, there is the purpose of enlightening others working closely with the respondents. I found the teachers in my school admitting that one reason for their preference for boys was that they felt they did not *know* the girls as well as they did the boys — and therefore they were suspicious and prone to stereotypes of them. Readable ethnography might 'humanize' girls in school once more, and give teachers a basis for understanding and interaction.

But at the final level I might want to move to a situation where ethnography for low status groups became a collaborative venture, where the group themselves decided what they wanted to do with the material, and could assess its immediate and long-term usefulness. We do not want sympathy or even empathy for women or for female pupils; we want in the long run for them to be able both to read and to 'do' ethnography for themselves.

Notes

1 I am not here getting involved in the usual distinctions between sex and gender, but will use the terms interchangeably in the cause of clarity rather than analytic device: for example, I would choose 'interaction between the sexes', but 'the problems of gender'. . . .
2 On sex differences in pupil deviance see Davies (1980).
3 See *Journal of Development Studies*, 17, 3, April 1981.

References

BRAKE, M. (1980) *The Sociology of Youth Culture and Youth Subcultures*, London, Routledge and Kegan Paul.
CORRIGAN, P. (1979) *Schooling the Smash Street Kids*, London, Macmillan.
DAVIES, L. (1973) 'The contribution of the secondary school to the sex-typing of girls', unpublished MEd dissertation, University of Birmingham.
DAVIES, L. (1978) 'The view from the girls', *Educational Review*, 30, 2.
DAVIES, L. (1979) 'Deadlier than the male?' in BARTON, L. and MEIGHAN, R.

(Eds) *Schools, Pupils and Deviance*, Driffield, Nafferton.

DAVIES, L. (1980) 'Deviance and sex roles in school', unpublished PhD thesis, University of Birmingham.

DAVIES, L. (1983) 'Gender, resistance and power' in WALKER, S. and BARTON, L. (Eds) *Gender, Class and Education*, Lewes, Falmer Press.

DAVIES, L. (1984) *Pupil Power: Deviance and Gender in School*, Lewes, Falmer Press.

DELAMONT, S. (1981) 'All too familiar: A decade of classroom research', *Educational Analysis*, 3, 1, pp. 69–83.

FRANKENBERG, R. (1976) 'In the production of their lives, men (?).... Sex and gender in British community studies', in BARKER, D. and ALLEN, S. (Eds) *Sexual Divisions and Society*, London, Tavistock.

FULLER, M. (1979) 'Dimensions of gender in a school', unpublished PhD thesis, University of Bristol.

FURLONG, V. (1976) 'Interaction sets in the classroom: Toward a study of pupil knowledge', in HAMMERSLEY, M. and WOODS, P. (Eds) *The Process of Schooling*, London, Routledge and Kegan Paul.

HARGREAVES, D. *et al.* (1975) *Deviance in Classrooms*, London, Routledge and Kegan Paul.

McROBBIE, A. (1978) 'Working-class girls and the culture of femininity', in Women's Studies Group, CCCS, University of Birmingham, *Women Take Issue: Aspects of Women's Subordination*, London, Hutchinson.

MEYENN, R. (1980) 'School girls' peer groups', in WOODS, P. (Ed.) *Pupil Strategies*, London, Croom Helm.

MORGAN, D. (1981) 'Men, masculinity and the process of sociological enquiry' in ROBERTS, H. (Ed.) *Doing Feminist Research*, London, Routledge and Kegan Paul.

OAKLEY, A. (1981) 'Interviewing women', in ROBERTS, H. (Ed.) *Doing Feminist Research*, London, Routledge and Kegan Paul.

ROBERTS, H. (1978) 'Women and their doctors: A sociological analysis of consulting rates', SSRC Workshop on Qualitative Methodology.

ROBERTS, H. (1981) 'Women and their doctors: Power and powerlessness in the research process', in ROBERTS, H. (Ed.) *Doing Feminist Research*, London, Routledge and Kegan Paul.

ROBINS, D. and COHEN, P. (1978) *Knuckle-Sandwich: Growing Up in the Working-Class City*, Harmondsworth, Penguin.

SPENDER, D. (1980a) *Man Made Language*, London, Routledge and Kegan Paul.

SPENDER, D. (1980b) 'Educational institutions: Where cooperation is called cheating', in SPENDER, D. and SARAH, E. (EDS) *Learning to Lose*, London, The Women's Press.

VARNIER, E. (1971) 'Educators and the mentally deficient', in RUSK, B. (Ed.) *Alternatives in Education*, London, University of London Press.

WILLIS, P. (1977) *Learning to Labour*, Farnborough, Saxon House.

WOLCOTT, H. (1975) 'Criteria for an ethnographic approach to research in schools', *Human Organisation*, 34, 2, pp. 111–27.

WOODS, P. (1976) 'Having a laugh: An antidote to schooling', in HAMMERSLEY, M. and WOODS, P. (EDS) *The Process of Schooling*, London, Routledge and Kegan Paul.

5 Qualitative Methods and Cultural Analysis: Young Women and the Transition from School to Un/employment

Christine Griffin

In January 1979 I began work on a three-year study of the transition from school to the labour market for young working-class women in Birmingham. Analyses of the empirical 'results' of this project are available elsewhere (see Griffin, 1982a; 1982b; in press), but this paper focusses on the methodological side of the research. I used mainly qualitative methods to develop an ethnographic cultural analysis of the young women's experiences. This paper looks at the potential advantages — and limitations — of such an analysis for research concerning gender relations and women's position in particular.

The Young Women and Work Project

The study was funded by the Social Science Research Council (SSRC) on the basis of a proposal written by Paul Willis and Stuart Hall, who was the director of the Centre for Contemporary Cultural Studies (CCCS) at that time. I applied for the resulting research fellowship out of an interest in the Centre's work, and in the position of young women. I also suspected that similar projects focussing on female experience would be few and far between.[1]

The first stage of the project involved visits to six Birmingham schools of varying size, student intake, organization and academic reputation. I visited mixed and single-sex (girls') schools; Roman Catholic, Church of England and non-denominational; as well as independent schools and those that had been grammar and secondary

97

Christine Griffin

modern schools before the shift to comprehensive education in 1974. As the sole research worker, I interviewed headteachers, careers officers, careers and form teachers as well as 180 school students. The latter included middle and working-class girls; fourth, fifth and sixth formers; Asian, Afro-Caribbean and white students; and some boys. I talked to more 'academic' sixth formers who hoped to move on to university or college; fifth formers taking CSEs or O-levels who were unsure whether to stay on or leave at 16; and 'non-academic' students taking few or no exams who were determined to leave school as soon as possible.

The second stage of the project was a longitudinal follow-up of twenty-five young white working-class fifth formers with few or no academic qualifications into their first eighteen to twenty-four months in the labour market. This involved a series of informal interviews in coffee bars, pubs and in the young women's homes; with their families and friends (mainly mothers, sisters and girl-friends); and ten work-place case studies. The latter covered 'women's jobs' in offices and factories, and 'men's work' in engineering, as well as interviews with unemployed young women. I talked to young women's employers, supervisors, co-workers, careers officers and Youth Opportunities Programme (YOP's) tutors.

The process of 'selecting' young women for the second follow-up stage was far from one-sided. It depended on the active cooperation of the participants, combined with the need to limit the breadth of the research in line with the time and resources available.[2] All of the young women were eager to talk about themselves and interested in the study, although one was unwilling to be visited at work, since she felt it would make her too conspicuous. Three employers refused my request to visit young women's work-places on the grounds that I would be 'in the way'. The only other barrier I encountered was in the family interviews. I had little difficulty in talking to female relatives and friends (usually in the kitchen, which was very much a female space), but the young women's fathers and elder brothers (if they lived with the family) proved to be the most elusive and unforthcoming, showing a wary interest in my presence.

Since this book focusses on fieldwork in educational settings, I shall be concentrating on the initial school-based stage of the research, only mentioning the work-place case studies where relevant. Access to the schools was negotiated through Birmingham's chief education officer, on the understanding that I would not be sitting in on any 'academic' lessons (those subjects in which students would be taking exams).[3] I then contacted individual headteachers with letters describing the aims and methods of the project. All of the heads agreed to take part, and my informal contacts with individual teachers (all women) at three of the schools proved invaluable sources of advice in approaching the heads. These contacts were an important factor in my decision to include these particular schools in the study.

I visited each school at least three times, and my first visit involved an informal chat with the head. This gave her/him a chance to 'vet' me before bringing in the careers or form teacher who would be organizing my visits. The first introduction to students would set the tone for subsequent interviews, so I asked teachers to describe me as: 'Chris Griffin who is doing a project about girls at school and at work.'

I was never introduced to students in front of a whole class, but set up my tape-recorder in a separate room. I could then introduce myself to students on my own terms, setting an informal atmosphere from the start, usually by laughing and smiling and adopting an informal conversational tone. I made it clear that I was not connected with the school or the Careers Service, and that the interviews would be treated in complete confidence, before asking the students' permission to tape their words. One young woman recalled this first interview just after she had left school, highlighting the status gap between students and older people who are automatically associated with teachers in school (cf. Willis, 1977).

> *Wendy:* It was a terrible atmosphere that first time at school, us all sitting there thinking "Is she a teacher?" 'Cos you assume that anyone who comes is a domineering sort of person, it's just not relaxed. We were taught to respect people, speak properly to them, but you can't respect and be relaxed [laugh].

Qualitative and Quantitative Methods

Before discussing my use of qualitative and quantitative methods in this project, I want to clarify the differential status of these methods in social science research. At the most basic level, qualitative and quantitative methods are sets of different research *techniques*, each with their own potential advantages and limitations. These various techniques can be (and often are) employed simultaneously in a given study, but they can take on a different status depending on the overall research approach or epistemology.

Broadly speaking, quantitative techniques involve codifying (i.e., quantifying) phenomena, using questionnaires, social surveys or structured interviews, for example. Such techniques allow social scientists to carry out large-scale comparative analyses like the government census. Qualitative techniques involve more open-ended, 'free response' questions based on informal, loosely-structured interviews, observation, or diaries. They are fairly time-consuming and often used in smaller-scale case study based research concerned with subjective experience and social meanings, such as Dorothy Hobson's research on young married women's experiences of unpaid housework and childcare (Hobson, 1978).

Cochrane and Billig (1980) have likened the relation between qualitative and quantitative methods to the tension between the depth and breadth of the analysis respectively. Although both sets of techniques have their own advantages and limitations, western social science has come to favour quantitative research as the main source of 'hard' and 'rigorous data'.

Williams (1979) has argued that quantitative techniques have dominated social science research since their use in conjunction with a logical positivist philosophy during the development of industrial capitalism. This positivist philosophy advocates the search for universal laws through the use of natural scientific methods. 'Facts' are assumed to exist external to the researcher, waiting to be discovered. The researcher is seen as an objective, apolitical and value-free being, who works at a necessary distance from the 'object' of study. As capitalism developed, quantitative studies adopting this apparently 'unbiased' positivist approach provided information on the health and strength (or lack of it) of British working-class people. These people were monitored because they formed the basis of the productive workforce, the armies that expanded and policed the British Empire, and the breeders of future generations.[4]

Quantitative positivist research still dominates western social science, relegating qualitative techniques to preliminary pilot studies, as sources of 'rich' anecdotal 'soft data'. Even when the potential value of qualitative techniques is recognized within the positivist paradigm, they are still seen as subordinate methods which could hardly be used as research techniques in their own right (see Campbell, 1978). Contrary to these assumptions, there is no hard and fast relationship between quantitative techniques and positivism. Karl Marx, for example, was a fierce opponent of positivism, but his scientific materialism was based on quantitative methods (see also the Counter Information Services reports which use government and other relevant statistics to examine the power structures of contemporary society: CIS, 1981a; 1981b).

The Young Women and Work project employed both quantitative and qualitative techniques, but not in a positivist context. It was relatively unusual in the use of mainly qualitative methods, which were based on interviews and systematic observation. Most of the interviews were taped, or recorded in as much detail as possible in fieldnote form. They were loosely structured around a series of key topics and questions to allow for a degree of flexibility.[5]

Both individual and group interviews in schools centred on these topics, with sufficient space for me to follow up particular areas, for example, if students had a grievance against a given teacher or the school. This also allowed students to discuss issues amongst themselves. This often happened during questions about their future status in family life and the labour market, managing the demands of marriage and/or motherhood, or surviving as independent single women. Some of these discussions became extremely heated, since the whole area was fraught with contradictions and confusion for many of the young women.

In another case, a group of Afro-Caribbean fifth formers began to discuss a series of recent confrontations with the police outside the school. Such conversations always occurred towards the end of the interviews, when the students had relaxed a little and developed a degree of trust in my promise of total confidentiality. These discussions did not always fall within my list of pre-set topics, and I could amend this list as the research progressed. As a white woman in her late twenties with a highly academic education, I could hardly predict all of the main concerns of young white and black working-class women. The use of qualitative methods meant that the research did not have to rely on my preconceptions, nor on material from comparable studies, of which there were very few.

In all research studies where people are the 'subjects', their views of the research worker(s) and of the research itself will affect their responses and behaviour. It is just as impossible to eradicate these influences as it is to remove the researcher's assumptions about the participants. Rather than deny, ignore or minimize these effects, I have tried to recognize and understand them as a part of the research analysis (cf. Willis, 1980). Young women often turned my questions around, asking how I had felt on leaving school, how I had found my first job and so on. During the later stages of the research, young women used their continuing contact with me to find out about ex-schoolfriends with whom they had lost touch since leaving school.

A positivist approach might treat these questions as irrelevant or unwanted intrusions, or as potential sources of 'data contamination', but I saw them as part of the reciprocal nature of the research process.

Research is not (or at least should not be) a one-way process by which social scientists coax information out of 'subjects' only to disappear and analyze the 'data'. All research, regardless of the methodologies used, places specific responsibilities on research workers with respect to their 'subjects': the participants. This involves taking people's words and actions seriously, although not necessarily liking them or taking their words naively at face value.[6] This responsibility also extends to the political context in which research material is written up or presented. Social scientists involved in work with black communities should be aware that their work might be used by the police or the Home Office Immigration Authority to the detriment of black people, or taken up by racist groups and reinterpreted according to their own objectionable criteria (Race and Politics Group, 1982). Research does not occur in a political vacuum, despite the positivist argument that an 'objective' and 'value-free' approach is possible which can transcend political 'biases' and divisions.

The project involved systematic observation as well as informal interviews. This was most important in the work-place case studies where it was often too loud or too busy to talk, and where relevant episodes could not always be recorded on tape. I did not use true participant observation, since I could not have worked alongside young women on typewriters, data processors or sewing machines in the more skilled jobs.[7] Quite apart from the disruption which this would have caused, I would have been doing unpaid work in a situation of rapidly rising youth unemployment. Although few of the work-places were unionized, shop stewards and other employees would hardly have welcomed my presence. Participant observation does have the advantage of allowing researchers to share some of the participants' experiences, and to 'blend in' to their lives to a limited extent (cf. Willis, 1979), but it was inappropriate in this case.

I used the non-participant 'fly-on-the-wall' technique to observe the pattern of the working day in various work-places, either sitting in a corner or walking around the office or factory floor. My presence was explained as 'seeing what X's job involves' for the project on 'young women leaving school to start their first full-time jobs'. Once the initial novelty had worn off and everyone knew who I was, pressure of work usually meant that I was more or less ignored. Several managers and employees remarked that they had soon forgotten about my presence. As one office supervisor (Ms Stewart) said: 'I hope you haven't been bored. I forgot all about you. Mind you, I suppose that's a compliment to you, isn't it? [laugh]'

All of the fieldwork involved some observation, but the work-place case studies relied less on taped interviews than did the school and home visits. It was therefore especially important to keep comprehensive and accurate fieldnotes during the work-place studies. I paid frequent visits to the women's toilets throughout the fieldwork, scribbling out notes frantically before writing them up in full at the end of each day. The literature on social science methodologies tends to be highly theoretical (e.g. Giddens, 1976), and seldom mentions that the actual experience of such fieldwork can be extremely tiring both mentally and physically.

Whilst the project relied primarily on qualitative techniques, I did use some quantitative analysis and research materials. The responses of the 180 school students to specific questions about domestic work, part-time jobs and family structures were collated in quantitative form and subjected to fairly basic statistical analysis. I also used relevant quantitative material from Finn's work (1981), from Birmingham Careers Service records, and from local and national government statistics on the labour market. This information was used to put the qualitative work in a wider national political context, since this material was the primary focus of the ethnographic cultural analysis.

Ethnographic Cultural Analysis

This section looks at how the research material was analyzed; at those features which differentiated this cultural analysis from a positivist social scientific approach; and at their advantages for the study of the transition from school to un/employment for young women.

Most of the school interviews were recorded on tape and transcribed later by part-time secretarial workers, whose wages were included in the research grant.[8] I kept comprehensive fieldnotes throughout the fieldwork, even after taped interviews in case of equipment failure (a wise precaution as it turned out). These fieldnotes were all dated, giving details of place, context and who was present, as well as dialogue, including my own contributions, and relevant events and episodes.

However comprehensive these fieldnotes were, a degree of selectivity was inevitable, particularly when whole working days

Christine Griffin

were spent 'in the field' in offices or factories. In these cases I recorded those incidents which I judged to be relevant, surprising, or those which seemed to illustrate commonly-occurring themes. I also included my own initial interpretations of the events, and more subjective reactions, such as 'felt at ease' or 'terrified'.

I kept several 'Fieldnotes' files: notes from my visits to schools, work-places, and a 'family life and leisure' file; a 'Method' file, including my own reactions and developing ideas on research methodology, participants' views of me and of the project; and a 'Theory' file, containing notes towards a theoretical framework, and points about relevant texts. Not all of these notes have been incorporated into the final research analysis, but they have proved invaluable in developing that analysis and in writing this paper. These fieldnote files are a record of the reflexivity of the research process, of my continual examination of my own position and of the project's progress.

Following the tape transcription, I went through all of the fieldnotes and transcripts to categorize the material according to a series of topic headings. These were designed to cover the main research areas (see note 5); to be exhaustive with the minimum of overlap; and to be fairly manageable with negligible loss of detail. This categorization was recorded on a card index system which shaped the final analysis. It included additional topics arising from the fieldwork, such as the prevalence of male domestic violence, racist attacks and sexual harassment.

This initial categorization generated more interpretative ideas towards the development of a theoretical framework, all of which were recorded at the time, however vague and seemingly incomprehensible. Since this process began in the second year of the study, such initial analysis could be acted upon and incorporated into the continuing fieldwork. For example, leisure played an important part in the young women's lives in and outside the school and the work-place, and particularly in relation to pressures to be heterosexual and 'get a man' (Griffin et al., 1980). As the research progressed I was able to focus more on young women's leisure time and on the various social meanings of 'leisure' as compared to waged work and unpaid housework and childcare (Griffin, 1982a; 1982b).

This is one example of what has been called 'theoretical sampling' (see Glaser and Strauss, 1967; Willis, 1980), in which theory is developed throughout the fieldwork via the continual interaction between research 'in the field' and the generation of a theoretical framework. In this way theoretical analysis was not a discrete event which took place outside the 'field' when the work was written up, but was an integral part of the research process.

I have tried to balance the simultaneous pressures of 'making the strange familiar and the familiar strange'; to maintain my responsiveness to new insights, my capacity to 'be surprised', and my willingness to examine and 'see beyond' my own preconceptions. All research workers bring their own set of expectations and assumptions to a project, and I am no exception. Willis (1980) has not been alone in arguing that the positivist promise of 'objective' and 'value-free' research is illusory. It is important to recognize and examine (as far as possible) one's own expectations from the outset, in what Willis has called a 'theoretical confession'.

Although I came to the project with a fairly open mind, I did have certain expectations about the fieldwork. I was surprised and intimidated by the tense atmosphere in some schools, since my last prolonged visit to a school had occurred some ten years before, when I was a sixth former. I knew that I would be treading an uneasy line between staff and students, but I had forgotten just how wide this gap could be in practice.

As a woman concerned with young women's experiences, there were certain areas of shared knowledge which helped me to establish an informal rapport with female participants, such as laughing at how 'stupid and useless' boys and men could be, or at the contents of some romantic novels and magazines. Whilst this shared knowledge was an advantage, it could also hinder the examination of my own 'commonsense' assumptions, as Lynn Davies points out (see Chapter 4). Although I did have a degree of shared experience in common with the female students, this was limited by differences in class, age, race and social context which could not be discounted. The reflexivity of the research process rested on that tension between 'being surprised' by unusual or unexpected events, and dismantling 'commonsense' ideas (both my own and other people's) which tended to pass without being questioned (see Lawrence, 1981).

I employed qualitative techniques to provide an ethnographic account of the young women's lives using a form of cultural analysis. Ethnography has its origins in social anthropology, in studies based on qualitative participant observation techniques which have tended to be overly descriptive. Much of this research has involved white academics, and produced patronizing studies of supposedly 'primitive' black communities in parts of Africa and Asia.

Cultural analysis developed out of this somewhat suspect tradition via the National Deviancy conferences in North America and

Britain, and the more recent studies of youth subcultures (see Hall *et al*, 1980). This brought ethnography out of its relatively descriptive mode, defining culture as 'the shared principles of life, characteristic of particular classes, groups or social milieux. Cultures are produced as groups make sense of their social existence in the course of everyday experience' (Education Group, CCCS, 1981, p. 27).

Cultural studies in Britain has developed a form of ethnographic cultural analysis based on qualitative methods, which concentrates on specific cultural processes 'as they are lived'. This has aimed to move beyond the youth subcultures studies which have focussed on descriptive accounts of particular 'gangs' or styles, to develop analyses of broader processes such as the transition from school to the labour market (see Willis, 1977; Hebdige, 1979). Unfortunately, such cultural analyses have tended to retain the subcultural emphasis on the experiences of young white working-class men (see McRobbie, 1980 for a feminist critique of this work).

Cultural analysis provides a means of understanding individual experience in a group context. We are both determined by and potential determinants of social forces. People are neither passive reflections of stereotyped images and ideas, nor acquiescent victims of oppressive social conditions. Conversely, we are not all active 'social agents', able to make 'free choices' and rise above the most harrowing social conditions through sheer effort, willpower or 'individual resourcefulness' (see Griffin *et al.*, 1980 for a critique of this approach). Qualitative cultural analysis tries to maintain that tension between the individual as active social agent, the product of a given 'life history', capable of making positive decisions and choices, and the individual as influenced by specific social structures and ideologies. The stress on the cultural as it ties the individual to the group is the key to holding on to both sides of this particular relationship.

When I used this form of cultural analysis, I was aware that it had been developed to explain the experiences of mainly white and working-class men, as had the very concept of 'culture'. I also knew that other women working on girls' and women's schooling had expressed serious reservations about the potential value of cultural analysis. Walden and Walkerdine (1982) and Davies (1979) have questioned the relevance of concepts such as 'culture' and 'identity' to an understanding of female experience. The former have identified specific 'discursive practices' in a Foucauldian analysis of mathematics education for girls. Davies has preferred a form of interactional analysis which looks for the various 'social scripts' associated with given roles and social positions. McRobbie has worked within the cultural studies framework, maintaining a feminist critique and developing her own analysis of a white working-class 'culture of femininity' (see McRobbie, 1978).

My own approach falls between Davies' analysis and McRobbie's cultural framework (Griffin, in press). I also felt the pressure to fit young women's experiences into the dominant cultural paradigm, and to identify 'feminine' cultural forms. At first I too searched for female equivalents to Willis' 'lads' and 'earoles', striving to identify female pro- and anti-school cultures, and the cultural links between school and the world of full-time employment (see Willis, 1977). I tried in vain to fit the young women's experiences into this 'gang of lads' format, but their lives were far too complex.

I found no neat link between young women's attitudes to school, their status as 'good girls' or 'trouble-makers', their expectations about full-time employment, and their eventual positions in the labour market. Berni, for example, defined herself and her four girlfriends as 'mad', and teachers referred to them as 'trouble-makers'. They all detested the 'swots' and 'pets' who hoped to leave school and get office jobs. Berni's first priority was to leave school as soon as was legally possible: 'any job will do'. She ended up with two CSEs and a job as an office junior, spending her leisure time as a 'weekend punk'.[9]

My difficulties with this form of cultural analysis did not arise because Paul Willis' arguments were misguided: they simply did not apply to these young women's lives (cf. Davies, 1979). The latter did not go around in large groups or 'gangs' with fairly static memberships and recognizable styles or identities. Their 'culture' was based on close, sometimes intense, friendships which were continually shifting, usually involving three or four, perhaps only two, young women. Although the structure of these groups differed from that of their male counterparts, they still operated with some 'shared principles of life' (e.g., the importance of 'having a laugh'). So I did not abandon cultural analysis altogether, but tried to use it without tying the notion of culture to a 'gang of lads' model. Like Lynn Davies, I saw young women as able to adopt a range of different (though limited) strategies in a given situation, which would have varying social meanings and implications depending on the young women's position.

So a female student might use a sullen, uncooperative stare to undermine a teacher's authority, but because girls receive less attention than boys in school, this form of silent resistance could work against them (see Griffin, 1982a; Spender, 1980). When they adopted more vocal and visible forms of resistance, young women tended to be written off by teachers (and male students) as a 'bunch of giggling girls' (cf. Stanworth, 1981). The dominant images of female deviance in school centred not on aggressive 'macho' disruption, but on uncontrolled sexuality (Griffin, 1982b).

As the research progressed, I realized that many of these methodological issues concerned my status as a woman interested in young women's lives.[10] The qualitative cultural analysis had particular advantages because of this focus on female experience. Whilst I was making tenuous connections between these areas, debates about 'feminist research' took on an increased visibility. In the final section I want to take a brief look at these debates, and at their implications for the Young Women and Work project and other similar studies.

Qualitative Cultural Analysis and Feminist Research

I was forced to recognize the political implications of the research from the outset. Whilst Paul Willis admitted that he had never been asked 'why only boys?', teachers, employers, young people and some (male) researchers often asked me why I was talking mainly to young women. Exclusively male studies pass without comment, accepted as perfectly normal, whereas my work was seen as unusual from the start. I was frequently assumed to be a feminist, simply because I was a woman interested in young women's lives.

I was careful to present a suitably 'feminine' appearance (no monkey boots or dyed pink hair), and I never mentioned feminism because of the overwhelmingly negative media representations of 'women's lib'. Despite my precautions, one headmaster of a small mixed comprehensive took me aside to inform me exactly why 'this equal opportunities thing is a waste of time'. The headmistress of a large girls' comprehensive made similar assumptions about the 'political' nature of the research, but her 'little talk' was more supportive. She told me of the barriers to women's promotion in teaching, and her opinion of the project: 'Girls have such a low self-image, and so do women teachers, I'm all in favour of your study.' Like so many of the women I talked to, she prefaced her more 'controversial' (i.e., feminist) statements with the disclaimer, 'I'm not a women's libber but. . . .'

The negative media image of feminism as either silly or potentially threatening (to whom?) also presents it as relevant only to white middle-class women. I found that feminist ideas and campaigns had considerable influence and support amongst young white and black working-class women, as well as their mothers and (female) work supervisors. When I visited Jeanette in her job as an office junior in a small printing shop she introduced me by striding into the middle of the floor, raising a clenched fist and shouting: 'This is Chris, she's doing a project on me — women's lib!' We had never discussed feminism explicitly, and I could hardly discount Jeanette's action as an example of my presence 'contaminating the field'. Had I ever entertained any misguided hopes of passing as an apolitical, inconspicuous observer, they would have had to dissolve with every shake of Jeanette's fist.

Since I could hardly avoid the gender-related political implications of the research, my ideas about methodology were influenced in part by the developing debates about feminist research in and outside of the women's liberation movement (e.g., Eichler, 1980; McRobbie, 1982; Stanley and Wise, 1983). There is still considerable discussion as to exactly what 'feminist research' might entail, and who can (and cannot) do it, which I have no space to cover here. All research is 'political' in some sense, regardless of whether it addresses social 'problems' or policies, but I want to focus on the importance of gender relations in the research process.

Social science teaching and research have been dominated by white middle-class men since their inception. This is evident in the uneven gender distribution in research and teaching hierarchies; in the 'nature of traditional academic practice; and in the types of research which receive most funding. An increasing proportion of (mainly white and middle-class) women has moved into the social sciences since the expansion in higher education during the late 1960s. Despite their position at the lower levels of the academic career hierarchy, these women have had considerable impact on social science, supported by the 'second wave' of twentieth century feminism (Stanley and Wise, 1983).

Feminist academics have objected to the sexist language used in many studies which either ignore or marginalize women, and judge them according to a norm of male experience. Social science has been criticized for its emphasis on rational objectivity, its rigid hierarchical structure, and the individualistic methods of generating and sharing knowledge (Spender, 1980; Roberts, 1981). Feminists have not been alone in criticizing social science on these terms, but they have focussed on the way that this has denied and distorted women's experiences, presenting a specific 'male' view of the world.

Christine Griffin

These critiques of traditional social science and debates about feminist research practices have had considerable impact, and women's experiences should no longer be discounted as 'subjective', or 'deviant' in comparison to the male norm. Feminists are arguing not only for more jobs, more research that is relevant to women's lives, and more women's studies courses, but also for a radical transformation of social science research and teaching, theory and practice. No social scientists should be able to ignore the gender dimensions of their work, any more than the implications for race, class or age relations.

I have already mentioned some of the advantages of qualitative methods and cultural analysis, and these were particularly relevant for a study of young women's position. Many older people (I include myself and other feminists and researchers here), and especially those who make decisions about young people's lives, see young working-class women as 'silly giggling girls', 'jailbait' or future 'supermums'. Social science research has kept these young women silent and invisible (on anything other than male terms), and done little to challenge or transform these assumptions (McRobbie, 1980). Qualitative cultural analysis has the potential to move beyond these preconceptions, with its stress on 'knowing the internal dynamics of the situation as experienced by the participants' (Willis, 1980).

Whilst qualitative methods and cultural analysis have particular advantages for research concerning women's lives, they are not the *only* appropriate methods in this respect. Quantitative research can provide valuable insights into women's — and men's — positions. I have argued that qualitative techniques should be treated as research methods in their own right, and not as subordinate to the collection of 'objective' quantitative data. These different methods should be used with an awareness of their relative strengths and weaknesses, in the context of an approach that recognizes the political implications of 'doing research'.

Notes

1 My suspicions were confirmed in 1981, when the SSRC asked a colleague to resubmit a research proposal on the grounds that it was 'sexist' to focus mainly on young women's experiences. She was compelled to include interviews with young men in the name of 'balance'. One wonders whether Halsey (Halsey *et al.*, 1980) or any of the numerous other male social scientists who have concentrated on boys' and men's position have ever faced similar accusations of 'sexism'.

2 Although I interviewed young Asian and Afro-Caribbean women (and some young men) in schools and work-places, I followed young white women into the labour market. As a white woman, I decided that it would be more appropriate for me to look at white racism (both my own and that of white participants), as it structured the lives of young white and black women. The recent 'ethnic minority' studies have constructed black cultures and black people as a problem, and I wanted to turn this around and focus on a more obvious source of racist 'inequalities': white people and white cultures.

3 In most cases I interviewed students during careers or 'social education' lessons, which is an indication of the value placed on 'academic' (i.e., exam) lessons and students. I asked teachers to send along students who were taking few or no exams (depending on the school). The main drawback in having teachers decide who should be interviewed occurred in more 'academic' schools where teachers were reluctant to send me the so-called 'low ability' students. In these cases I had to persevere in making my interests as clear as possible.

4 Other analyses have suggested that positivist quantitative research is often used by dominant groups to render the experiences or very presence of oppressed groups invisible, or to distort their position (see Lawrence, 1981 for a look at the racism of 'ethnicity studies'; and Spender, 1980 on women's relative invisibility).

5 These topics included students' experiences of school, teachers, friendship groups, expectations of full-time waged work, unemployment, present and future family life, domestic work, leisure, part-time jobs, etc. I did not use a pre-set interview schedule or sit with a list of questions in front of me, but I did operate with a predetermined (and memorized) set of key questions.

6 I am grateful to Mick Billig for pointing out that not all qualitative research involves developing an empathy or rapport with the participants (see Billig, 1978 in which the interviewees were members of the National Front).

7 Most young working-class men move into jobs which fall into a fairly clear hierarchy based on differential skill levels. Young women's jobs have no equivalent structure, since where their work is skilled (e.g., typing, shorthand, sewing), this is seldom reflected in the pay, promotion prospects or on-the-job training provision (see Griffin, in press).

8 I only transcribed a few of the less audible tapes myself, although I checked through all the transcripts. Most of this extremely tedious transcription was carried out by Liesel Rosindale, Mary Ballard, Ann Lane and Deirdre Barker, to whom I am very grateful. The contributions of Lynn Davies, Sue Scott and John Wakeford to this book all refer to the complex hierarchies within research work, and to women's position in the lower paid, lower status secretarial and administrative jobs.

9 This was in 1979 and 1980. Everyone mentioned in this paper is referred to by a pseudonym.

10 My growing involvement in youth work with girls and young women as a worker on a Girls' Night at a Birmingham youth club led me to consider the links (or lack of them) between 'academic' research and

youth work or teaching 'practice'. I was also involved in a group of feminist youth workers and/or research workers who were meeting regularly to discuss the process of writing up research and youth work projects.

References

BILLIG, M. (1978) *Fascists: A Social Psychological View of the National Front*, London, Academic Press.

CAMPBELL, D. (1978) 'Qualitative knowing in action research', in BRENNER, M. *et al.*, (Eds) *The Social Context of Method*, London, Croom Helm.

COCHRANE, R. and BILLIG, M. (1980) 'Social problems in the real world', paper presented at BPS (Social Psychology section) conference, Canterbury.

COUNTER INFORMATION SERVICES (1981a) 'Women in the eighties', London, CIS pamphlet.

COUNTER INFORMATION SERVICES (1981b) 'Anti-report', London, CIS pamphlet.

DAVIES, L. (1979) 'Deadlier than the male? Girls' conformity and deviance in school', in BARTON, L. and MEIGHAN, R. (Eds) *Schools, Pupils and Deviance*, Driffield, Nafferton.

EDUCATION GROUP, CCCS (Eds) (1981) *Unpopular Education: Schooling and Social Democracy in England since 1944*, London, Hutchinson.

EICHLER, M. (1980) *The Double Standard: A Feminist Critique of Feminist Social Science*, London, Croom Helm.

FINN, D. (1981) 'New deals and broken promises', unpublished PhD thesis, Centre for Contemporary Cultural Studies, Birmingham University.

GIDDENS, A. (1976) *New Rules of Sociological Method*, London, Hutchinson.

GLASER, B. and STRAUSS, A.L. (1967) *The Discovery of Grounded Theory*, Chicago, Aldine.

GRIFFIN, C. (1982a) 'Cultures of femininity: Romance revisited', stencilled paper, CCCS, Birmingham University.

GRIFFIN, C. (1982b) 'The good, the bad and the ugly: Images of young women in the labour market', stencilled paper, CCCS, Birmingham University.

GRIFFIN, C. (in press) *Typical Girls? The Transition from School to Un/employment for Young Working Class Women*, London, Routledge and Kegan Paul.

GRIFFIN, C. *et al.* (1980) 'Women and leisure', paper presented at 'Leisure and social control' conference, CCCS, Birmingham; also in HARGREAVES, J. (Ed.) (1982) *Sport, Culture and Ideology*, London, Routledge and Kegan Paul.

HALL, S. *et al.*, (Eds) (1980) *Culture, Media, Language*, London, Hutchinson.

HALSEY, A.H., *et al.* (1980) *Origins and Destinations: Family, Class and Education in Modern Britain*, Oxford, Clarendon Press.

HEBDIGE, D. (1979) *Subcultures: The Meaning of Style*, London, Methuen.

HOBSON, D. (1978) 'Housewives: Isolation as oppression', in WOMEN'S STUDIES GROUP, CCCS (Eds) *Women Take Issue: Aspects of Women's Subordination*, London, Hutchinson.

LAWRENCE, E. (1981) 'Common sense, racism and the sociology of race relations', stencilled paper, CCCS, Birmingham University.

McROBBIE, A. (1978) 'Working class girls and the culture of femininity', in WOMEN'S STUDIES GROUP, CCCS, *Women Take Issue*, London, Hutchinson.

McROBBIE, A. (1980) 'Settling accounts with subcultures', *Screen Education*, 34, pp. 37–49.

McROBBIE, A. (1982) 'The politics of feminist research: Between talk, text and action', *Feminist Review*, 12, pp. 46–57.

RACE and POLITICS GROUP, CCCS (Eds) (1982) *The Empire Strikes Back: Race and Racism in 70s Britain*, London, Hutchinson.

ROBERTS, H. (Ed.) (1981) *Doing Feminist Research*, London, Routledge and Kegan Paul.

SPENDER, D. (1980) *Man Made Language*, London, Routledge and Kegan Paul.

STANLEY, L. and WISE, S. (1983) *Breaking Out: Feminist Consciousness and Feminist Research*, London, Routledge and Kegan Paul.

STANWORTH, M. (1981) *Gender and Schooling: A Study of Sexual Divisions in the Classroom*, London, Women's Research and Resources Centre.

WALDEN, R. and WALKERDINE, V. (1982) 'Girls and mathematics: The early years', University of London Institute of Education, Bedford Way Papers no. 8.

WILLIAMS, R. (1979) *Politics and Letters: Interviews with New Left Review*, London, New Left Books.

WILLIS, P. (1977) *Learning to Labour: How Working Class Kids Get Working Class Jobs*, Farnborough, Saxon House.

WILLIS, P. (1979) 'Shop floor culture, masculinity and the wage form', in CLARKE, J. *et al.* (Eds) *Working Class Culture*, London, Hutchinson.

WILLIS, P. (1980) 'Notes on method', in HALL, S. *et al.* (Eds) *Culture, Media, Language*, London, Hutchinson.

WOMEN'S STUDIES GROUP, CCCS (Eds) (1978) *Women Take Issue: Aspects of Women's Subordination*, London, Hutchinson.

6   Working through the Contradictions in Researching Postgraduate Education

Sue Scott

As with most social practice, doing research is usually an untidy, multifaceted and often contradictory process. In this chapter, which is one of three accounts of the Postgraduate Research Project, hereafter called the Project,[1] I hope to illustrate the significance of this for understanding some aspects of the research process.

When sociologists and researchers write about their work, there is a tendency for it to be located within one of two models. The traditional research report attempts to be a statement of facts, involving descriptions of the theories and methodologies used and the results obtained. More recently, there has been a call, which is to be welcomed, for us to 'come clean' about the problems involved in our research, to admit to our failures and to failures of method and theory.[2] This itself, however, too often develops into a confessional mode, as if the problems we encounter are lamentable, and if eradicated would lead us to 'the truth'. I want to suggest here that not only are problems and contradictions an inevitable part of the process of research, but that the results of our research are centrally achieved through these contradictions, and this includes many of the useful results. I will not suggest that all problems are good for research, that would be foolish, but I do want to suggest that working through the contradictions in the research process can be stimulating and offer the opportunity for insight and understanding which the simple eradication of or attempted ignoring of the contradictions would not create.

Not only do I feel that the contradictions evident in my own position as a woman researcher within higher education, most notably those between assumed equality and actual marginality, helped me to understand better the positions and accunts of the people I interviewed (since many of them were in similarly contradictory positions), but that this in itself is useful in an examination of the research process in general. I feel strongly that the acceptance of the fact of contradiction within research itself can lead to a fuller understanding of the data, or at least to understandings which are significantly different from those attainable if the process is seen to be straightforward.

Before I go on to look at the research process itself, I think it is worthwhile setting it in its place in terms of the contradictions inherent in the Project from the very start, which moulded the conduct of the research in important ways. The processes of appointment and setting up of the projects when discussed at all in research reports (which is rare) are usually bald statements of 'fact', and yet they may often be as important as the research process itself. Research is, after all, the application of methodologies and theories to the social world by members of that social world, by individual people and groups of people. So knowledge of the fact that three named individuals carried out the research is of little use to the reader unless something is known of their positions, attitudes and emotions, and in particular of the history of their embarcation on the research process.

Setting Up

I first became aware of the Project in a conversation with John Wakeford at the 1978 British Sociological Association's (BSA's) Annual Conference, when he told me that it was likely that the Social Science Research Council (SSRC) would fund some research that he had been considering into the postgraduate research process in the social sciences. The research stemmed from debates within the BSA and between members of the BSA Executive and the SSRC. My impression was that John was asking whether I would be interested in working on the Project, although I was unsure of the exact status of our conversation. At the time I was a part-time postgraduate in the Department of Sociology at Lancaster, and John was postgraduate convenor, so I already knew him and had found him sympathetic and helpful. The funding was duly granted by the SSRC and the post was advertized in November 1978, and although I had had further discussions with John about the Project I still had to decide whether to apply. At this time I had several part-time teaching jobs all over Lancashire, and my thesis work was suffering. I needed a job, and welcomed the thought of doing a structured piece of work with other people, but I knew that my own work would grind to a halt if I had a full-time job which entailed a great deal of travelling, and I was worried about this because I still felt that having a PhD was the only way to become a 'proper' academic. I also worried that my interest in the research was insufficient — I was interested in a vague way in the situation of part-time postgraduates, my own experience not having been entirely unproblematic, but I did not feel that this was a sufficiently academic level of interest.

Actually getting the job was also potentially problematic, because although I certainly did not see my appointment as a foregone conclusion, I knew that some colleagues would see it that way, so that even if I were appointed, I did not feel that I could feel fully satisfied with my position. Even though the post was advertized externally and several people were interviewed, and even though I did have three years' experience as a researcher, the fact of my appointment was still, I felt, problematic, both for my own self-esteem and for my relationship with the department.

There were tensions between the department and the Project from the outset, which focussed on the widespread view that John was 'empire-building', primarily, I think, because the department viewed itself, somewhat hopefully, as a democratic unit, and John had had the nerve to organize the research unilaterally, with the support of the BSA.[3] Also, no-one in the department had ever held a large research grant with attached staff before, and people were unsure how to react. John did involve the whole department in the appointment of the research staff, but there was disagreement over my fellow researcher Mary Porter's appointment, and John having the final say, as research director, reinforced some people's prejudices against the Project, and actually brought about the very situation which they had been concerned about in the first place; that is, a lack of integration between the Project and the department.

All this, coupled with the suggestion that John had deliberately chosen two women to work with because they were less threatening,[4] served to make me nervous about the Project from the start. It could also have caused problems in my relationship with Mary, since I chose not to tell her of the ill-feeling in the department over her appointment, thinking that she had enough to deal with without having her relationships in the department rendered problematic at the very beginning. I am not sure that this was a good idea, and when Mary did find out some time later, she was understandably upset although, thankfully, it did not seem to affect the relationship we had by that time developed. Two other factors were important. First,

Mary was appointed as a research assistant on a lower scale than I was, which on the one hand reinforced my greater research experience, but on the other highlighted a hierarchy which ran contrary to our attempt to set up an equal team. Secondly, the views of colleagues in the department, that the research was trivial (summed up by one person's comment a few weeks into the project, asking whether we had finished it yet), fed into my own insecurity about what I 'should' be doing, and what constituted 'proper' academic work.

The situation I have outlined is, although particular to the Project, not, I am sure, wholly without precedent; I have yet to hear of an entirely unproblematic academic appointment. However, the process of setting up the Project itself set up contradictions through which the actual work of the Project took place. In brief, for me, the most important were these. We were supposed to be integrated into an academic department, but we were not, either physically (our office was some distance away from the department, on the other side of the campus) or academically. On the one hand this created a feeling of marginality, but on the other created a strength in the Project, and, after a while, a determination to show that it *was* useful and academically viable. The fact that we were technically members of staff, but were rarely treated as such, had similar effects. We set out to be an equal team, and to an extent our work was based on this premise and dependent on it, but we were not, at least in the beginning, either in levels and types of experience or in structural terms; on the one hand this made me feel wary at the outset of imposing my own ideas on Mary and having John's ideas imposed on me, but on the other concentrated our minds on the implications of this inequality so that we at least attempted to take it into account. I was, at the outset, committed to 'theory', while the Project seemed to me to be simple data-gathering. On the one hand this meant that it was some time before I began to treat the Project's work 'seriously', but on the other freed me from the invidious necessity of squeezing that work into a rigid framework, allowing me to be flexible in my approach to the work.

The Research

The object of the research, in very general terms, was to study the context and process of postgraduate research in the social sciences,[5] and, in particular, to attempt to isolate some of the more important constraints, both within and external to academic life itself, on part-time self-funding students. John's research proposal centred on a qualitative methodology in an attempt to discover, through semi-structured interviews with a broad spectrum of students and supervisors, what those directly involved in the postgraduate research process considered to be the major areas of concern. Our theorization and analysis were to be 'grounded' in the actual understandings of our interviewees rather than in any pre-existing theoretical framework and the post-hoc squeezing of the data into pre-codified patterns and categories. The choice of a qualitative methodology was, I think, wise, and proved useful, although at times, faced with the criticism and occasional anger of some of our fellow sociologists, it took on the semblance of a revolutionary act.

On reflection, I think that the major contradiction with which we worked throughout the Project was that between our chosen methodology and the ghost of positivism, which I certainly felt as an almost real presence at my shoulder. I often felt almost besieged by empiricism; at seminars and in papers we gave throughout the research there was a constant demand for numbers, a constant dismissal of our qualitative data not on their own merits but as a 'failure' to quantify. Annoying though it was to be often placed in the role of acolyte to John's Anti-Christ,[6] it was the contradiction in this area, between positivism and our chosen methodology, which we ourselves built into the research, that I found most problematic and subsequently most interesting. First, the quantity of interview data we collected was almost unmanageable; we collected so much data that we left ourselves too little time to reflect on and analyze it. I am left with the nagging feeling that there are transcribed interviews which I carried out that I have not even re-read, let alone analyzed. Partly, this was due to a pressure which I certainly felt (whether it came from my own insecurities or from outside pressures) to collect 'representative' data, that is from as many departments as possible, and partly it was because having vast quantities of transcript data was to an extent a defence against our empiricist inquisitors, so that we could say, look, this does not just come out of our heads, it's all down on paper, in black and white. For a long time I measured the success of the Project in terms of the quantity of interviewing, such that interviewing became the raison d'être rather than analysis. I now think that we interviewed far too many people, and that past a certain number of interviews, the returns in usable data and insights became progressively less. I do not think we would have found out anything more useful than we did if we had interviewed every postgraduate in the country, which is what it felt as if we were trying to do at times.[7]

Sue Scott

Allied to this was another aspect of the contradiction between our methodology and the positivist tradition, which was concerned with our use of tape-recorders in the interviewing. Rather than seeing the use of tape-recorders as a sort of extra memory, storable and recoverable, the technique began to take over, so that we began to assume that the tapes would somehow provide us with the 'truth' of the interview. In a sense I became merely an extension of the tape-recorder rather than the other way about, a channel through which the data ran from its individual sources to the reservoir in our filing system. In retrospect I would have been happier and kept more in touch with the data if I had been writing interview notes, but the quantity of interviewing would have made this almost impossible.

All this happened, I think, because we did not feel safe with the methodology, we did not for a long time fully believe our own defence of qualitative methods and our practice suffered because of it. Also, by half way though the Project, my knowledge of qualitative methods had increased to the level where I was beginning to doubt whether what we were doing actually qualified for that description in a full sense. Our interviewing was supposed to be informal, structured only by a series of very generalized subject areas. The use of tape-recorders, however, tended both to formalize the interview itself and split the interviews, reifying the recorded data at the expense of other aspects of the interview relationship. In most interviews, the recorded data were perhaps three-quarters, sometimes less, of the actual interview. The remainder — introductions, the establishing of some sort of rapport, the after-taping conversation, and importantly our own feelings and understandings of the interview — became actually, if not theoretically, less important. This had the effect of hiding the researcher, so that our own understandings became only secondary data, to be recovered from the unreliable data bank of the memory rather than from the objective fact of our transcripts.

This became increasingly problematic as we began to realize the very specific nature of doing sociological research on the process of sociological research. Primarily it became obvious that not only the interviews but also our work situation and indeed much of the rest of our lives, both academic (in terms of our attendance at conferences) and even social, was actually participant observation. We could not tell where the data stopped and the rest of our lives started. Now I think this is the case, to varying degrees, in all research, but it is effectively hidden by most methodology. In doing sociological research on sociological research, it became obvious, and we should have been able to use this and even concentrate on it, but because we started with tape-recorded interviews we were to a large extent unable to blend the information in our files with our participant observation data except after the event in written commentaries such as this.

There were other aspects of the interview process which were difficult. I have already mentioned, and discuss in more general terms later, that my anxieties as to whether the research was 'proper' academic work, and the reasons for this, were central to my appreciation of the task in hand at the beginning of the Project. Actually doing the interviewing, by comparison, seemed to be the least of my worries; after all, it was simply a matter of going out and talking to people and recording what they said. It was not 'proper' academic work precisely because it was so simple and straightforward. My naivety, or rather my belief that the interviewing would be similar to the sort of interviewing I had already experienced, was soon shattered. I soon became painfully aware of the complexity of the interview process in this instance, and of the seemingly endless minor and major contradictions within it. First to come was a partial realization of why I felt interviewing was not 'proper' academic work. It was not 'proper' academic work because it was women's work. Our initial reading around the interview process produced such gems as: 'It is quite clear that certain sorts of data are made more readily available to personable young women' (Dingwall, 1980), and: 'I do not advise the interviewer to pretend to adopt views of which he [sic] does not approve. He [sic] will, however, do well to remember that a coquette is in a much better position to learn about men than a nun' (Wax, 1971). Interviewing is down-graded because it is the time-consuming part of research which other people (usually women) are paid to do.[8] Interviewing is a service job and is seen by many men as women's work; after all, establishing rapport is what we women do so naturally and so well! Interviewing is also far removed from the processes of individualized (and male-centred) research, the angst-laden process of critique and counter-critique, the pulling out of devastating intellectual blockbusters from the tortured mind that still lies behind our understandings of the research process.

I started interviewing torn between an outraged resolution that *I* certainly was not going to be either a coquette or a 'personable young woman', and a residual feeling that the interviewing process really was not an academic task. Many of the interviews, particularly those we carried out with male supervisors and postgraduates, reflected this view of interviewing as a menial task, and this was often linked to their conceptions of our positions as young women. Whilst I certainly enjoyed interviewing and found it a very useful research tool, it was also the case that I was often aware, because of the personalized rather than formal nature of the process, of being patronized, both as an interviewer and as a woman. Many of our interviewees treated the interview as just an opportunity for a chat, and many of the men imposed a definite male/female power relationship over the interview process.[9] While this was annoying, and the devaluation of the qualitative methodology did not do much at times for my personal esteem, it often had a desirable side-effect, in that many people revealed much more than I think they would have in a more formal situation precisely because of this devaluation; since the interview was not important or threatening in either a personal or a sociological sense, people often felt more able to be open about what they felt and about their personal beliefs and preoccupations.

It was, of course, to return to a point I raised earlier, extremely important that we were interviewing sociologists, that we were, at least in a simple sense, interviewing our peers. There were, I think, two major areas of difficulty here. The first was that I never felt as if I was developing an expertise in a particular area of work. I could never feel as if I was an 'expert' in postgraduate research. All of the people I interviewed were either doing or had done postgraduate research; it was not as if I was finding out about anything that people did not think they knew all about anyway. The second difficulty was perhaps more important, and concerned the ethics of our relationship to the sociological community.

During the course of the research, we attended, both in personal capacities and as members of the Project, several conferences, study group meetings, summer schools, and so on. At the beginning I tended to think that our data came only from our sample, but, of course, my attendance at conferences and the like made me aware that almost everything I did in this respect became data. I never actually felt that I was spying on people, but, since people inevitably talked about their experiences at events such as this, I was always having to remind myself and other people that when they started to talk about their experiences in departments that were part of our sample, their views would inevitably become data. They would, of course, remain confidential, but nevertheless, it was never comfortable for me to be in such a different and very specific relation to what was for others simply conversation and gossip. On the other side of the coin, the information which I had gathered from interviewing was, of course, confidential, and several times I found myself with knowledge about particular departments and individuals which would have been of use to people to whom I was talking in a social context. I never felt comfortable about that either.

It did not occur to me until quite late in the Project that this placed me in quite a powerful position. It was so problematic for me that it was not until a member of a department on our sample said he wished he had the information about sociologists and departments in his head that I had in mine, that I recognized that that must be how many people understood my position. On reflection, I still do not think the information I have makes me powerful, for three particular reasons. First, and quite simply, would anyone take any notice of what I said anyway, even if I did 'spill the beans'? Secondly, on a more ethical level, should I expose the problems within social science, and sociology in particular, at a time when it is under attack on an ideological level and in financial terms? Thirdly, and on a personal level, if I did construct an exposé of the attitudes and behaviours in sociology, would I ever work again? Surprisingly, many of my colleagues in sociology did not appear to appreciate these problems, and I was forever being cornered at conferences and invited to 'tell all', as if all information about other people's lives in sociology was public property.

Now it sounds as though what I have done so far here is to suggest that the Project was fatally flawed and did not produce anything very much in the way of useful information. Far from it. What I want to do now is to suggest that the contradictions I have described, both in my own position and in the methodology of the research, were actually useful as well as problematic, and that working through them was considerably more useful in the inter-pretation of the data than either ignoring them or attempting to abolish them. I also want to suggest, tentatively at the moment, that this might be true of all research.

Simplistically, the contradictions in my own position helped me to see how what departments and supervisors say they do for their students may be interpreted quite differently by the students them-selves, and from the contradictions within the research itself I learned how the theories about, and practices in, postgraduate research may be very, very different. But surely, I hear the cry, it would be hopelessly naive to believe anything else. Of course, I had a theoreti-cal or simply a 'commonsense' understanding that these things would be evident, and I had some notion of why. What I found out was a great deal about *how* such things occurred, not on a theoretical but on a practical, day-to-day level.

The Results

I do not intend here to present a list of the 'findings' of the Project. No such list exists, nor could it, given the complexity of the research process we studied and of the data generated. Nor have I space here to go into more than a few of the more important examples of the process which I call 'working through the contradictions'.

It is probably worthwhile here, before I do that, to state a little more clearly what I mean by contradiction. There is, I think, a danger in any research, that it can become purely problem-oriented, often in line with a preconceived set of theoretical understandings. Now I do not support the view that there is good in anything if only you look for it (I cannot find anything good in rape or nuclear war), but the other side of the coin, the discovery of problems which are more important to the researcher and the theory used than to the re-searched, is terribly insidious. Of course, we started with a set of understandings that postgraduates would experience difficulties in certain areas, such as funding and supervision, and I am sure that if we had used survey methods we could have arrived with relative ease at a 'top ten' of postgraduate problems, but what we found using a qualitative methodology was a situation of extreme complexity which such a top ten would have hidden and distorted. It would have hidden the fact that some postgraduates said they did not have any problems at all, that others found the whole situation intolerable, that most found some situations problematic but others did not and that some even found a particular situation a problem one week and not a problem another. It would also have hidden the fact that the categories themselves are complex. When we talked about bad supervision, or problematic supervisory relationships, we found that this not only encompassed a whole range of different problems, from sexual harassment to academic bullying, but that what was bad supervision for one person (e.g., leaving the student to get on with it) was actually good supervision for another, and vice versa.

The use of the term 'contradiction' then is an attempt to encompass this complexity, and there are three important aspects of its use here. First, contradiction (e.g., between the aspirations and objectives of supervisor and student) may not necessarily be prob-lematic, depending on how the relationship is handled. Secondly, contradiction implies a two-way power relationship between indi-viduals as well and not simply a structural dyssymmetry as in its use in Marxist theory. Thirdly, it implies a relationship which can be at the same time both problem and challenge, closure and opening.

Let me take as an example a contradiction which I recognized in myself as it was described to me by many of the feminist postgraduates I interviewed, that is, that many feminists, although openly critical of the academic enterprise, also lack confidence in their academic abilities. So, for instance, one interviewee spent half an hour ripping apart the academic machismo, stilted writing styles and rank elitism of her colleagues, and the next half an hour telling me of her feelings of inadequacy, her worries that her work was not sufficiently academic. Now we could, and many women I talked to did, identify this as a problem, either as an individual 'failure' to reconcile theory and practice such that the critique of academia has 'failed' to develop into a complete rejection of it, or as a failure of feminist theory itself. I think, however, that even as descriptions of events, let alone as prescriptions for action, these answers are insufficient. As a personal response to a perceived anomaly, neither abandoning the academic enterprise nor attempting personally to push back the frontiers of feminist theory is adequate, for what we have here is not a simple problem but a contradiction. This contradiction raised many questions and responses to those questions which are of relevance to feminism and to academic life in general as well as to postgraduate research in particular, which, I suspect, would have been overlooked in a quantitative survey and in the understanding that such contradictions need to be 'resolved' in a simplistic sense. First there seems to me to be no *necessary* reason why a critique of academia and at the same time worrying about one's academic competence is *essentially* problematic, although in our talks with women this link was often explicitly described as such. The link becomes problematic because there is no position which feminists (unlike, for instance, Marxists) can easily take up within academic research, except perhaps for those we create for ourselves, in social life in general. Academia is not as problematic a part of late capitalism as it is concerned in men's dominant social position. Again, and importantly, the anomaly becomes problematic because we expect our feminist critique of academia to ease our worries about its effects, including our worries about academic credibility, as if our assertion of power in the critique takes a similar amount of power away from our academic overlords. This zero-sum conception of power is all too prevalent and often leads to just such apparent personal 'failures' of will. Worrying about academic credibility is a result of the exercise of power by the academic mandarins, and is neither a personal failure nor a failure of feminist theory but the result of a tactical misalignment. When we criticize something, we *feel* its power as well as understanding it, and we must develop tactics which deal with the former as well as explanatory theories of the latter. The simple explication and critic-ism of accepted structures and behaviours is not enough but should be allied to positive strategies as to how to deal with the complexity of our individual responses to situations and events.

Of course, worries about academic credibility were not confined to feminists, to women, or indeed to those who were overtly critical of aspects of the academic enterprise. If there was anything approaching a universal within our results, it was this. At first, I think, I tended to dismiss this as not particularly interesting; after all, in a sense, you would have to be either massively egotistical or in a position to define the academic for this not to be the case, and any hierarchical institution is bound to create self-doubt as well as oppositional attitudes in its 'lesser' members. However, a combina-tion of the sheer quantity of reports of self-doubt and of my own feelings of not being a 'proper' academic, prompted me to try to offer other explanations and to pry a little deeper.

It became obvious that at the same time as the notion of academic excellence and the PhD as a necessary rung in the academic career structure was increasingly being thrown into doubt in the wake of education cuts and the almost total drying up of academic career possibilities, people were much more ready to doubt their own academic credibility. People who knew that they were building a sugar castle, that there would be no academic job at the end of their studies, were apparently perversely more worried about their academic credibility than if they were still involved in competition for jobs. I had half expected that the job situation would have resulted in an increased lack of will or at least less worry about academic excellence, a sort of 'well if I'm not going to get a job anyway, why should I worry about my work, I'll just do what I want.'

Partly, I think, this can be explained in terms of departmental responses to SSRC (now ESRC) guidelines, such as they are, on postgraduate study. While departments were in theory only grud-gingly falling into line with those guidelines, in actuality they began to fall over themselves to grab the 'best' students, and students who could be relied on to follow the SSRC pattern of research, and, fundamentally and importantly, complete on time.[10] This meant that some departments often interviewed large numbers of students, upwards of twenty, for a single award, and made it known in no uncertain terms to the successful that they were expected to do it right and do it on time. These demands have placed increasing pressure on students. Being one of a very limited number of chosen students may be an ego-boost for a while, but it soon becomes a weight on the shoulders and magnifies the inevitable difficulties of the academic enterprise into personal and departmental failure to deliver the goods. For part-timers, who are anyway often viewed as simply those who have failed to be full-time, the pressures are different but often as great.

Again, when jobs were more freely available, the importance of doing credible research and finishing it on time was much less; many of those in lecturing jobs now were appointed during their last year of research and completed their PhDs only after a lengthy period of employment. It was enough then simply to be doing research; to be accepted as a PhD student meant that you were good enough as well to progress to a tenured lecturing post. To get one of the few lecturing jobs nowadays you have to be a certified grade-one genius with a proven ability to push back the frontiers of sociological theory. Or that's how it seems to many postgraduates. The response is either to give up, and worry about your academic credibility, or to push yourself harder and harder, to be one of the chosen, and worry about your academic credibility.

The Final Contradiction

I spent three and a half years working on the Project, and in that time we generated a considerable quantity of information, even though at times doing qualitative work on postgraduate education at a time when even the most rational academics seem to be obsessed with completion rates often felt like trying to run up the down escalator. Even given that the Project was successful in that sense, and that we ourselves enjoyed the work and think it has been useful and extremely informative, the final contradiction is that the policy recommendations that we could undoubtedly make would, I am afraid, fall on stony ground. This was reinforced for me when I attended the SRHE (Society for Research in Higher Education) Leverhulme Conference on Postgraduate Study, where I discovered that all but a handful of the participants assumed that postgraduates were all 21-year-old men who could not possibly 'choose' a research topic and would be happy to be trained for industry or academia. I only wish the conference had taken place three years ago; it would have focussed my mind wonderfully. Even those policy recommendations which may have some possibility of being implemented in the future do not, I am afraid, escape from contradiction. It is not beyond the bounds of possibility, for instance, that some move will be made to offer some form of minimal funding, possibly in the form of the payment of fees, to part-time postgraduate students. While this would, I suspect, be welcomed in most quarters, we cannot forget that this move could also be seen as a controlling mechanism, for along with the offer of finance there would surely come a demand for some sort of control over what is researched and how it is done.

In this chapter, I have not told the 'truth', either in the sense of offering an objective description of the process of the research, since I believe this to be impossible anyway, or even in a colloquial sense. The problem with much of what I found to be the more interesting information which the Project generated is that it is too specific to be used. Departments and individuals, if I give too much detail, would be instantly recognizable, and I have not been able to do more than generalize in many cases (even though I have come across many instances of individual supervisors, for instance, who should not be allowed anywhere near a student) because I am unsure about the ethics of the situation and, also, I have no great desire to be sued for libel.

What I have attempted to do is to open up some of the more intractable problems I encountered in doing the research, with the intention of suggesting that many of the problems we encounter are not solvable in a simple sense, that if we start out in our research by attempting to think of all the problems we may encounter and devising strategies to minimize their importance, we may at the same time minimize both the scope of our efforts and the results we obtain. Some contradictions are useful, particularly if we strive to work through them rather than against them.

Notes

1 This account would most usefully be read together with John Wakeford's account in this volume (Chapter 7), and Mary Porter's account, 'The modification of method in researching postgraduate education' (Porter, 1984).
2 See particularly the introduction to Bell and Newby (1977).
3 See John Wakeford's account in this volume (Chapter 7).
4 I think it worth stating that in my opinion this criticism was entirely unfounded.
5 We also examined a number of chemistry departments for comparative purposes (see Porter, 1984).
6 I make this point because some people assumed that we (Mary and I) were mere carriers of John's ideas and had no commitment of our own to qualitative methods.

7 For a useful discussion of the process of saturation in qualitative interviewing see the chapter by D. Bertaux in Bertaux (1982).

8 For a more detailed discussion of this process see Scott and Porter (1983).

9 For a more detailed discussion of this see Scott (1984).

10 The question of what the criteria are for selecting a good postgraduate student was raised for me again recently when I read a reference which an ex-tutor had written for an intending student which, after a couple of paragraphs on his academic promise, concluded by saying that he was also an extremely good long-distance runner — staying power is obviously the name of the game.

References

Bell, C. and Newby, H. (Eds) (1977) *Doing Sociological Research*, London, Allen and Unwin.

Bertaux, D. (Ed.) (1982) *Biography and Society*, Beverley Hills, Calif., Sage.

Dingwall, R. (1980) 'Ethics and ethnography', *Sociological Review*, 28, 4, pp. 871–91.

Porter, M. (1984) 'The modification of method in researching postgraduate education', in Burgess, R.G. (Ed.) *The Research Process in Educational Settings: Ten Case Studies*, Lewes, Falmer Press.

Scott, S. (1984) 'The personable and the powerful: Gender and status in sociological research', in Bell, C. and Roberts, H. (Eds) *Social Researching: Politics, Problems and Practice*, London, Routledge and Kegan Paul.

Scott, S. and Porter, M. (1983) 'On the bottom rung: A discussion of women and women's work in sociology', *Women's Studies International Forum*, 6, 2, pp. 211–21.

Wax, R. (1971) *Doing Fieldwork: Warnings and Advice*, Chicago, University of Chicago Press.

For other useful material on ethnographic work and the study of postgraduate education see:

Brenner, M. *et al.* (Eds) (1978) *The Social Contexts of Method*, London, Croom Helm.

Dexter, L.A. (1970) *Elite and Specialised Interviewing*, Evanston, Northwestern University Press.

Faraday, A. and Plummer, K. (1979) 'Doing life histories', *Sociological Review*, 27, 4, pp, 773–98.

Glaser, B. and Strauss, A.L. (1967) *The Discovery of Grounded Theory*, Chicago, Aldine.

Platt, J. (1976) *The Realities of Social Research*, London, Chatto and Windus for Sussex University Press.

Roberts, H. (Ed.) (1981) *Doing Feminist Research*, London, Routledge Kegan Paul.

RUDD, E. (1975) *The Highest Education: A Study of Graduate Education in Britain*, London, Routledge and Kegan Paul.

RUDD, E. and HATCH, S. (1968) *Graduate Study and After*, London, Weidenfeld and Nicolson.

SCOTT, S. and PORTER, M. (1981) 'Postgraduates, sociology and the cuts', in *Transactions of the 1980 BSA Conference*, London, British Sociological Association.

STANLEY, L. and WISE, S. (1983) *Breaking Out — Feminist Consciousness and Feminist Research*, London, Routledge and Kegan Paul.

7   A Director's Dilemmas

John Wakeford

While you are young you will be oppressed, and angry, and increasingly disagreeable. When you reach middle age, at five and thirty, you will become complacent and, in your turn, an oppressor; those whom you oppress will find you still disagreeable, and so will all the people whose toes you trod upon in youth. It will seem to you then that you grow wiser every day, as you learn more and more of the reasons why things should not be done, and understand more fully the peculiarities of powerful persons, which make it quixotic even to attempt them without first going through an amount of squaring and lobbying sufficient to sicken any but the most hardened soul. If you persist to the threshold of old age — your fiftieth year, let us say — you will be a powerful person yourself, with an accretion of peculiarities which other people will have to study in order to square you. The toes you will have trodden on by this time will be as the sands on the seashore; and from far below you will mount the roar of a ruthless multitude of young men in a hurry. You may perhaps grow to be aware what they are in a hurry to do. They are in a hurry to get you out of the way.
Oh young academic politician, my heart is full of pity for you now; but when you are old, if you will stand in the way, there will be no more pity for you than you deserve; and that will be none at all. (Cornford, 1953)

I should not have entered the world of research contracts with such naiveté. Despite the fact that nearly all my previous work had consisted of investigation in person or sometimes supervision of the individual work of students, I should not have underestimated the extent to which this was a different world, a world in which my perception of academic research and the management of scholarship would need realignment, and my understanding of one critique of academic institutions would be vividly deepened.

True, few accounts of academic work include examination of research directorship. Halsey and Trow (1971) published a monumental study, *The British Academics*, without reference to it. Many methods texts analyze the research process independent of its social and political context. However, six years previously I had been asked to review what seemed to me then a relevant but rather far-fetched analysis of the fate of American universities by Robert Nisbet (1971). His main theme had been that the historic ideal of the pursuit of knowledge for its own sake — referred to as the 'academic dogma' — the cornerstone of the traditional university for several centuries was in the process of being undermined and betrayed from within. Gone, he suggested, is the community of teacher/scholars in American universities, as unselfishly dedicated to the pursuit of knowledge for its own sake as to enabling their pupils to acquire it. Gone too are the academic standards and allegiances once presumed to permeate such communities. What was the main source of this malaise? — the direct funding by governments, industry and foundations of individual members of faculty for the purpose of creating institutes, centres, bureaux and other essentially capitalistic enterprises within universities. In Britain too, I pointed out in my review, as Arblaster (1974) and E.P. Thompson (1970) have demonstrated, the state had continuously extended its control over social science research not only through directly commissioning research but also through the political control of the Research Council.

I had become dimly aware that the process identified by Nisbet (1971) as taking place during the expansion of American universities might be mirrored in Britain. But it is only now (in the 1980s) as we stagger from crisis to crisis, economy to economy, successive governments cutting research funding, postgraduate work and, at an accelerating rate, higher education finance as a whole, that the full significance has become apparent. Institutions which have, in some cases for centuries, withstood the forces of state, business and commerce, enthusiastically latch on to the new academic capitalism, competing (with the assistance of public relations departments) in the pursuit of new consultancies, selling their expertise and knowledge for profit, and undermine their authority and claims as autonomous centres of learning. Why should educational researchers, or chemists or systems analysts, defer to the trivialities of academic processes when judicious attention to the current problems of the minister or ministry, international commissions and multinational enterprises, can produce such high economic returns and prestige? Resources, graduate students, secretaries, are gathered to make a private retinue no senate or academic board could sanction out of University Grants Committee (UGC) funds, all justified in the interests of meeting the institution's financial and strategic targets. So, with higher education under threat, the new academic bourgeoisie is being uncritically welcomed — directing rather than conducting sometimes several research assignments conspicuous by their sheer bulk, evading teaching responsibilities, hiring assistants to carry out the real work, meanwhile wintering in some institute and emerging only to attend international conferences or to lunch with senior civil servants. Even when it is only a minority who operate on a sustained and substantial scale, in this last decade of economies most British academic institutions positively reaffirm their policy of underwriting faculty's willingness to plunge into the direct or indirect service of those who can afford to pay. Who has heard of a university refusing to sanction any proffered ministry or industrial grant? Any such move would almost certainly be criticized as an attack on academic freedom.

But such thoughts did not cross my mind as I prepared my Social Science Research Council (SSRC) submission for support for 'A Sociological Investigation of Part-Time Study for Higher Degrees in Sociology and Social Administration'. I was at the time (1978) holding office in the British Sociological Association (BSA) and responsible for arranging bi-annual meetings between our Executive Committee and some representatives of the Sociology and Social Administration Committee of the Social Science Research Council. Out of a general concern for postgraduate work in general and the promotion of opportunities and finance for people — particularly women — to work part-time for higher degrees (who at the time were not being attracted to BSA summer schools), I suggested that this topic be on our agenda. Subsequently the meetings endorsed the suggestion for an investigation in this area, and through a series of coincidences and misunderstandings the BSA Executive Committee allocated me the responsibility of writing the application for funds and obtaining my university's counter-signature as a recognized body for administering the research.

I had no specific academic interest in this topic, although I had some previous involvement in studies of public schools, student withdrawal and the power structure of universities, but I felt that there was the need for some research, partly to provide ammunition in later negotiations with the Social Science Research Council for greater support and postgraduate awards for part-time students whose difficulties had not been properly recognized.

On the other hand, academic prestige is largely based on research and publication performance, and my application for £40,000, being the first of this order in the department, caused my colleagues' concern. Logan Wilson forty years ago pointed out that such 'promotional activities' are not generally carried out by reputable academics. Those who do are in the opinion of their colleagues being sidetracked from the true purpose of scholarship, probably trying to compensate for incompetence in or indifference towards their own speciality, and in all probability have discreditable motives. So perhaps I should not have been so surprised when the day I called in to the department to check, sign and submit the application, I found a delegation of over half the staff of my department in my room. Nor should I have been surprised to be subjected to a lengthy and hostile cross-examination on my research proposal. The exact reasons for the protest were never made clear to me, except that, because of the BSA Executive's decision and SSRC deadlines, there had as yet been no formal report of my application on the departmental agenda. The worries expressed, mainly in the third person, focussed on the effect the research, the funds and the new staff would have on the academic reputation of the department. I had joined the academic bougeoisie, and although the majority of our colleagues thereafter showed not even a polite interest in the content of our work, and no reluctance to apply for funds for their own projects, the appointment of research staff and a selection of a postgraduate student for a studentship 'linked' to the research gave rise to intense interest. In one case this was on the grounds of what a circular referred to as 'authoritarian decision-making with the collusion of the Head of the Department' and the 'curious pattern to these attempted and actual appointments, that is, that they are all women', in another because I was unwilling to propose the addition to the short list of a late applicant for the studentship who had applied only two days before the interview of the previously short-listed candidate.

Such accounts as have appeared of the organization of research work invariably commend a collaborative ethos. They imply that it can be assumed that productivity and efficient performance of assigned duties can be obtained if the director treats the research workers as colleagues in a 'team' — a piece of deception so fundamental that as Platt (1976) and later Hanmer and Leonard (1980) demonstrate any residual trust is soon undermined. Roth illustrated this in relation to survey research in 1966, and, whatever the gloss, research workers soon recognize that the 'team' is a myth, and that the director is more accurately described as a research entrepreneur, in some cases merely 'backer' or 'broker'. Research directors have generally negotiated the terms of the financial support with the sponsor and the administering institution, are held responsible by both for the general conduct, the financial control of the work and for writing interim and final reports. There is therefore an inevitable conflict of interest between director and research workers vividly portrayed by Roth (1966), Wax (1971), Hanmer and Leonard (1980) and others. Directors generally have secure tenured jobs and are well-paid. The staff we appoint are generally on ill-paid short-term contracts. Directors have all the perks and symbols of established members of the organization — our own room, rights and sup-plementary resources. Research staff in contrast have to negotiate for premises and access, which are often provided grudgingly — some-times requiring protracted discussions about 'principle'. In our case the university administrators were often helpful, but the relative position of research staff was clearly identified in the wording of their contracts of employment, the remoteness of the room to which they were allocated and the difficulties they had in becoming recognized in the department and the university as eligible to be members of the university and departmental committees, exacerbated by the practice of the SSRC and the university administration of officially recogniz-ing only the director for most administrative purposes. (It was assumed, for instance, that I personally and not the research staff would select and appoint the project secretary.)

Platt explores research workers' ideas of 'democracy' in their work organization — but as one of her respondents points out: 'democracy all depended on [the director] surrendering rank, it was a concession, and he could pull rank any time he wanted.' As Hanmer and Leonard (1980), in their biting indictment of the organization of research, point out:

> Women [research workers] may be confused by democratic organisation — the fact of sharing all the tasks and having pleasant, trusting working relationships — and to forgetting the differential power between members of the project 'team'.

I did in fact attempt to modify the hierarchy endemic in the overall structure, and tried to work with and act in response to the requests of the research staff, from the outset assuring them that within the conditions of the grant I would not want to interfere with their work, nor issue directions as to the way it should proceed.[1] I also tried to assure them that I would not take over the data or publish them, and that I saw myself as an agent facilitating research that the professional association and the Research Council considered important. The product has so far been almost entirely authored by and attributed to the research staff, but I sense colleagues still wait for me to revert to the traditional pattern. Apart from the first few months when I was on study leave and helped the research workers in initial negotiations, we all recognized that my other responsibilities would prevent me from being a full member of the group and from carrying more than a token share in the fieldwork.

Despite comments from colleagues that this was a facade, I believe I personally made a serious attempt to avoid reproducing in the research process the general social and familial subordination of women — the pattern accurately identified by Hanmer and Leonard (1980). Nevertheless, the central dilemmas of the research director are not personal but concern the structure of power and control. Platt's study (1976) indicated the importance of the 'lack of experience' of research directors in the unhappy state of sociological research, and directors are faced with formidable decisions and constraints. Their sponsor will have insisted on particular conditions or even specified research goals, and almost certainly laid down strict financial rules. Institutions have regulations, contracts, procedures. Colleagues make demands. How should I and my fellow tenured colleagues have reacted to a paper from the departmental research staff, suggesting that members of the department had the obligation at least to attempt to find research funds to continue their employment? Academic capitalism had, it dawned on us, transformed our position. A new breed of academic was being formed in us and the norms of our academic community were being transformed.

The dilemma rarely faced is: who is to control the theoretical and methodological dimensions of the research? The research council model assumes that this is to be the director. However, are research associates, fieldworkers, whose future is more closely tied to the outcome of the project, and who have carried most of the actual research, to have no contribution, no rights? Platt (1976) found it 'rather surprising that no director expressed hostility, or even ambivalence, about the extent to which his [sic] own previous research idea had been taken over and twisted by junior team members; intellectual possessiveness was low, or at least remained unexpressed.' While I held the view that they would only do good research when they had the freedom to follow their ideas in whatever way seemed best to them, to adopt pseudodemocratic practices is merely dishonest or diversionary. In any case the research director's promotional responsibilities — particularly if he or she is to try and secure a steady income for the department — may conflict with attempts at devolving control. The alternative, spelled out by Payne and others, is cynical:

> The alternative is for the director to make continued employ-
> ment strictly contingent on compliance with his [sic] require-
> ments. If he is to succeed then he must adopt research modes
> which can readily be bureaucratized, particularly survey type
> enquiries. He must also discourage staff from acquiring
> sufficient experience to contest his position or be distracted in
> to career channels. Typically the director resorts to the large
> scale employment of young women graduates as 'hired
> hands', their selection orients conventional attitudes and
> modes of life. The director can, then, reasonably expect that
> within a few years they will retire to raise a family and will
> not, therefore, have particular reason to pursue career ends or
> seek a stake in the credit for the research. (Payne *et al.*, 1981,
> p. 251)

The director's dilemmas therefore largely rest on the policies and structure of academic institutions and the funding of research. It is ironic that the majority of research is carried out by people with so little personal investment in the outcome and whose energy is more directly applied to incidental activities and interests or even modifying the nature of the task. No wonder Wax (1971) insisted that we should not make or let others do our fieldwork and Mills (1959) advocated avoiding the dilemmas altogether.

Note

1 For the views of the research workers on this project see Mary Porter's account in Porter (1984) and Sue Scott's contribution to this volume (Chapter 6).

References

ARBLASTER, A. (1974) *Academic Freedom*, Harmondsworth, Penguin.
CORNFORD, F.M. (1953) *Microcosmographia Academica*, Cambridge, Bowes and Bowes.

HALSEY, A.H. and TROW, M.A. (1971) *The British Academics*, London, Faber.

HANMER, J. and LEONARD, D. (1980) 'Men and culture: The sociological intelligentsia and the maintenance of male domination: or superman meets the invisible woman', in ABRAMS, P. and LEUTHWAITE, P. (Eds) *Transactions*, London, British Sociological Association.

MILLS, C.W. (1959) 'On intellectual craftsmanship', in *The Sociological Imagination*, New York, Oxford University Press.

NISBET, R. (1971) *The Degradation of the Academic Dogma*, London, Heinemann.

PAYNE, G. *et al.* (1981) *Sociology and Social Research*, London, Routledge and Kegan Paul.

PLATT, J. (1976) *The Realities of Social Research*, London, Chatto and Windus for Sussex University Press.

PORTER, M. (1984) 'The modification of method in researching postgraduate education', in BURGESS, R.G. (Ed.) *The Research Process in Educational Settings: Ten Case Studies*, Lewes, Falmer Press.

ROTH, J.A. (1966) 'Hired hand research', *The American Sociologist*, 1, 4, pp. 190–6.

THOMPSON, E.P. (1970) *Warwick University Ltd*, Harmondsworth, Penguin.

WAX, R. (1971) *Doing Fieldwork: Warnings and Advice*, Chicago, University of Chicago Press.

WILSON, L. (1942) *The Academic Man*, London, Oxford University Press.

8 The Whole Truth? Some Ethical Problems of Research in a Comprehensive School

Robert G. Burgess

With the development of empirical research in the social sciences over the past twenty years some concern has been expressed about what is investigated, how data are collected and analyzed and the way in which research data are disseminated. A brief glance at social science books and journals in the USA will find numerous articles devoted to these issues which has resulted in a detailed debate on the ethics of social research.[1] As in almost all social settings, academics have simplified the situation and polarized the positions that can be adopted. In these terms, the focus of the debate has been 'open' as against 'closed' or covert research. It is argued that if researchers are 'open' in the conduct of their investigations then they tell the truth, inform individuals about what they are doing, honestly report their findings and never subject their informants to risk or harm. Meanwhile, those who engage in 'closed' or covert research are seen as spies who violate the principle of informed consent, lie to their informants and deceive them, invade privacy, harm individuals both socially and psychologically and jeopardize the future of further research in the social sciences. Indeed, in order to overcome some of these problems professional associations have established 'codes of ethics' (American Anthropological Association, 1971) and in the USA Institutional Review Boards have been established in universities and research institutes to exercise some control over research and researchers (cf. Olesen, 1979).

Meanwhile, in Britain there has been less activity both publicly and within academic circles (although the British Sociological Association had regularly considered ethical issues and since 1968 has published a statement of ethical principles, British Sociological Association, 1982[2]). In 1963 Barnes published an article that raised some of the main ethical questions involved in the conduct of fieldwork (Barnes, 1963), but no further British material became widely available until Barnes published a series of lectures given in India in 1975 (Barnes, 1977) and a further text that considered issues relating to privacy and ethics (Barnes, 1979). Around this time, Homan, who had done covert research on old time Pentecostalists, was subject to criticism from Dingwall (1979) and Barbour (1979) who sent letters to the editor of *Network* (the newsletter of the British Sociological Association) to complain about Homan's work. In particular, Dingwall suggested that it was wrong for the *Sociological Review* to publish an article on Homan's research that had been based upon covert fieldwork (Homan, 1978), and had involved deceit as he argued it would prejudice the work of other sociologists who might wish to conduct research with this group. Indeed, Dingwall came out clearly on the side of 'open' research. Furthermore, when Homan published an article on covert methods in the *British Journal of Sociology* (Homan, 1980) it was followed by a rejoinder from Bulmer (1980) who pointed out that while he could not say covert research was never justified, the merits and demerits of this approach had to be carefully considered. It is to this debate that Bulmer has recently returned in a collection of British and American essays that provide an assessment of the merits of covert participant observation (Bulmer, 1982). Here, various writers discuss celebrated cases of covert fieldwork in the USA, including the study of a sectarian group by Festinger *et al.* (1956) and the study of homosexual activity in public restrooms (Humphreys, 1970). In addition, there are British studies on the police (Holdaway, 1982) the National Front (Fielding, 1982), and Pentecostalists (Homan and Bulmer, 1982). In this collection, in common with many others, there is no discussion or illustration of the ethical issues involved in educational studies, which is somewhat surprising given the recent upsurge in ethnographic studies of schools and classrooms (Hammersley and Woods, 1976; Woods and Hammersley, 1977; Woods, 1980a; 1980b). Indeed, even in specialist collections devoted to the ethnography of schooling there is no mention of research ethics (Spindler, 1963; 1974; Popkewitz and Tabachnick, 1981; Spindler 1982). It is, therefore, the purpose of this chapter to consider some of the ethical problems that I confronted whilst conducting an ethnographic study of a purpose built, co-educational Roman Catholic comprehensive that I called Bishop McGregor School (Burgess, 1983). In turn, attention will be focussed on research experience and the ways in which that experience confronts and confounds simple dichotomies and abstract debates that are found in the British and American literature and how compromise is an essential component in fieldwork practice.

Studying Bishop McGregor School: The Researcher's Experience and Research Design

As Stacey (1982) has noted, researchers now relate not only their research biographies but also their own biographies as a means of highlighting the reasons that lay behind the selection of a particular area of social investigation in sociological study. Indeed, it is this approach that has been taken by authors of educational studies in Shipman (1976) and Burgess (1984a). In my own case it would be easy to root my study of Bishop McGregor School within the theoretical tradition of symbolic interactionism, and the fieldwork tradition of the Manchester School of social anthropologists and sociologists (Gluckman, 1942; Mitchell, 1956a; 1956b; Turner, 1957; Pons, 1969). In turn I could point to the applicability of this approach to the study of social situations in industrial societies such as 'communities' (Frankenberg, 1957), factories (Lupton, 1963; Cunnison, 1966) and schools (Hargreaves, 1967; Lacey, 1970; Lambart, 1970). Yet, this over-simplifies the situation and therefore it is essential to dig deeper within my own biography.

At the age of 11 I was allocated to a secondary modern school where I remained for five years, taking ordinary-level GCE examinations before proceeding to a grammar school for advanced-level work. This was followed by three years at a college of education studying for the Teachers' Certificate and then three years at a university where I studied sociology before going to teach social studies and sociology at a secondary modern school. It was only after being a full-time school teacher that I returned to university as a full-time postgraduate student to do research. This brief resumé of fifteen years of my life is only of significance and interest in this context in as far as it can illuminate the way in which I formulated my school study that brought together sociological interests that were informed by personal and professional experiences.

At the time I began my research (October 1972) there were no ethnographic studies of comprehensive schools, no studies of co-educational schools and no detailed studies of children who did not succeed in the school system other than the study by Hargreaves (1967) which did not examine the lowest group, 4E in Lumley

Secondary Modern School. Added to this the government had announced that the school leaving age was to be raised to 16 and I considered that this was virgin territory for a PhD candidate such as myself as it was a major talking point in the press and among teachers and pupils in the school from which I resigned. When I went to Warwick University to begin my studies I decided that I wanted to incorporate my professional interests into my work alongside my sociological concerns. However, at that stage it was not my intention to study a Roman Catholic comprehensive school.

The time spent on reading and research design was punctuated by interviews with education officials in a number of local authorities and attendance at teachers' meetings out of which came an invitation to visit a school. As I sat beneath a fireplace in a crowded meeting, squashed between two teachers, a middle-aged man on my left whispered, 'who are you and where do you come from?' I told him my name and explained that I was doing research at Warwick University. 'Interesting', he replied, 'my name is Geoff Goddard and I run the Bishop McGregor Comprehensive School.' It rolled off his tongue and I remember thinking that he had obviously introduced himself that way many times before. At the end of the meeting he gave me the school telephone number saying that if I would like to look around his school I should give him a ring.

Towards the end of that term I telephoned to arrange a 'look around' Bishop McGregor School; 8 December 1972 was fixed for the visit which I assumed would consist of a brief word with the headmaster before being foisted on some unsuspecting teacher with a 'free' lesson. However, it turned out very differently. The whole morning was devoted to a discussion between the head and myself, partly about his school (which at that time was in its fourth year), about his plans for the school and the work that was being done with pupils he regarded as non-academic, that is, pupils he considered would have little chance of passing public examinations. Alongside this discussion I was questioned about my professional training, my qualifications and my teaching experience. It was very informal but resembled a mini-interview. (In retrospect, I realize that I was being vetted before the head offered the school as a research site.) At the end of the morning I was invited to take lunch with several teachers and then in the afternoon two pupils (selected at random) were requested to show me around the site before I was taken back to the head's study where I was invited to come back to the school again 'to teach, observe, meet the staff, discuss sociology, offer a social studies course, meet the pupils, accompany them on a visit out of school, talk to them about the university and "get your feet wet".'[3] Such was the beginning of the Bishop McGregor School study. I now had a site where I could conduct fieldwork and I therefore started to consider ways in which I could incorporate the school into my research design.

While I was in McGregor School I had learned that they had a special department that worked with non-academic pupils called the Newsom Department.[4] I had some experience of such pupils as some of my peers in the secondary modern school I attended had been taught in a similar area. I had also taught pupils who were regarded as non-academic and who were not entered for public examinations while I had been training to be a teacher, while I was engaged as a supply teacher and during the time when I was a permanent full-time teacher.

I decided that this experience together with my sociological interests would be useful in focussing attention on these pupils in the Department at Bishop McGregor School (cf. Burgess, 1982). It would give me a base from which to move within the school. Accordingly, in the spring term 1973 I wrote a brief proposal to begin work in Bishop McGregor School where I offered to take on some teaching duties in the Newsom Department on a part-time basis. I decided to design my proposal in this way as I was convinced that I wanted to make use of my former teacher status while doing research and this would allow me to take a participant role. Furthermore, I had been told by the headmaster at Bishop McGregor that 'people are always welcome at McGregor provided that they're prepared to work their passage.'

I decided to tell the teachers at Bishop McGregor School that I was doing research as well as teaching, while the pupils were only to be told that I was a new part-time teacher in the Newsom Department. I decided on this course of action for several reasons. First, I wanted to get a teacher's perspective of the school. I did not want to be seen as a student or a visitor. Secondly, I knew from my previous experiences as a teacher that other teachers were suspicious of researchers who only had an academic understanding of 'education' and who were unable to demonstrate their skills as practitioners. Thirdly, I was aware from my earlier experiences as a pupil and as a teacher that if I first went to the school as a visitor I would not get a teacher's perspective, especially if I entered classes where it was usual for pupils to 'perform' for visitors. Finally, I knew that many teachers disliked having any other adult in the classroom when teaching and especially where 'difficult' classes were involved (cf. Shaw, 1969).

Naively I decided that my research would be 'open' as far as teachers were concerned and 'closed' as far as pupils were concerned. However, this was too simple a dichotomy, for as Roth has remarked:

> there is a tendency to oversimplify the issue — to pose 'secret research' against 'non-secret research' and then put forth the technical or moral advantages and disadvantages of each. Actually, the ends of the continuum from 'secret' to 'non-secret' probably do not exist.... All research is secret in some ways and to some degree — we never tell the subjects 'everything'. (Roth, 1961, p. 283)

The truth of this statement was to be revealed in the course of my research when the lines between 'non-secret' and 'secret' research became blurred.

'Open' and 'Closed' Research in Bishop McGregor School

Although I provided a brief document about myself and my work in the school, I found that throughout the first term I had to explain my position to all the teachers I encountered as it appeared that the head had not circulated my document to his staff despite the fact that he had originally agreed to do so. I found that many roles were attached to me. Some teachers thought I was a new permanent member of the staff, others thought I was a course evaluator, while one teacher asked me if I was an inspector from the Department of Education and Science who was examining the School's Newsom course. On each occasion I indicated that I was doing some part-time teaching in the Newsom Department and taking substitution lessons while doing research. Even this account was not sufficient. For some teachers such as the Head of the Mathematics Department I was just 'a visitor' and I am sure that he never saw me in any other role throughout my sixteen-month stay in the school (cf. Burgess, 1984b). Meanwhile, the Head of the Newsom Department told me 'You're one of us. You understand the kids and the work we do with them.' Indeed, she explained that she had told the pupils that I was a new permanent part-time teacher.

The pupils did not, at first, query my explanation that I was a new part-time teacher who would teach them in the summer term. However, pupils like their teachers engage in informal observation in order to orientate their daily actions (cf. Threadgold, 1980) and at McGregor they were no exception. One day I saw Terry Nicholls who was a key member of the Newsom group wandering around the school grounds during the middle of a lesson. I stopped him and asked where he was going; he replied, 'nowhere'. At this remark, I felt as a teacher I should ask what he thought he was doing to which he replied: 'I was gonna ask you that question. When I've been out of lessons I've seen you wandering about. You can't have much teaching to do.' I said nothing. In truth I was scared that I had 'blown my cover' for he continued: 'Let's put it like this if you split on me I shall tell Mr Goddard [the head] that you are always out of lessons.' While this was the only direct challenge I received, it was enough to make me feel uncomfortable. I decided that I could not continue my part-time teacher role and walk freely around the school when I was not teaching. As a result I spent a considerable amount of my non-teaching time in the staff room. I told this story to several teachers and discussed with them the possibility of telling the pupils I was doing research. However, Sylvia Robinson, the Head of the Newsom Department, commented: 'I don't think you should tell them [the Newsom pupils] that you are here doing research otherwise they'll think you're trying to find out if they're mental.' She elaborated on this remark by explaining that many Newsom pupils had been seen by the educational psychologist throughout their school careers and would probably think that I was engaged in a similar activity. Furthermore, she indicated that Newsom pupils were very willing to talk candidly to Newsom teachers about the school, about their courses and about other teachers once one had gained their trust.

I continued teaching throughout the summer term and con-tinued to talk to teachers about revealing my research role to pupils. However, they argued that my teacher status was the only way in which I was going to get a teacher's perspective of the difficulties involved in working with the Newsom group and at this stage I was happy to be convinced by this argument. At the end of the summer term I had a meeting with the headmaster to discuss the progress of my work and to consider whether I should continue my research in the school. He agreed that I could continue to do fieldwork within the school as he had received no objections from teachers about my research. At this point I felt obliged to raise a question about the extent to which the research was 'open'. I indicated that not all teachers appeared to know about my research as even at the end of the summer term individuals were still making enquiries about what I was doing in the school. The headmaster said that he did not want to make an announcement about my research at any staff meeting and suggested that we might arrange an informal meeting for those who were interested during the new school year.[5]

However, pupils' rights were not introduced by the head: it was assumed that they would cooperate with my work (cf. Fuller, 1984). Accordingly, I raised this issue by explaining that the pupils did not know what I was doing and appeared to accept me as a part-time teacher, apart, that is, from Terry Nicholls. When I related the story of my encounter with Terry in the school grounds, Mr Goddard laughed and said: 'Terry doesn't think that I'm a real teacher or some of the staff let alone you.' However, it was evident from his manner that he was not concerned about whether the pupils knew about my research role. As far as he was concerned it was more important that I had been acceptable to the staff because: 'You've come in and done a share of teaching and you've not always had the best classes either.'

While my teacher self appeared to be acceptable to many of the teachers, I was still dubious about my role as far as the pupils were concerned. I realized that if I was going to systematically interview all the pupils in the next academic year there would come a time when I would have to tell pupils about my research. When I returned to the school in the autumn term I was, therefore, convinced that I would have to discuss my research with the pupils.

In the week before the autumn half-term I was walking around the classroom during one of my Newsom lessons when I noticed Terry Nicholls was not working so I asked:

RB: Why aren't you working?
Terry: What's the use of this work?
RB: What do you think you ought to do?
Terry: I wanna do as little as possible for as long as possible.
   I wanna do as little as I can. Anyway this work don't give
   you any qualifications. It don't get you anywhere.

I could not deny this. I said nothing, but my silence prompted further questions from Terry: 'What subjects do you teach besides this? What qualifications do you have?' I explained that I had qualifications in sociology and in geography, but Terry continued, 'It's not important to have these qualifications to teach Newsom.' At this remark Peter Vincent chipped in: 'What's the sense of teaching Newsom with those qualifications? You don't have to be clever to teach Newsom. I don't think you're a proper teacher. What else do you do?'[6] I sensed that this was my opportunity to bring my research into the 'open'. I had now been in the school for one and a half terms and I felt much more secure in my position so I asked: 'Why do you think I'm not a proper teacher?' Peter replied: 'Newsom isn't proper teaching.' I did not reply, but Diane Lane persisted with the questioning: 'What else do you do in this school?' At this point in my fieldnotes I wrote as follows: 'Here I came up against a central research problem. I initally set the research up as partly open and partly "closed": "open" to the staff but "closed" to the pupils. In this instance I wondered whether I should tell the truth or tell a lie.' I decided to tell the truth as my notes record the following response to Diane's question:

> *RB:* I teach Newsom and some substitution lessons two days each week.
> *Diane:* What do you do when you're not here?
> *RB:* I'm at Warwick University.
> *Diane:* What do you do at the University?
> *RB:* I work on a project.
> *Diane:* What project?
> *RB:* A research project about Bishop McGregor Comprehensive School, Merston.

At this remark the group of pupils looked amazed. For once the group was quiet. Their silence was broken by Patrick McConnell who remarked that he thought I was doing something else as I had said I was part-time. He went on to say that he had always wondered what else I taught in the school. Indeed, he remarked how he had noticed that I was always interested in the pupils' point of view unlike some of the other teachers. Questions then followed about doing research, about how much I was paid and about writing a book, as I indicated in my responses that I was writing about what the Newsom pupils thought about their schooling. Sarah Molinski then asked, 'Will we be named?' I explained that in the book she would probably be called 'Joan Smith', to which she replied, 'That's not fair. I think you ought to put our names in it. We ought to get mentioned.' After this there were further questions which took up the remaining part of the lesson. In the afternoon, I arranged to see the headmaster to explain what had occurred in the lesson in case he had enquiries from parents about what was happening at the school. However, to my knowledge no such queries were ever raised.

Now I was concerned in case the pupils treated me differently from other Newsom teachers. However, I subsequently found that while my research was periodically mentioned I was still addressed as 'Sir' and treated to a similar set of stories about the school that pupils exchanged with other Newsom teachers. Indeed, the activities in which pupils engaged in my classroom did not change, and I found that pupils did not treat me in the way that they treated visitors who came into the school. However, when I asked the pupils what they would have done if they had been told I was doing research, Diane Lane replied that they would have treated me differently from the Newsom teachers. She said that they would have treated me like a visitor; other pupils agreed with her assessment. On this basis it would appear that establishing myself in the teacher role had given me access to a teacher's perspective of Newsom classes. However, my sociological colleagues looking on will now ask: do the ends justify the means? Do the benefits outweigh the risks? Is such an approach ethical? While these questions raise central issues in the research process, they imply that such research activities involve deception and are not as honest as 'open' research.

However, as Barnes (1979) among many other commentators has indicated, such a stance on ethical issues is inappropriate given that fieldwork is not like biomedical investigations where ethical problems are frequently discussed in these terms. Indeed, Wax (1980) had commented:

> Fieldwork is ... a complex interaction between researcher and hosts and is constructed in a process of give-and-take (or exchange and reciprocity) and so it cannot be assimilated toward the model of a biomedical experiment where the researcher is free to outline what is to be done to the passive subjects. (Wax, 1980, p. 273)

In these terms, fieldworkers are constantly engaged in taking decisions about ethical issues in *both* 'open' and 'closed' research; they are involved in arriving at some form of compromise whereby the impossibility of seeking informed consent from everyone, of telling the truth all the time and of protecting everyone's interests is acknowledged. It is, therefore, to a consideration of some of these issues that we now turn as they are common to both 'open' and 'closed' research.

Informed Consent

The principle of 'informed consent' was developed during the Nuremberg war trials where individuals were charged with conducting medical experiments during the Second World War. This principle states that in research:

> The voluntary consent of the human subject is absolutely essential. This means that the person involved should have legal capacity to give consent; should be so situated as to exercise free power of choice, without the intervention of any element of force, fraud, deceit, duress, over-reaching or any other ulterior form of constraint or coercion; and should have sufficient knowledge and comprehension of the elements of the subject matter involved as to enable him to make an understanding and enlightened decision. (Nuremberg Code, 1949, reprinted in Reiser *et al.*, 1977, pp. 272–3)

At first glance it may appear that I upheld this principle as far as teachers were concerned but not as far as the pupils were involved. However, this over-simplifies matters. As I have noted, teachers often asked about my research in my first term in the school but even here some doubt can be expressed about informed consent. When asked what I was doing, I talked about research in the Newsom Department and in the school. However, nobody ever asked, 'will this conversation be included in your study?' Indeed, had they done so I would have found it difficult to respond as the changing direction of field research often means that the researcher is unsure what will be included and what will be excluded from the final research report. In conversations in the staff common room, in meetings, at social gatherings and at parties it would have been impossible constantly to remind individuals that they were being studied.

Whenever I was asked about what constituted 'doing research', I explained that I included all conversations in my research notes. However, only a few teachers showed any concern, while others considered their remarks well outside the orbit of any study. This point was illustrated in a conversation in the staff common room between Don Williams and June Harper. I had been chatting to these teachers during the lunch break when the conversation turned to Maggie Rolls (their head of house). Don indicated that he had received a letter from her indicating that he must either accept her authority or leave the house. June wanted to know some of the details in Maggie's letter, but Don declined saying, 'He's making a study of all this.' However, June replied, 'He's not interested in this. He's not going to report this back to Maggie.' Fortunately, neither of them asked if I would make direct use of this conversation in my study as I would have had to have said that I did not know.

Meanwhile some teachers defined my study to include any information about teachers and pupils. One of my key informants,

Sylvia Robinson, always came to tell me what was going on in the school.[7] She told me what happened on days when I was outside school, she talked to me about aspects of school policy that had been discussed at meetings that I did not or could not attend, attributing remarks to particular teaching staff. Furthermore, she always updated me and any other teacher within earshot of the latest gossip in the school. However, one day when she was about to tell me something that she claimed nobody else knew she prefaced it with the remark: 'Of course, I'm only telling you this because I know it's your job to collect all the gossip.' In these circumstances, information was being transmitted to me that was later incorporated into my study once I had cross-checked it with other teachers. Although many teachers recognized that she would gossip to others about their activities, I wonder about the extent to which they appreciated that the things she and other colleagues told me would find their way into my study and eventually into print.[8] Certainly, I never told Sylvia or any other teachers or pupils that they were my key informants for that would have been even more problematic. Yet in these circumstances some consideration needs to be given to the extent to which they were engaged in covert research activities on my behalf.

Among the pupils I was studying, the research only became 'open' after one and a half terms. In this respect, I had to get their permission retrospectively to utilize all the data that I had gathered. Furthermore, while the Newsom pupils knew that I was doing research, there were some 1200 other pupils who were not informed about my research activities. In these terms, covert research activity continued after the research was nominally 'open' to all teachers and pupils and as such is open to question. I was particularly aware of this as I travelled to and from the school on public service buses. To many of the pupils and passengers I was no doubt viewed as a teacher as I boarded the bus with pupils and other teachers from the school. However, when incidents occurred on the buses between pupils and passengers I faced a dilemma. If I became involved pupils might accuse me of not being a real teacher; a risk that I could not take as passengers might wonder what was happening at the school. Fortunately, such a situation never occurred but it illustrates how even a potentially 'open' research situation was partially 'closed' and posed a major dilemma for a nominally 'open' researcher.

Truth Telling and Lying

Another dimension of the research situation involves truth telling and lying, honesty and deception. While we might take the statement made in the court room: 'I swear to tell the truth, the whole truth and nothing but the truth so help me God', as a reasonable dictum to follow, we need to consider the extent to which truth is socially constructed. Indeed, lies may be told in different circumstances — to protect peers, to maintain confidentiality and in crises (cf. Bok, 1978). It is, therefore, to a consideration of such situations in which truth telling and lying are issues for the researcher that we now turn.

On the basis of my observations, conversations with teachers and my own participation in teaching Newsom classes I was aware that teaching in the Newsom Department was a difficult situation, that pupils were regarded as difficult and that success was rare or short-lived. While this was freely acknowledged by my colleagues in conversations in the staff common room, I soon found that the situation was presented in very different terms when reports were made of the teaching during Newsom Department meetings with the headmaster. One such meeting is reported in my study where I found that the teachers discussed their work in very different terms:

Sylvia talked about swimming classes and outside visits that she had organized for her classes. She reported that pupils were becoming much more 'mature' and 'responsible' — a direct result of the courses provided by the department. In particular, she singled out Peter Vincent and Terry Nicholls who were regarded by other teachers as notorious trouble makers. She claimed they were settling down to their work and becoming much more mature. This was agreed by other teachers, although in private they were prepared to report their misgivings about it.

Terry Goodwin talked about the girls' group she had taken for home economics. Part of this course was said to include continental cookery and first aid. Terry thought first aid was very popular as the pupils could combine practical work with some written work to gain an examination certificate. She reported that most pupils had enjoyed the written and the practical work and had successfully gained certificates.

Keith Dryden was next. He supported the views already advanced. He said that he found all the Newsom pupils were 'nice kids' who were prepared to get as much as they could out of their courses. It was then my turn to say what I was doing. I realised that the strategy was to provide an edited report that was positive about the pupils. I talked about the success I had with outside visits and how the pupils had produced a reasonable amount of written work. I claimed that the success of the course could be attributed to the fact that I had the opportunity to get to know my group as people rather than pupils. This report was warmly received by the others, especially since I had talked about 'people' rather than 'pupils' — the terms that they utilised themselves. (Burgess, 1983, p. 226)

Here I had told a direct lie and my colleagues would have known this to be the case on the basis of my conversations with them in the staff common room. Like many of the others in the room, I was finding Newsom teaching 'tough going' as the pupils were giving me a 'rough ride'. Yet in this meeting I felt obliged to lie. My colleagues were engaged in a strategy whereby they rationalized their activities and those of their pupils when they met with the headmaster. Furthermore, as several of the teachers later explained, it was important to relay success to the head as they considered this would be used in judgments that were made about their career prospects. On this basis, I had felt obliged to tell a lie to support my colleagues as the truth or even a version of the truth would, I feel, have destroyed the rationalization which they used about their teaching and may have harmed them in terms of their future careers.

A further set of incidents in which I told lies or failed to tell the truth concerned matters of confidentiality. During my fieldwork I read confidential documents, and teachers and pupils told me about various matters 'in confidence'. In these terms, I considered that it was most important to keep my word to individuals to whom I had sworn confidence. Among the documents that I read within the school was a sheet that showed the allocation of scale posts to individual teachers and the distribution of points for posts of responsibility among houses and departments.[9] Such information was confidential and never made publicly available to the teachers. The result was that there was much speculation about posts of responsibility and numerous conversations took place in the staff common room about the possibility of promotion. At these times individuals pieced together information that they had gleaned from conversations with the head about their own promotion prospects, from gossip that they had heard about the posts which individuals held and from guesses they made about the distribution of points within the departments. In these conversations, I was often silent although I could, on the basis of my data, have corrected inaccuracies and updated their information. To do so would, no doubt, have increased my popularity with teachers but at the same time destroyed my credibility with the headmaster who might have prevented me from reading further confidential documents in the school office. In this instance I was deferring to the power of my sponsor. However, when individual teachers talked to me about promotion, I entered into the discussion without directly giving them any information. For example, when Keith Dryden (a member of the Newsom Department) asked my views about going to the head to seek promotion I encouraged him without indicating that I knew that the head did have points in reserve. Similarly, during the same term, when Sylvia Robinson told me that she had been to ask for promotion but had been told by the head how he was in a difficult position with no points in reserve, I sympathized with her version of the story. On the basis of my knowledge and her version of the interview with the head, it appeared that she had been told a lie as at this time the school records indicated that there were six points in reserve. However, I did not pursue this matter with Sylvia or with any other teacher.

Similarly, when pupils talked to me in confidence, I did not transmit their remarks to teachers or fellow pupils. When I interviewed pupils I was often asked what would happen to the tape-recordings that I made and whether the teachers would get to hear them. In these cases, I promised that I would not tell the teachers whatever they told me, and that I would not play their tape (or for that matter any tape-recording) to the teachers. When teachers asked me what individual pupils had said about them, I would not transmit the information. However, whenever pupils indicated that they had no objection to me talking to teachers about their views, I would consider using what they had said in conversation. Nevertheless, even in these circumstances I needed to make judgments about the possible harm that might be done. As a consequence, when pupils told me that I could discuss something they had told me, I would always evaluate the information as I was not prepared to be used for political ends. Similarly when teachers told me that I could tell the headmaster about their views on school organization and their ideas for reorganization, I decided against such action. I was not prepared to act as 'a go-between' for various groups and individuals within the school.

A third instance in which lies were told was in the daily routine

of fieldwork. As many of the basic fieldwork textbooks (cf. Schatzman and Strauss, 1973; Douglas 1976) advise, I asked naive questions.
Such questions were frequently used when I knew the answers to my
questions or when I merely wished to confirm actions or activities
that I had either observed or had discussed with me by another
informant. A classic example of this kind of questioning occurred in
situations which were defined by the participants as crises (cf.
Burgess, 1983, pp. 84–119). When teachers or pupils asked if I had
heard about activities that had occurred, either I denied knowledge of
them or I told the individuals concerned that I was unclear about the
situation being discussed. I did this as I was particularly interested in
the different perspectives that participants adopted and the different
ways in which definitions of situations were constructed.

Another dimension to telling lies in crisis situations concerned
the protection of friends and colleagues. At the end of the summer
term the headmaster issued a 'secret document'; this was supposed to
be confidential to his senior staff (the deputy head, the senior mistress
and the house heads). This document outlined plans to get all pupils
away from the site on the last day of term without any disruption in
the form of uniform tearing and associated activities that had spilled
over into neighbouring streets at the end of previous terms.[10] In the
house to which I belonged, Ron Ward, the head of house, freely
discussed the document with all house staff and allowed two of us,
who were part-time teachers, to read the document so that we would
not be confused with the routines that were adopted in the school
during the final week of the term. However, he did not make clear
that the document was intended to be confidential, nor did he ask us
not to discuss this document.

As I had always been given copies of all material issued in the
school I went to the school secretary later that morning to get a copy
of this document. Immediately I asked for a copy of the document
she asked how I knew about it. I indicated that Ron Ward had told
me about it. However, sensing its confidentiality I did not tell the
secretary that Ron was reading out portions of the document to
house staff nor that he had allowed another part-time teacher and
myself to read it. Immediately following this encounter, I went to
warn a friend of mine about the status of this document as I had
discussed some of the details with him which had not been discussed
by our house head. In each of these situations I either omitted to say
anything or did not tell the truth in order that no harm would come
to my colleagues. Similar strategies also had to be considered as far as
data dissemination was concerned.

Data Dissemination

The ethical problems that surround the publication of data have been well summarized by Fichter and Kolb (1954), by Becker (1964) and by Platt (1976). These commentators indicate that the main issues involved are: loyalty to those who sponsor the study and those who are studied, violation of secrecy and privacy, and harm to the individual. In these terms, the researcher is involved in taking decisions about what shall be included in and excluded from the research report and ways in which confidentiality can be maintained. During my research I was alerted to some of these difficulties when I presented my material during meetings and when I showed the headmaster copies of my study in draft. It is to these issues that I now turn.

Two years after the fieldwork had been completed I gave an oral presentation of some of my data. My presentation focussed on life in the Newsom classes and I took extracts from my fieldnotes and records from teachers' diaries to use as illustrations of the activities that occurred in Newsom classes. The picture I depicted included a situation where a Newsom pupil had sat in a classroom and proceeded to dye his hair in the middle of a lesson. On hearing this the headmaster remarked, 'I find it impossible to believe that any member of this staff would allow this to happen in a lesson.' Several teachers disputed the head's remark and quoted instances of other activities within classrooms. However, it was evident that they carefully avoided any reference to their own teaching in McGregor School, and to work by other teachers in the school. Here the examples were constructed out of their experiences *before* coming to McGregor School or *other* teachers' experiences in *other* schools. Meanwhile, the teacher in whose classroom this incident had occurred looked distinctly uncomfortable throughout the discussion. He did not verify my account nor did I call on him to do so. Instead, I maintained a situation of anonymity for the teacher, the pupil concerned and the subject that was being taught. At the end of this seminar the teacher concerned came to talk to me about my example. He thanked me for not saying who it had involved or what subject was being taught and explained that he felt unable to verify my account as he was currently seeking promotion and thought that such an account if verified would jeopardize his chances, especially given the reaction of the headmaster.

This situation concerned me. I knew that I could have provided more detailed accounts about Newsom work. I had descriptions of my own and accounts from other teachers where pupils smoked, swore at and with teachers, and where little school work was done. I was concerned about how I was going to keep loyalty to teachers and pupils who had allowed me to witness these activities or had recorded them in diaries or discussed them with me, while at the same time communicating the experiences to a wider audience. While I would not say that this was the only reason for the time it took to finally present my PhD thesis, I would say that it was one of the contributing factors; although the report by Swinnerton-Dyer on the completion of PhD theses does not appear to take such factors into account (HMSO, 1982). Indeed, I spent some time considering the ways in which I could disseminate my data and protect my informants. It might be argued that I could have written up quickly and placed a block on my thesis. While this would have contributed to an improvement in SSRC (now ESRC) completion rates it would not have satisfied my desire to disseminate my findings more widely. It was, therefore, seven years after the fieldwork was completed that I showed the headmaster draft copies of my chapters on Newsom teaching. By that time the teachers concerned had all moved to posts in other schools and as a consequence I felt easier about it. In presenting my data I had disguised the names of all the teachers and pupils in my study, but because there were only four members of the Newsom Department, it was possible for the head and for other teachers in the school to have a reasonable chance of identifying them. Indeed, on occasions, I have found that the head has called individuals by name other than the pseudonym when discussing my study. In some cases he has guessed correctly, while in others he has been incorrect. However, I have never confirmed or denied any of the guesses that have been made as I would hope that this would result in my data being used neither for nor against my former colleagues. In turn, I have changed some of the courses that they taught and some of the situations in which they were located in the hope of preserving their anonymity. However, I have not like Tomlinson (1982) changed the sex of the persons concerned as I thought that this would destroy evidence on gender-specific behaviour; I feel this would be to engage in deception particularly if the evidence is used by other writers in commenting upon gender and education (cf. Delamont, 1980). However, the reaction I received is of interest as it illustrates some of the difficulties involved in disseminating data.

When I visited the head to discuss the last chapter in my study, which was devoted to the Newsom course (Burgess, 1983, pp.

208–35), I noticed that he was visibly annoyed. He said that he was hurt because I had not told him about the ways in which Newsom pupils were *actually* taught. He argued that he did not know that this pattern of teaching occurred in the Newsom Department. Furthermore, he maintained that I should have told him what was happening as seven other groups had passed through that department since my fieldwork was completed and, he argued, if that was the course they were getting, it could hardly be described as an 'education'. I claimed that I had felt a responsibility to the teachers and I asked, 'what would you have done if I had shown you this chapter a term after I had completed my fieldwork?' to which he replied, 'I would have wanted to sack the bloody lot of them, but I know that I couldn't because I needed those teachers.' At this point, he went on to discuss how these teachers did at least keep Newsom pupils away from other staff who would be ready to complain to him if they had had to teach them. I indicated that his immediate reaction had proved the point I was making about the need for confidentiality, but he maintained that I was still culpable.

This situation is instructive in several respects. First, I had allowed some considerable time to elapse before I released my data in order to protect my informants, but this had been subject to criticism. Secondly, I had disguised the names of teachers and pupils, but some guesses had been made as to who the individuals were. Thirdly, there is an issue here that concerns the pupils. While nothing can be done about the activities of former pupils, action can be taken against their successors. I am aware that my material can be read with a view to considering how pupil behaviour can be controlled and more 'education' provided. In such situations the teachers' activities may be out of professional concern for the 'education' of pupils, but in turn this may result in some curtailment of the strategies that pupils adopt to come to terms with their schooling (cf. Davies in this volume, Chapter 4).

It is evident that whatever precautions are taken to protect those who are involved in a field study, nothing is foolproof. In the preface to a study of a work situation, Cavendish (1982) outlines the problems concerning the dissemination of detailed field data and the constraints imposed by the British libel laws. On this basis, researchers have to take a series of decisions that will maintain confidentiality but will further our knowledge of social institutions and social processes, while protecting the informants, the institution and the researcher. In short, compromise is essential.

Robert G. Burgess

Conclusion

On the basis of my research in a co-educational Roman Catholic comprehensive school I have tried to extract from my research experience elements that will shed some light on ethical considerations that need to be discussed on research in general and field research on education in particular. The experiences that I have discussed are not examples of exemplary conduct. Indeed, my confession to having engaged in 'closed' as well as 'open' research might well earn me a place in the methodologists' 'chamber of horrors' where I will be subject to some 'torture'. However, I would hope that my field experiences go some way towards demonstrating that there are similar problems concerned with 'open' and 'closed' research and that no 'solutions' are instantly available to a set of seemingly intractable problems. Indeed, as field researchers we need to make public the ethical and political problems that we encounter in our research if we are to understand how compromise is to be achieved and how knowledge can be advanced alongside the protection of our informants.

Acknowledgements

I would like to thank all the participants at the second Ethnography of Educational Settings Workshop held in July 1982 for their comments on an earlier draft of this chapter. In addition, I am indebted to John Barnes, Hilary Burgess, Len Threadgold, Margaret Threadgold and the Headmaster of Bishop McGregor School who provided detailed comments on an earlier version. The fieldwork on which this chapter is based was made possible by a postgraduate studentship from the SSRC.

Notes

1 For a selection of the main articles in the USA in the 1960s see *Social Problems*. Many of these articles were reprinted in section six of Filstead (1970). For a review of issues in the 1970s see, for example, Cassell and Wax (1980).
2 For a commentary on this statement of ethical principles see Burgess (1981) and Burgess (1984b), Chapter 9.
3 This statement, together with all other extracts from my fieldwork, is taken from my fieldnotes unless otherwise stated.
4 In Bishop McGregor School the Newsom Department provided courses

for pupils for whom the maximum expectation of success in public examinations seemed likely to be three CSE (Certificate of Secondary Education) grade fives or less.

5 For a discussion of one of the seminars given to teachers during the subsequent academic year see the section of this chapter on data dissemination.

6 For a discussion of these data see Burgess (1984c).

7 For a discussion of key informants in ethnographic work see Burgess (1984b), pp. 73–75 and for a specific discussion of the use of key informants in this study see Burgess (1985).

8 For a discussion of the problems of transmitting data in print from an informant's point of view see Scheper-Hughes' (1981) commentary on the publication of her field study (Scheper-Hughes, 1979).

9 Scale posts and points for posts of responsibility carried additional money that was paid above the basic scale. For a discussion in relation to Bishop McGregor School see Burgess (1983), pp. 62–6.

10 For a discussion of this incident see Burgess (1983), pp. 101–14.

References

AMERICAN ANTHROPOLOGICAL ASSOCIATION (1971) 'Statements on ethics: Principles of professional responsibility', reprinted in WEAVER, T. (Ed.) (1973) *To See Ourselves: Anthropology and Modern Social Issues*, Glenview, Ill., Scott, Foresman and Company.

BARBOUR, R. (1979) 'The ethics of covert research', *Network*, September, p. 7.

BARNES, J.A. (1963), 'Some ethical problems of modern fieldwork', *British Journal of Sociology*, 14, pp. 118–34, reprinted in FILSTEAD, W.J. (Ed.) *Qualitative Methodology: Firsthand Involvement with the Social World*, Chicago, Markham Publishing Company.

BARNES, J.A. (1977) *The Ethics of Inquiry in Social Science*, Delhi, Oxford University Press.

BARNES, J.A. (1979) *Who Should Know What?* Harmondsworth, Penguin.

BECKER, H.S. (1964) 'Problems in the publication of field studies', in VIDICH, A.J. *et al.* (Eds) *Reflections on Community Studies*, New York, Harper and Row.

BOK, S. (1978) *Lying: Moral Choice in Public and Private Life*, Hassocks, Harvester.

BRITISH SOCIOLOGICAL ASSOCIATION (1982) 'Statement of ethical principles and their application to sociological practice', Originally published in 1968, revised 1970 and 1973).

BULMER, M. (1980) 'Comment on the ethics of covert methods', *British Journal of Sociology*, 31, 1, pp. 59–65.

BULMER, M. (Ed.) (1982) *Social Research Ethics*, London, Macmillan.

BURGESS, R.G. (1981) 'Ethical "codes" and field relations', paper prepared for the 41st Annual Meeting of the Society for Applied Anthropology held at the University of Edinburgh, April.

BURGESS, R.G. (1982) 'The practice of sociological research: Some issues in school ethnography', in BURGESS, R.G. (Ed.) *Exploring Society*, London, British Sociological Association.

BURGESS, R.G. (1983) *Experiencing Comprehensive Education: A Study of Bishop McGregor School*, London, Methuen.

BURGESS, R.G. (Ed.) (1984a) *The Research Process in Educational Settings: Ten Case Studies*, Lewes, Falmer Press.

BURGESS, R.G. (1984b) *In the Field: An Introduction to Field Research*, London, Allen and Unwin.

BURGESS, R.G. (1984c) 'It's not a proper subject: It's just Newsom', in GOODSON, I.F. and BALL, S.J. (Eds) *Defining the Curriculum*, Lewes, Falmer Press.

BURGESS, R.G. (1985) 'In the company of teachers: Key informants in the study of a comprehensive school', in BURGESS, R.G. (Ed.) *Strategies of Educational Research: Qualitative Methods*, Lewes, Falmer Press.

CASSELL, J. and WAX, M.L. (Eds), (1980) 'Ethical problems of fieldwork', special issue of *Social Problems*, 27, 3, pp. 259–378.

CAVENDISH, R. (1982) *Women On the Line*, London, Routledge and Kegan Paul.

CUNNISON, S. (1966) *Wages and Work Allocation*, London, Tavistock.

DELAMONT, S. (1980) *Sex Roles and the School*, London, Methuen.

DINGWALL, R. (1979) 'Letters to the editor', *Network*, May, p. 7.

DINGWALL, R. (1980) 'Ethics and ethnography', *Sociological Review*, 28, 4, pp. 871–91.

DOUGLAS, J.D. (1976) *Investigative Social Research*, Beverly Hills, Calif., Sage.

FESTINGER, L. *et al.* (1956), *When Prophecy Fails*, New York, Harper and Row.

FICHTER, J.H. and KOLB, W.L. (1954) 'Ethical limitations on sociological reporting', in FICHTER, J.H., *Social Relations in the Urban Parish*, Chicago, University of Chicago Press.

FIELDING, N. (1982) 'Observational research on the National Front', in BULMER, M. (Ed.) *Social Research Ethics*, London, Macmillan.

FILSTEAD, W.J. (Ed.) (1970) *Qualitative Methodology: Firsthand Involvement with the Social World*, Chicago, Markham Publishing Co.

FRANKENBERG, R. (1957) *Village on the Border*, London, Cohen and West.

FULLER, M. (1984) 'Dimensions of gender in a school: Reinventing the wheel?' in BURGESS, R.G. (Ed.) *The Research Process in Educational Settings: Ten Case Studies*, Lewes, Falmer Press.

GLUCKMAN, M. (1942) *An Analysis of a Social Situation in Modern Zululand*, Rhodes-Livingstone Paper No. 28.

HAMMERSLEY, M. and WOODS, P. (Eds) (1976) *The Process of Schooling*, London, Routledge and Kegan Paul in association with the Open University Press.

HARGREAVES, D.H. (1967) *Social Relations in a Secondary School*, London, Routledge and Kegan Paul.

HMSO (1982) *Report of the Working Party on Postgraduate Education* (Swinnerton-Dyer Committee), London, HMSO.

HOLDAWAY, S. (1982) '"An inside job": A case study of covert research on the police', in BULMER, M. (Ed.) *Social Research Ethics*, London, Macmillan.

HOMAN, R. (1978) 'Interpersonal communication in Pentecostal meetings', *Sociological Review*, 26, 3, pp. 499–518.

HOMAN, R. (1980) 'The ethics of covert methods', *British Journal of Sociology*, 31, 1, pp. 46–59.

HOMAN, R. and BULMER, M. (1982) 'On the merits of covert methods: A dialogue', in BULMER, M. (Ed.) *Social Research Ethics*, London, Macmillan.

HUMPHREYS, L. (1970) *Tearoom Trade*, London, Duckworth.

LACEY, C. (1970) *Hightown Grammar: The School As a Social System*, Manchester, Manchester University Press.

LAMBART, A.M. (1970) 'The sociology of an unstreamed urban grammar school for girls', unpublished MA thesis, Manchester, University of Manchester.

LUPTON, T. (1963) *On the Shop Floor*, Oxford, Pergamon Press.

MITCHELL, J.C. (1956a) *The Kalela Dance*, Rhodes-Livingstone Paper No. 27.

MITCHELL, J.C. (1956b) *The Yao Village: A Study in the Social Structure of a Nyasaland Tribe*, Manchester, Manchester University Press.

OLESEN, V. (1979) 'Federal regulations, institutional review boards and qualitative social science research: Comments on a problematic era', in WAX, M. and CASSELL, J. (Eds) *Federal Regulations: Ethical Issues and Social Research*, Boulder, Colorado, Westview Press.

PLATT, J. (1976) *Realities of Social Research*, London, Chatto and Windus for Sussex University Press.

PONS, V. (1969) *Stanleyville: An African Urban Community under Belgian Administration*, London, Oxford University Press for the International African Institute.

POPKEWITZ, T.S. and TABACHNICK, B.R. (Eds) (1981) *The Study of Schooling: Field Based Methodologies in Educational Research and Evaluation*, New York, Praeger.

REISER, S.J. *et. al.*, (1977) *Ethics and Medicine*, Cambridge, MIT Press.

ROTH, J.A. (1961) 'Comments on "secret observation"', *Social Problems*, 9, pp. 283–4.

SCHATZMAN, L. and STRAUSS, A.L. (1973) *Field Research: Strategies for a Natural Sociology*, Englewood Cliffs, N.J., Prentice Hall.

SCHEPER-HUGHES, N. (1979) *Saints, Scholars and Schizophrenics: Mental Illness in Rural Ireland*, Berkeley, Calif., University of California Press.

SCHEPER-HUGHES, N. (1981) 'Cui bonum — for whose good? A dialogue with Sir Raymond Firth', *Human Organization*, 40, 4, pp. 371–2.

SHAW, K.E. (1969) 'Why no sociology of schools?' *Education for Teaching*, 69, pp. 61–7.

SHIPMAN, M. (Ed.) (1976) *The Organization and Impact of Social Research*, London, Routledge and Kegan Paul.

SPINDLER, G.D. (Ed.) (1963) *Education and Culture: Anthropological Approaches*, London, Holt, Rinehart and Winston.

SPINDLER, G.D. (Ed.) (1974) *Education and Cultural Process: Toward an Anthropology of Education*, New York, Holt, Rinehart and Winston.

SPINDLER, G.D. (Ed.) (1982) *Doing the Ethnography of Schooling*, New York, Holt, Rinehart and Winston.

STACEY, M. (1982) 'The sociology of health, illness and healing', in BURGESS, R.G. (Ed.), *Exploring Society*, London, British Sociological Association.

THREADGOLD, M.W. (1980) 'The use of teacher-based research for school policy', *Insight*, 3, 3, pp. 11–14.

TOMLINSON, S. (1982) *The Sociology of Special Education*, London, Routledge and Kegan Paul.

TURNER, V.W. (1957) *Schism and Continuity in an African Society: A Study of Ndembu Village Life*, Manchester, Manchester University Press on behalf of the Institute for African Studies, University of Zambia.

WAX, M.L. (1980) 'Paradoxes of "consent" to the practice of fieldwork', *Social Problems*, 27, 3, pp. 272–83.

WAX, M. and WAX, R. (1971) 'Great tradition, little tradition and formal education', in WAX, M. *et al.*, (Eds) *Anthropological Perspectives on Education*, New York, Basic Books.

WOODS, P. (Ed.) (1980a) *Teacher Strategies: Explorations in the Sociology of the School*, London, Croom Helm.

WOODS, P. (Ed.) (1980b) *Pupil Strategies: Explorations in the Sociology of the School*, London, Croom Helm.

WOODS, P. and HAMMERSLEY, M. (Eds) (1977) *School Experience: Explorations in the Sociology of Education*, London, Croom Helm.

9 Speaking with Forked Tongue? Two Styles of Observation in the ORACLE Project

Maurice Galton and Sara Delamont

> So many princes visited Argus in the hope of marrying either Aegeia, or Deipyla, the daughters of King Adrastus, that, fearing to make powerful enemies if he singled out any two of them as his sons-in-law, he consulted the Delphic Oracle. Apollo's response was: 'Yoke to a two-wheeled chariot the boar and the lion which fight in your palace'. (Graves, 1960; pp. 15–16)

This opaque advice was a typical pronouncement by the Pythia, prophetess of Apollo at Delphi. King Adrastus interpreted it to mean that his two daughters should marry two fugitive princes, Polyneices of Thebes (whose emblem is the lion) and Tydeus of Calydon (emblem the boar), pledging to restore them to their kingdoms. Thus the seven marched against Thebes. As there were seven scholars working on the ORACLE transfer studies, and the transfer studies consisted of an attempt to yoke two normally antagonistic research methods together, the Adrastus *motif* seems an appropriate one to lead us into a consideration of what the ORACLE project meant for its participants.

The ancient Greek oracles took many forms, and supplicants sometimes had to go through complex rituals before receiving enlightenment. There was an oracle of Trophonius (son of one of the Argonauts) at Lebadeia where the supplicant had to be purified for several days, eat the flesh of a sacrificial ram, drink from the water of Lethe and descend into a large pot. Once inside the large pot the enquirer after truth was hit on the head, dowsed in water and finally returned, dazed and senseless, to the house of the Good Genius. During the whole uncomfortable process, the supplicant must carry two honey cakes for the serpent ghost of Trophonius.

Maurice Galton and Sara Delamont

Graves (1960) chooses to interpret this procedure as a kind of mock death, but to an experienced ethnographer it sounds like the process of fieldwork. We have to be initiated into strange environments, eat strange foods and appease strange shades. In this paper we describe some of our attempts to consult our ORACLE, and our struggles to yoke together two different approaches to classroom research and organize them to pull together to produce a rich portrait of classroom life in England. Our difficulties in doing this, and avoiding the production of only Delphic utterances, are recounted below. We describe harnessing the lion of 'systematic' classroom observation (data collection with a pre-specified coding schedule) and the boar of ethnographic methods. The paper is divided into six sections. First we provide a brief description of the ORACLE project, with an emphasis on its methods. Then we discuss the difficulties involved in producing a reflexive account of the methodology for this volume. A straightforward narrative on the management of the transfer studies follows. Then the fourth section reflects on the relative status of the two kinds of observational data; the fifth deals with the induction and training of classroom observers. The sixth part considers the power which was placed at the disposal of one author (Delamont) by her control of the final account.

The ORACLE Project

ORACLE (Observational Research and Classroom Learning Evaluation)[1] was 'the first large-scale, longitudinal study to use observation techniques' in Britain (Galton et al., 1980, p. 1) Funded by the Social Science Research Council (now Economic and Social Research Council), it ran from 1975 to 1980 at the University of Leicester School of Education. The results of the five-year programme have appeared in four books to date, with a fifth yet to appear (Galton et al., 1980; Galton and Simon, 1980; Simon and Willcocks, 1981; Galton and Willcocks, 1983; Galton and Delamont, forthcoming). It is not possible to describe every aspect of this large research programme in one paper, and so we concentrate on the two kinds of observational data collected. The computing techniques, the teacher-based group work, and the testing programme, are not discussed, and the interested reader is referred to the appropriate publications.

ORACLE was focused mainly on the top primary age range (9–11 year old children) learning from different teachers. However, the project ran in three different LEAs, where three different three-

Maurice Galton and Sara Delamont

Graves (1960) chooses to interpret this procedure as a kind of mock death, but to an experienced ethnographer it sounds like the process of fieldwork. We have to be initiated into strange environments, eat strange foods and appease strange shades. In this paper we describe some of our attempts to consult our ORACLE, and our struggles to yoke together two different approaches to classroom research and organize them to pull together to produce a rich portrait of classroom life in England. Our difficulties in doing this, and avoiding the production of only Delphic utterances, are recounted below. We describe harnessing the lion of 'systematic' classroom observation (data collection with a pre-specified coding schedule) and the boar of ethnographic methods. The paper is divided into six sections. First we provide a brief description of the ORACLE project, with an emphasis on its methods. Then we discuss the difficulties involved in producing a reflexive account of the methodology for this volume. A straightforward narrative on the management of the transfer studies follows. Then the fourth section reflects on the relative status of the two kinds of observational data; the fifth deals with the induction and training of classroom observers. The sixth part considers the power which was placed at the disposal of one author (Delamont) by her control of the final account.

The ORACLE Project

ORACLE (Observational Research and Classroom Learning Evaluation)[1] was 'the first large-scale, longitudinal study to use observation techniques' in Britain (Galton et al., 1980, p. 1) Funded by the Social Science Research Council (now Economic and Social Research Council), it ran from 1975 to 1980 at the University of Leicester School of Education. The results of the five-year programme have appeared in four books to date, with a fifth yet to appear (Galton et al., 1980; Galton and Simon, 1980; Simon and Willcocks, 1981; Galton and Willcocks, 1983; Galton and Delamont, forthcoming). It is not possible to describe every aspect of this large research programme in one paper, and so we concentrate on the two kinds of observational data collected. The computing techniques, the teacher-based group work, and the testing programme, are not discussed, and the interested reader is referred to the appropriate publications.

ORACLE was focused mainly on the top primary age range (9–11 year old children) learning from different teachers. However, the project ran in three different LEAs, where three different three-tier school systems existed, and it was also decided to compare the resulting transfer processes. Local Authority A had first schools, 9–13 middle schools and 13–18 upper schools. Local Authority C had first schools, 8–12 middle schools and 12–18 comprehensives. Local Authority B had a three-tier system of 5–11, 11–14, and 14–18 schools. In the main phase of the research, pupils were studied in the 5–9, 8–12, and 5–11 schools, and in the transfer phase we followed ORACLE children into the 9–13, 12–18 and 11–14 schools.[2]

As Galton *et al.* (1980, p. 1) describe it, the major objective of the ORACLE programme was: 'to study the relative "effectiveness" of different teaching approaches across the main subject areas of primary school teaching.' This was done by observing teachers and pupils in the classroom, and by administering tests of achievement to the pupils. The major results of these observational and test data are presented in Galton *et al.* (1980) and Galton and Simon (1980). The classroom observation which lies at the centre of the ORACLE project was done with two pre-specified coding systems originally developed by Deanne Boydell (1978): the Teacher Record and the Pupil Record. The first three ORACLE books use these observational data exclusively. In the fourth volume (Galton and Willcocks, 1983) the focus is on school transfer, and the ethnographic data collected are introduced. In the transfer studies the two schedules designed originally by Boydell were still used but there was also a substantial commitment to participant observation or ethnography. Essentially, the difference between the two in terms of methodology turns on pre-specification and standardization. The ORACLE observer using the Teacher and Pupil Records is handling a standardized research instrument which *must* be carried out in the same way across different classrooms, teachers and schools. Considerable effort throughout the project went into preventing observer 'drift' away from reliability and keeping them on the straight and narrow. This has been documented by Jasman (1980) and Croll (1980) and does not need reiteration here.

In this paper we have focused on how the ethnographic work was done, and how it fitted into the transfer studies. These ORACLE transfer studies can be seen as one attempt at the *rapprochement* between 'systematic' and 'ethnographic' research which is frequently called for (e.g., McIntyre, 1980).

The five-year period during which ORACLE was funded allowed some of the sample children to be observed for three years of schooling, changing teachers in their primary or middle school and then moving up to a middle or secondary school where they met a wide range of different subjects and teachers. This spread allowed the research team to replicate their work on primary teaching *styles* on two samples of teachers, to discover whether pupils' work patterns were subject to change when they met a different teacher (they were), and to study the process of school transfer in some detail. This last objective was particularly suitable for ethnographic methods.

On transfer, our sample pupils in Local Authority A entered one of two 9–13 middle schools (Gryll Grange or Guy Mannering); in Local Authority B one of two 11–14 high schools (Maid Marion or Kenilworth); and in Local Authority C one of two 12–18 secondary schools (Melin Court or Waverly). Therefore these paired schools were matched in terms of intake, neighbourhood and so forth, but in each pair the first named used mixed-ability teaching while the second had streaming and/or banding. Our sample pupils were divided among the various first year classes, and mixed with pupils from classrooms and schools not included in the ORACLE project. They also met a curriculum with specialist, subject-based teaching, even in the 9–13 schools. The observation with the Teacher and Pupil Record was confined to English, maths, and one newly introduced subject (either science or a foreign language). The ethnographic research took place across the whole curriculum, embracing rugby, cooking, religious education and metalwork, as well as English, maths, French and science.

There were four good reasons for using participant observation in the first month of our sample's time at middle or secondary school. First, we wanted to try combining ethnographic research methods with the Teacher and Pupil Records to discover how far there were compatible findings. Secondly, we felt that the initial encounters between teachers and new pupils were peculiarly susceptible to ethnographic observation (Ball, 1980). Thirdly, we were interested in mounting a team effort in ethnographic research, where different observers studied the same classrooms. Finally, we felt it was the only efficient way to follow up the sample pupils, once they had been spread round new classes (see Galton and Willcocks, 1983, p. 1).

The subject matter of this paper is, then, the relationship *within the transfer studies* between the deployment of the Teacher and Pupil Records and the use of ethnographic methods. It does not describe the methodology of the ORACLE project as a whole, nor should it be taken to represent the whole of the transfer studies. Nor has writing it been an easy task, as the next section discusses.

Reflecting on ORACLE

ORACLE was a team effort as the introductions to the four volumes (Galton *et al.* 1980; Galton and Simon, 1980; Simon and Willcocks, 1981; Galton and Willcocks, 1983) show clearly. There were two directors (Maurice Galton and Brian Simon), three full-time researchers (John Willcocks, Anne Jasman and Paul Croll) and seven classroom observers employed part-time. There were two secretaries (Jaya Katariya and Diane Stroud). Deanne Boydell, who had devised the two observation instruments, acted as a consultant to the project. Sara Delamont undertook two periods of ethnographic observation and has written up that material. All of these people have a legitimate perspective on ORACLE and could produce an account of it. This paper is a view shared by Galton and Delamont on one aspect of the work: observation in the transfer studies.

The production of accounts about how cooperative research was done by part of a team is always hazardous, and sometimes offensive. The precedent set by the paper (Bell, 1977) on the restudy of Banbury (Stacey *et al.*, 1975) included in Bell and Newby (1977) is an obviously unhappy one. Bell's paper emphasizes interpersonal conflict rather than methodological concerns. We have deliberately eschewed the *mea culpa* or 'true confessions' style of account, in favour of a methodological discussion. We have not named any individual in the team in connection with any of our retrospective criticisms of the transfer study, believing any mistakes are our own. We have tried to highlight areas of concern to future research projects which will enable them to do better classroom studies. Even so, we recognize that our perspective on the ORACLE transfer studies may not be shared by other members of the team. We wish to emphasize that reading this paper is no substitute for studying the five volumes of results and discussion.

There are also important differences in social science perspective between the two authors of the paper. Delamont is an anthropologist by initial training and a practising sociologist of education. Galton's background is in chemistry, and his educational research has been psychological in inspiration. Our discussion of methodology will, inevitably, reflect a difference of opinion about what count as data, and what should be done with those data collected.

An illustration of what this paper does and does not do arises when we consider the methodological concept of triangulation. The rest of this section discusses triangulation in the ORACLE transfer project to exemplify the scope, focus and approach we have adopted in preparing this paper.

Triangulation in ORACLE

It is possible to characterize the ORACLE transfer studies in the six schools as examples of two kinds of triangulation, and this is done briefly in Galton and Willcocks (1983). Cohen and Manion (1980) separate three kinds of triangulation:

1 between method triangulation;
2 investigator triangulation;
3 within method triangulation.

Between method triangulation means using different research methods to surround, or get a grip on, a particular problem. Thus, in the ORACLE transfer studies (Galton and Willcocks, 1983) we studied the issue of pupils' anxieties about changing schools using ethnographic observation, interviews with pupils, interviews with parents, a psychological test of anxiety and essays written by pupils. These four different data-gathering methods (observation, interviewing, psychological testing, and pupils' written accounts) allow us to state conclusively that transfer anxiety is a transient phenomenon.

Investigator triangulation involves using several different interviewers, or observers, or test administrators, to gather data on the same topic, to reduce investigator idiosyncracies. In the ethnographic observation we always had at least three researchers working in each pair of schools, so that our account of any one school was drawn from fieldnotes produced by at least three separate people (see Galton and Willcocks, 1983). The use of several observers during the transfer studies gave us triangulation between researchers. Within the ethnographic work, however, there was not systematic triangulation of the kind advocated by Denzin (1970).

It would be possible to claim that between method and investigator triangulation were fundamental principles of the ORACLE transfer studies from the beginning of the project. We *could* claim that all along we had been engaged in these two forms of triangulation. It would be especially tempting to make such a claim in a volume of this kind. However at no point in the life of the ORACLE project was the concept used, and the research was *not* designed with this notion in prospect. Therefore, to claim, retrospectively, that the ORACLE transfer studies were designed as triangulated enquiry would be dishonest. In this paper we have eschewed being wise after the event, and especially making sociological capital out of such retrospective wisdom. This general approach has been adopted throughout the paper.

Managing the ORACLE Ethnography

This section presents the 'natural history' of the ORACLE ethnography from the perspective of Galton and Delamont. The pupils involved in the study in Local Authority A transferred to the 9–13 middle schools (Gryll Grange and Guy Mannering) in September 1977. The pupils in Local Authorities B and C made their transfer in September 1978. Thus, the timetable of the ethnographic research allowed us to use the study of the 9–13 schools in September 1977 as a pilot study for 1978, when the rest of the pupils transferred into the 12–18 and 11–14 schools. Thus by 1978 we had a fistful of ideas from the 1977 study which we could use as 'foreshadowed problems' or 'sensitizing concepts' in 1978. Sara Delamont lived in digs in the town, where one part-time researcher lived. Delamont and the 'hired hand' spent all of September in the two schools, visiting each on alternate days. That is, Delamont spent Monday at Gryll Grange, Tuesday at Guy Mannering, boxing and coxing with the other observer. Maurice Galton observed in the schools on at least two days per week as well in September, and then paid occasional visits during the remainder of the school year. In 1978 Sara Delamont lived in digs in Local Authority C, and worked with another local 'hired hand', augmented by visits from Maurice Galton. Meanwhile, one of the full-time workers from Leicester and another 'hired hand' dealt with the two schools in Local Authority B (Maid Marion and Kenilworth), also augmented by Maurice Galton. The three 'hired hands' were fully trained in two systematic techniques, but were not 'trained' ethnographers. Indeed, all the researchers used had very different academic and research backgrounds. Sara Delamont was the only experienced ethnographer, while all the other observers had been trained as teachers and were experienced as classroom observers with the Teacher and Pupil Records. Maurice Galton had done systematic observation with the Science Teacher Observation Schedule (Eggleston *et al.*, 1976) before launching ORACLE.

While the ethnographic observation was deliberately intended to be more flexible and responsive than the systematic observation, it was not our intention to send observers into the six transfer schools with completely blank minds and blank notebooks. In the 1977 study of the two 9–13 schools we had a shortlist of 'foreshadowed problems' derived from our reading of other school studies. These were of two kinds: some vaguely 'theoretical' ideas we had derived from the literature, and some 'commonsense' ideas derived more from our 'members' knowledge'. Among the more 'theoretical' ideas, we were interested in utilizing Bernstein's (1971; 1974) ideas on classification, framing and visible versus invisible pedagogies; the beginnings of labelling, and the notion of 'coping strategies' (Woods, 1980). More concretely, we asked all observers to look carefully at pupils' 'adjustment' to their new schools, sibling comparisons, staff-room discussions of pupils, bullying and the schools' responses to it, and to compare 'theory' and 'practice' in such areas as curriculum balance, pupil groupings, allocation of teachers to classes, and so on. For example, in Local Authority A we had found that allocation of children to Bands at Guy Mannering School was more closely related to primary school attended than ability or heads' reports, and so we asked the observers in Local Authorities B and C to examine Band allocation, class allocation and so forth. How far the observers took any notice of these 'foreshadowed' problems is, in retrospect, unclear, because of the diverse nature of the observers and the rather unsystematic training given (see below).

In each town there were regular meetings among the observers to discuss their 'findings' (although they were brief and not minuted). No systematic attempts were made to standardize or harmonize fieldnotes or diary-taking, and the resulting documents vary enormously in length, depth, social scientific language-use and the extent to which judgments are made explicitly, for example, one observer's only record of a maths lesson at Kenilworth (11–14) School:

> I find Mr Mairs a very pleasant man who gets on with his job easily and confidently. However his lessons are tedious to observe. The children get on with their work with the minimum of fuss; they go up to him individually for help; and consequently very little happens which is striking or noteworthy.

Such a record is more judgmental than either of us would like. However, we found surprising similarities in accounts of the same classrooms, observed by the three researchers who studied each of them. These convergences were greater than Delamont had anticipated. (Indeed, she had feared a set of contradictory or incompatible records.) Naturally, ethnography does not generate inter-observer reliability of the kind demanded, and achieved, with the Teacher and Pupil Records (Croll, 1980).

The production and management of the fieldnotes varied between the observers. Maurice Galton describes his practice as follows:

> I actually wrote my notes during class and during the periods between lessons I recorded other impressions of the class-room. Going over these at night I then dictated a fuller version. It may be of interest to put in a word about this supplementation of my class record.

Sara Delamont kept her fieldnotes in spiral-bound shorthand pads, which have neither been transcribed nor seen by anyone else, and an 'out of field' diary, which she had typed by the ORACLE secretaries and circulated. Other observers wrote their notes legibly, and they were either typed or merely photocopied by the secretaries. Once the fieldnotes were gathered, those taken by the other five observers were handed over to Sara Delamont, who has analyzed them and written up the material. This was considered to be the only practical course, but also has the effect of giving a coherence and common focus to the resulting account which may be exaggerated. Accordingly we have chosen this issue as one for further elaboration below, where we raise it as one problem associated with triangulation between observers.

The next section deals with a second unresolved issue from the transfer study: the between method triangulation.

Reconciling the Irreconcilable?

The 1970s saw many classroom researchers call for *rapprochements* between quantitative and qualitative methods (Stones, 1978; Mc-Intyre, 1980; Wragg, 1975). Some projects, notably the Beginning Teacher Evaluation Study (BTES) reported by Denham and Leiberman (1980) and ORACLE, did attempt to gather both ethnographic and schedule-based data. More recently, Bennett's (1982) work in infant schools has used the two approaches. The act of gathering more than one type of data — though it shows good interdisciplinary intentions — does not in itself go any distance towards reconciling competing paradigms. The real problems associated with *rapprochements* come when the analysis is proceeding and when the results are to be presented to the outside world. Here the real problems of between method triangulation 'rise in green robes, roaring from the green hells of the sea, where fallen skies, and evil hues, and eyeless creatures be' (Chesterton, 1927). Or more prosaically, the research team's real problems begin.

When faced with the data on the transfer studies, which consisted of both qualitative and quantitative material, three possible methods of combining them are available:

1 The sets of data could be treated equally.
2 The qualitative data could be treated as more valid and the quantitative used to reinforce important and/or controversial points in the argument.
3 The quantitative data could be regarded as 'the facts' and the qualitative used to 'flesh them out', illustrate them, or 'humanize' them.

While the first option is the most desirable, it has not seemed attainable in educational research. Most projects have opted for either '2' (e.g., Nash, 1973) or '3' (as ORACLE and BTES do). We are not proud of this, nor do we recommend it, but we feel the process by which it occurred is illuminating for other researchers attempting between method triangulation.

Thus, while the main subject of this paper is the 'problems' which arose from linking the schedule-based and ethnographic observation, in an important way, for the fourth ORACLE volume at least we avoided it. We did not settle down with all our various sorts of data — the Teacher Pupil Records, pupil essays, pupils' test scores, pupils' 'personality' questionnaires, interviews with pupils and parents and the ethnographic materials — treat them equally, and deduce our main conclusions from them all. Rather the Teacher and Pupil Record data, and the pupils' test scores, were treated as *the findings*. Other material was used to illuminate or flesh out these results, or treated as variables dependent upon them. The fifth ORACLE volume is the one where the ethnographic research, plus the essays and interviews, will be the data. However, it is the fourth book (Galton and Willcocks, 1983) that is relevant here, where we have, *de facto*, relegated the role of ethnography to that of *illustrations*. We have not actually yoked the lion and the boar together, but have allowed the lion to determine the basic structure of the book.

How we organized *Moving from the Primary Classroom* around the systematic data is described first. The plan of this volume went through several modifications before reaching the published version (Galton and Willcocks, 1983). In 1980 a chapter plan was prepared in which the ethnographic material on transfer would occupy four chapters as follows:

1   Preparation for transfer (visits, parents' evenings, etc.)
2   First days in the new school
3   Curriculum, teachers and pupils
4   Sex roles in secondary school

All four of these chapters combined material on buildings and rooms, teachers, the curriculum and relations with peers. The first proposed chapter was drawn from observation of pupils' and parents' visits to the transfer schools in June, interviews with pupils about the transfer, and essays pupils wrote on their expectations of, and the reality of, their new schools. These materials showed that pupils had three major concerns about transfer: new teachers, new peers and new subjects. Some were anxious, some expectant, but all were aware of these three themes (see also Measor and Woods, 1983). Three chapters were then prepared on what happened in the early weeks after transfer among the pupils, between teachers and pupils, and in the curriculum.

Sara Delamont drafted rough versions of these four chapters in 1980 while other members of the project team were still analyzing project data and drafting Simon and Willcocks (1981). The four draft chapters drawing on the ethnographic materials and the pupil essays and interviews were discussed with the research team, before the chapters based on the schedules and tests were written. They were then put aside, until the rest of the research team were ready to write 'their' chapters. As Galton has explained it, an agreement about publication had been made among the five central members of the team (Simon, Galton, Jasman, Croll and Willcocks):

> This is the agreement which was made with all the researchers on the ORACLE project concerning their right to have a recognised piece of work published under their own name. Thus after *Inside the Primary Classroom*, the second volume was done with sections under joint names and this fourth (transfer) book was to be done with separate pieces for Croll and Willcocks. This meant, essentially, that they exercised their right to do what they wanted and it was in the light of their drafts that the book had to be re-jigged.

Once John Willcocks, Paul Croll and Maurice Galton had produced their chapters on the numerical findings, the book was replanned and Delamont redrafted her chapters. The data on transfer

Maurice Galton and Sara Delamont

between one class teacher and another at primary school, and the test results which showed pupils 'standing still' academically in their transfer schools, were made more prominent in the new plan. The ethnographic chapter on preparation for transfer was omitted altogether and held over for the fifth volume. The other three were 'rejigged' — not to change the substantive points, but to reorganize them. The material on all maths lessons was pulled together to show how maths lessons 'felt' to the ethnographers, because of the disturbing findings about the subject produced by the Teacher and Pupil Records. (Most girls are uninvolved in maths lessons and do very little work.) Similarly we drew all the English lessons together, to illustrate the numerical data on language and literacy. This involved moving chunks from one place to another, rather than extensive rewriting. The three chapters then went through another draft by Delamont, and the final preparation for the publisher was done by Galton without Delamont seeing that version at all.

The published chapters are, therefore, organized as follows:

1 A very common curriculum (material showing that the curriculum was similar in all six schools);
2 Teachers and their specialist subjects (including detailed material on maths, English and science);
3 Through the eyes of the pupil (material on pupil-pupil and pupil-teacher relations, from the pupils' viewpoint).

These three chapters show, from ethnographic data, how pupils face up to school transfer and what their new schools were like.

Overall, the numerical statistical data were seen as paramount, and the ethnographic data were the flesh on its bones. However, the team's interpretation of the statistical information may have been influenced by the ethnographic chapters they had already read. In general we found that the two observational methods produced very similar findings. That is, nothing that was said about the teaching of maths, English, science or French in the transfer schools drawn from the codings done with the Teacher and Pupil Record was challenged by the ethnographic findings. However, there were some features of classroom life in the transfer schools which were spotted by the ethnographic observation, but which, because the schedules had not been designed to include them, are not apparent from the quantitative data.

Two examples of such features are sex-stereotyping and sibling labelling. The ethnographers nearly all commented upon sex-stereotyping in classroom interactions, and all observers had recorded

174

incidents of it. However, the Teacher and Pupil Records were not designed to highlight such behaviour, and so the two sorts of observation do not produce the same results in this area. For example, one observer at Kenilworth (11–14) School heard the following in a music lesson with Mr Tippett.

> He began by saying that violins were like young ladies. They are fairly big at the top, they are small-waisted, and they have got ... er 'Big Bums!' came a suggestion from an unidentified child, 'Yes, that is right, large bottoms', said Mr Tippett.

The observer found this a noticeable example of sexual stereotyping — but the Teacher Record would only show such an interaction as 'Teacher Statement of Ideas, Problems' to whole class. Similarly the ethnographers found a good deal of sibling labelling. For example, a new teacher might look at the class list and ask; 'Beverly Wynn, are you Duane's sister? He's very good in geography when he's with us.' This again would not show up from either Teacher or Pupil Records.

In summary, the Directors of the ORACLE Project (Simon and Galton) felt vindicated, because while the schedules had provided a barrage of statistical information on classroom interaction, the ethnography has revealed many other facets of school transfer while confirming the central ones.

The Problem with Untrained Ethnographers

One issue of wider relevance for educational research than merely understanding how ORACLE was carried out concerns the preparation of the ethnographers before they entered the field. This issue is the proper induction and training of ethnographic researchers. With the benefit of hindsight, Sara Delamont should have organized formal training procedures for the observers before and during their fieldwork. Such induction into ethnographic approaches to data collection would have served both symbolic and practical functions, and the absence of any formal preparation for the qualitative data collection stands in sharp contrast to the training of the schedule-users.

Jasman (1980) has described the training procedures used to produce reliable and valid use of the Teacher and Pupil Records. The observers went through a two-week, intensive course using video-tapes and practice in actual classrooms. They were paid for this training, and achievement of appropriate standards was necessary if they were to take part in the project. Additionally, the observers were regularly brought into the School of Education and given refresher courses on the use of the schedule, to ensure that no observer 'drift' took place (Croll, 1980).

This induction is not only essential if systematic coding schedules are to be used; it also has symbolic significance for the observers. Such paid training showed that classroom research is a serious business which was to be learnt. We did not fully appreciate this when we planned the five-year ORACLE programme. By failing to budget time or money for an ethnographic training procedure, we implicitly signalled that the ethnographic approach was 'easier' than the schedules, and that taking fieldnotes was not a specialized technical skill. We may even have suggested, unwittingly, that we did not regard the ethnographic research as particularly important. Being wise after the event, we should have set up a training programme of at least a week, where researchers would be paid to learn the techniques.

Two issues of concern to future research teams arise. First, there are the consequences of our use of relatively unskilled observers; secondly, there are our thoughts on what ethnographic training might involve. We examine these in turn, with a view to helping future research projects learn from ORACLE.

The Familiarity Problem

The consequences, for the ORACLE transfer studies, of not training our ethnographers were that many of them met the problem of finding classrooms too familiar (Delamont, 1981), and some were not able to make detailed enough fieldnotes. The familiarity trap was described by Becker (1971, p. 10):

> We may have understated a little the difficulty of observing contemporary classrooms. It is not just the survey method of educational testing or any of those things that keeps people from seeing what is going on. I think, instead, that it is first and foremost a matter of it all being so familiar that it becomes impossible to single out events that occur in the classroom as things that have occurred, even when they happen right in front of you. I have not had the experience of observing in elementary and high school classrooms myself, but I have in college classrooms and it takes a tremendous effort of will and imagination to stop seeing the things that are

conventionally 'there' to be seen. I have talked to a couple of teams of research people who have sat around in classrooms trying to observe and it is like pulling teeth to get them to see or write anything beyond what 'everyone' knows.

Becker's diagnosis of the problem facing observers in educational settings appeared as a footnote to an article by Murray and Rosalie Wax (1971) in which they bemoaned the lack of 'a solid body of data on the ethnography of schools'. Since 1971 there has been a good deal of ethnographic research on education published (Hammersley, 1982; Smith, 1982) but, as one of us has argued elsewhere (Delamont, 1981), many studies have failed to make the familiar strange. Most of the ethnographic observers in the ORACLE transfer studies found the struggle against the familiarity too hard, because we had not trained them sufficiently to combat it. They are, however, in good company, for while we suspect Becker was ignorant of much contemporary research on classrooms such as Jackson (1968), Smith and Geoffrey (1968), Leacock (1969) and Hargreaves (1967), there is an important issue raised in his comment. Everyone in the ORACLE team had been to school, many of them had been teachers, and thus classrooms were 'so familiar'. When Becker says that getting researchers to see or write things which are insightful is like 'pulling teeth', he is expressing feelings familiar to many research supervisors and project directors. The very 'ordinariness', 'routineness' and 'everydayness' of school and classroom life do indeed confound many researchers, who do complain that they are bored, they cannot find anything to write down, and that 'nothing happens'. All ethnographic work is hard, but schools and classrooms do have a particular kind of familiarity — beautifully captured by Jackson (1968) — which make it especially tough. (Whether the demands of classroom observations with a coding schedule are more exhausting than those of ethnographic recording is a matter that needs researchers' attention).

Becker does, therefore, have a point which is revealed in ORACLE. It should not have been any kind of terminal diagnosis. The fact that the classroom is familiar does not mean that the researcher passively accepts the difficulty. Rather the task of the social scientist is *to make the familiar strange*. Becker's brief footnote does not address itself to solutions for the familiarity, but it is important to find some, rather than bleat about 'will and imagination'. In retrospect, we did not work hard enough at finding solutions for novice ethnographers.

The purpose of training ethnographers before and during the

ORACLE transfer studies, had we done so, would, therefore, have been to get them to make the familiar strange. Wolcott (1981) has pointed out how the traditional anthropological training in an 'exotic' strange culture 'made much behaviour stand out in bold relief'. He goes on:

> It is this experience (fondly recollected years later as 'culture shock') that prior generations of anthropologists have found so important and that perpetrates the strongly held preference for having students conduct their first major fieldwork in a cross-cultural setting. (Oddly enough, we have not system-atically encouraged our students in educational research to go and look at something else for a while. We keep sending them back to the classroom. The only doctoral student I have sent off to do fieldwork in a hospital was a nurse-educator who returned to her faculty position in a school of nursing!) (Wolcott, 1981, p. 260)

To inculcate culture shock in our ethnographers perhaps we should have paid them to practise ethnographic techniques in non-educational settings, such as hospitals, pubs, casinos, greengrocers, hairdressers or supermarkets. The difficulties of making British schools anthropologically strange are parallel to the difficulties experienced by ethnographers working in the USA discussed in Messerschmidt (1982).

Allied to the problem of familiarity is the adoption of cultural relativism during data collection. It is important to separate judgments, personal reactions and value statements about school life from the ethnographic record of the events. Personal reactions to events are a legitimate part of ethnography, but need to be clearly separate from the events themselves in the fieldnotes. Many of our observers found this difficult to do, and the importance of struggling to attain relativism should have been made clearer to them (Wolcott, 1975, offers a good discussion of this issue).

The results of Delamont's failure to budget for, and plan, training courses in 1977 and 1978 are most apparent in the unpub-lished fieldnotes taken by the 'systematic' observers. These observers were all fully trained in the Teacher and Pupil Records, had used them in the pre-transfer schools, and were going to use them again after the ethnography of the transfer schools. All of them knew the names of the ORACLE target pupils (and many of their classmates) from the earlier work. All of them reacted strongly to some features of the transfer schools and were unable to suspend those feelings. The fieldnotes of these researchers were generally sparse and summary, lacked the use of participants' natural language, mixed judgment and description, and showed a concentration of attention on a few 'academic' lessons. Delamont was the only observer to attend systematically and record at swimming, games, PE, assembly, house meetings and so on, because no-one told the others clearly enough that vital data might be obtained therein. Interestingly, Galton, who had seven years' previous experience with schedule-based observation, and was previously sceptical about ethnography, enjoyed being an observer with a notebook the most, and produced the fieldnotes Delamont found most similar to her own in focus, if not in style. (Galton has suggested that the reason our fieldnotes were similar in focus was that we spent more time talking together after school visits than any other pair of researchers.)

The contrast between what was recorded by an experienced and a novice ethnographer can be illustrated by the following extracts from notes taken in lessons *consisting of silent seat work* at Guy Mannering (9–13) Middle School. First, everything that an untrained observer managed or chose to record about an English lesson, taught by Mr Evans, which lasted 35 minutes:

> Children supposed to work in silence on essay 'a foolish thing I did'. Terence, of course, had done three foolish things in his life, according to his mum, and whispered them to Mr Evans who advised him on the most foolish. Dominico Grillo seems to get a fair share of friendly attention and Norris a lot of chivvying. [All names are pseudonyms.]

Silent seat work is one of the hardest lesson types to observe, especially if the overall discipline is tight. The dialogue between the teacher and individual pupils is whispered and sparse, there is little pupil-pupil talk, and the observer is largely forced to concentrate on imputing meaning to non-verbal behaviours. The following notes, which are the complete transcript of another observer's notes from an early meeting of Mr Evans and the same class, show how much more was written at the time. The notes were subsequently written into a longer and more elaborated account, but what was recorded in the lesson is reproduced here. All names are pseudonyms, and the author's abbreviations have been spelt out in full. Material added for the reader of the volume appears in square brackets:

Guy Mannering 13/9/77 (Tuesday)
2nd period after break — English

1   Pupils at this school are very good at opening doors for adults.
2   At 11.55 [the form] have to go back to Mrs Forrest.
3   Mr Evans tells them off for arriving in 'dribs and drabs'.
4   'You leave your last lesson all together, you should get here all together.'
5   Goes over [pupils] names — gets them right.
6   Mentions several siblings — 'You're a Pryce.'
7   Mair Pryce has long blonde hair [the girl he had just linked to her siblings in the school].
8   Gets two boys to give out books.
9   Green Book I *New Reading: An English Course for Schools.*
10   [Announces] Chapter 1 Nature's Joke — The Kangaroo.
11   After boys have given out books — giving one to me on his instructions, read aloud round the class — when a pupil makes a mistake, the next one reads.
12   Reading standards vary — some do several lines, some only do a phrase.
13   'What have you got to have to be a good reader?'
14   Terence 'concentration'.
15   Gives them a lecture on concentration. Then tells them that they must answer questions in sentences.
16   Goes over how to answer questions. [Pupils] reading [questions] in unison and [Mr Evans] checking the answers are known to all of them.
17   This room is obviously for geography — big globe, maps, sets of geography books.
18   Tells them about not starting [to write] till he has gone over setting out. So does — ruling off, not wasting space.
     Date — Sept 13th
     Stresses heading/capitals etc.
19   Terence has put his date on the wrong side.
20   No he hasn't.
21   Red-haired Rowena's hand is up again — wants to change her pen cartridge [Mr Evans moves around the room looking at individual pupils].
22   Finds Gavin has started. Tells him he's done it wrong, rule it off, and do it all over again. 'Do it my way.'
23   Asks ginger Sonia if she always prints — apparently she does — leaves her.
24   Tells them it is not a race — first person to finish may be the worst work.

25 Goes over the rules — Date on the right — 100% got that
    Leave a line — about 10 people forgot
    Heading*

26 Start. 1st Question is done on the board. 'Copy it' — then
    do [Question] 2 which he has begun.

27 This room has spare capacity too.

28 'Nice and tidy, Mitchell, good boy'.

29 Mr Evans goes round twice — then settles to mark books.

30 Stresses that they should ask if in doubt.

31 Tells off room 'cos someone is talking/humming.

32 Girl goes to front to ask for advice about line spacing.

33 'You're not here to giggle girl, you're here to work. I'll
    giggle if it's necessary.'

34 Silence reigns.

35 (At the beginning class was interrupted by 3 pupils from
    another room wanting a set of books.)

36 Gavin is obviously a very fast worker. He asked if they were
    to go on to Qu.3. Told probably not time — except he
    might — but mustn't forget to answer the questions (i.e. not
    just copy incomplete ones off the board).

37 'That's nice, Dominico.'

38 'Somebody told me you had influenza.'

39 'That's nice, good one. Take your time, now, don't go
    rushing it.'

40 'How do you spell "goes", Norris? You've got all the right
    letters.'

41 Tells them to pack up.

42 Terence and Marvin to collect books.

43 Tells girls to go.

44 [Pupils] return to form room.

We are in no sense claiming that the second transcript is a set of
model notes on a lesson. They are too sparse, and need to be written
into a narrative account the same evening. However, there are many
more pieces of information in them. There is teacher talk recorded
verbatim, there is more on the setting, the teacher's concern for the
presentation of work is clear, the opening and closing of the lesson is
apparent, some girls appear in the action, there are examples of sibling
location, sexual differentiation and the beginnings of pupil identities.
However, many features of the action have been left implicit by the
author, including the register being called at the beginning and the
first perambulations of Mr Evans. Also these notes are still too sparse

and are only an aide-memoire for an observer to amplify later the same day. We should have had all our researchers not only writing this much in the lessons, but using such notes as the basis of much longer narratives subsequently submitted to the project secretaries. (Although, we recognize, the implications of this are a need for much greater secretarial 'back up' than ORACLE had.)

Accepting the need for training, we now turn to a consideration of how such a training programme might be run.

Training Ethnographers

It is not clear that training for ethnographic observation can be done. Harry Wolcott (1981) has raised the intriguing question: are observational skills 'caught' or 'taught'? In a discussion of his own socialization as an ethnographer, and attempts he has made to run courses in observational methods, Wolcott argues that too often the question of *what to look for* is dominant, and the more important issue, *how to look*, is neglected.

Wolcott describes six ways in which courses in ethnographic methods become sidetracked into a range of issues but never actually tackle how to observe. First, Wolcott suggests, courses become sidetracked into discussing the role of the observer in the field and 'we lose sight of what and how one actually observes.' Secondly, there is discussion of avoiding 'narrowing our research focus too much and too soon' and remaining flexible, which distracts from how observation is done. Discussion of note-taking becomes concerned with where and when to record, but 'we do not talk specifically about what to put in them.' Consideration of observer bias leads to calls for it to be made explicit, but 'we never call for similar explication of what and how the observer actually observes.' Fifthly, discussion of objectivity rarely turns, Wolcott argues, into how involvement or detachment affect observation. Finally, he concludes, although his seminar groups read ethnographies, they 'find it devilishly hard to know precisely what they were observing that prompted one thing and not another to come to their attention.'

Wolcott goes on to describe how he became an experienced observer over his career, and concludes that in a new field setting: 'I have a sense of what to do, but I have not found an adequate way to convey it to someone else.' Wolcott is sceptical of courses specifically designed to train ethnographers, or indeed other observers for classrooms, suggesting that unless the trainer issues specific and detailed instructions about what is to be observed, different people continue to attend to different things.

There are, however, several things we could have done. Were we starting an equivalent project in 1983 there are good materials available we would use. Today there is an excellent textbook (Spradley, 1980) which breaks ethnographic projects down into twelve stages, and discusses each with ample examples. We would now spend a fortnight taking our observers through Spradley's book, carrying out the suggested exercises. This text would be supplemented by the materials on ethnography produced as part of the Open University Course DE304 [Block 3 Part 5; Block 4 Part 3] and the TV programmes associated with those Blocks. These too contain practical exercises. Neither of these is specifically educational, which is an added advantage. As background reading, we would now recommend Hammersley and Atkinson (1983) and would feel more confident in our researchers.

In 1977 and 1978 we merely produced a short reading list of a few key texts on interpretive methods (McCall and Simmons, 1969; Schatzman and Strauss, 1973) and a few ethnographies (Sharp and Green, 1975; Stubbs and Delamont, 1976). We did not check up on the researchers to see if this reading had been done, let alone if its messages had been absorbed. Although Delamont (1976, p. 112) had already stressed the importance of wide reading for classroom researchers, this was not made explicit enough to the rest of the team, and the ORACLE ethnography does not meet the standards Delamont (1981) has set on this criterion.

Our next methodological issue is concerned with authorship: with what happens to the data once gathered.

The Author's Privilege?

The final theme arising from the ORACLE transfer studies which has general relevance for other teams of researchers concerns the production of accounts for publication. Several descriptions of research done by teams (e.g., Platt, 1976; Bell and Newby, 1977) have reported disagreements over assigning credit for work done between authors and eventual publications. In ORACLE the five full-time researchers shared all royalties equally, but the credits on publications reflected the amount of writing and editorial work done. Thus in Galton and Willcocks (1983) Sara Delamont and Maurice Galton have their names on three chapters each, while Paul Croll and John Willcocks are credited on two each. Galton and Willcocks prepared the final typescript and so appear on the cover. Revelations about squabbles over money or credits inside a project team sometimes makes good reading for voyeurs but rarely give insight or help to future researchers. Here we want to raise a more fundamental issue about the extent to which the person or persons who produce the account of a team ethnography actually determine the nature of the account to a significant extent.

The analysis and writing up of an ethnography have been less discussed in the literature on research methods than data collection or the negotiation of access to the research setting. Spradley (1979; 1980) is unusual in discussing how to write up an ethnography as well as how to conduct one. The lack of reflexiveness about the production of ethnographic accounts is discussed by Atkinson (1982) and is given serious consideration in Hammersley and Atkinson (1983). Here we wish to describe how the data on the transfer schools were handled in the ORACLE project and show the dilemmas that were raised. We do not have solutions for the dilemmas we reveal.

The analysis of the ethnographic material from the six transfer schools was based on Delamont reading all the observers' notes and diaries several times, indexing them to locate examples of significant events, and then preparing drafts of chapters which were discussed with some of the permanent members of the research team (Galton, Simon, Croll and Willcocks) at meetings in Leicester. There were several reasons why this was practical, but the consequences have to be understood.

Three of the observers used to gather ethnographic notes (Tann, Lea and Greig) were part-time workers, paid by the hour to gather data. Their contracts did not include writing time, and they had all left the project by the time (1980/81) the relevant volume came to be prepared for Routledge. They could not be expected to write up that material. Willcocks and Galton were permanent team members, but when the analysis and writing up fell due, they were fully engaged on preparing earlier ORACLE volumes, and other chapters of the book on transfer. Delamont had the experience with 'soft' data and the spare writing capacity, so she prepared the three chapters of Galton and Willcocks (1983) which depend on ethnographic data.

This has several consequences. First, there were genuine differences among the team over *stylistics*. Delamont prefers pseudonyms for teachers, pupils and schools; other team members prefer 'Pupil 312', 'Teacher Maths 12', and 'School 3C'. While this may seem trivial, it actually reveals differences about the 'scientific' status of ethnography, the 'readability' of the research and so forth which go deeper than a dispute over which nomenclature to use. Krieger (1979, pp. 175–8) is one of the few authors to write about this discussing her study of a radio station in California. She wanted to produce a text with a coherent narrative, and so had 'the problem of developing characters who would be capable of carrying its narrative.' To make her characters live for the reader, she decided they had to have 'their own personal, or "real" names, as well as names indicating something of their relationship with the station.' Delamont felt like this about the ORACLE school ethnography: some other members of the team did not. Galton and Willcocks therefore altered the drafts, and the book appears without pseudonyms. Instead of Gryll Grange (9–13) the book talks about APT, signifying Local Authority A Primary School Type.

Perhaps more serious is the issue of *power*. Because Delamont writes the accounts of the ethnography, her version of reality is the one which is offered. Other members of the team can query it, but do not have the same access to the data, or time to construct an alternative. The account of everyday life in the schools is probably more *sociological*, more conscious of sexism, and more grounded in other ethnographic work than it would be if written by anyone else involved in the project.

It seemed important to mitigate the effects of this power that had been given to Delamont as far as possible. The main strategy adopted was to make sure that whenever any point was made, it could be illustrated and/or substantiated by extracts from at least three observers' notes. It also seemed important to use at least one extract from every one of the six researchers and to make sure that all six schools were represented in the account, including the two not studied in person by Delamont. This would probably have been impossible if Delamont had not had some acquaintance with the two 11–14 schools from occasional teaching practice supervision.[3] We decided that we would not identify particular researchers as authors of individual extracts or comments.

We are convinced that ours was the only practical way of handling the writing of the ORACLE ethnography, but we are acutely aware that there are no clear ground rules for handling such a decision.[4] Should the 'hired-hand' ethnographer own her own fieldnotes? And who, if anyone, should veto the account — researchers or researched? We are not quite sure.

Maurice Galton and Sara Delamont

Conclusion

This paper has offered the reader some of our experiences in doing the ORACLE transfer studies. Whether we have emulated Adrastus and yoked the lion and the boar, or merely collapsed, stunned like the supplicant approaching the oracle of Trophonius, we leave to the reader. We have, however, raised three serious issues which all researchers planning cooperative, team projects, could do well to consider: between method triangulation, the training of ethnographers, and the powers vested in the authors of reports compared to the hired hands.[5] When the next team sets out to march on Thebes, we hope they will have learnt from our experiences.

Notes

1 The ORACLE project was funded by the SSRC at the University of Leicester from 1975 to 1980, directed by Brian Simon and Maurice Galton. We are grateful to the SSRC for the funding, to the schools where data were collected, and to Mrs Myrtle Robins and Val Dobie for typing this paper.
2 In this paper all LEAs, schools, teachers and pupils have pseudonyms. We have named the researchers involved, but as in our other publications we have not added names of particular researchers to specific aspects of the data.
3 At issue here is the question of 'members' knowledge, and its role in making sense of ethnographic data. It is possible that Delamont could not have written accounts of the two 11–14 schools (Kenilworth and Maid Marion) if she had never seen them herself.
4 Galton has commented that our final paragraph is ironic: because if we had done it all more carefully and got all the observers to write extended fieldnotes and had more meetings to discuss drafts, etc., the main result would have been to delay the book considerably, first because the typist would have been under greater pressure and also because of the drafting and redrafting problems. We think that team studies are preferable to ones done by individuals for obvious reasons but they do require considerable resources.
5 The whole issue of 'hired-hand' research was scrutinized by Roth (1966) and he raises many issues pertinent to ORACLE that we have not analyzed here.

References

ATKINSON, P. (1982) 'Writing ethnography', in HORST JURGEN HELLE (Ed.) *Kulter and Institution*, Berlin, Duncker and Humblot.

BALL, S. (1980) 'Initial encounters', in WOODS, P. (Ed.) *Pupil Strategies*, London, Croom Helm.

BECKER, H. (1971) footnote, in WAX, M. *et al.* (Eds) (1971) *Anthropological Perspectives on Education*, New York, Basic Books, p. 10.

BELL, C. (1977) 'Reflections on the Banbury restudy', in BELL, C. and NEWBY, H. (Eds) *Doing Sociological Research*, London, Allen and Unwin.

BELL, C. and NEWBY, H. (Eds) (1977) *Doing Sociological Research*, London, Allen and Unwin.

BENNETT, S.N. (1982) unpublished paper, presented at the IAAP conference, Edinburgh, July 1982.

BERNSTEIN, B. (1971) 'On the classification and framing of education knowledge', in YOUNG, M.F.D. (Ed.) *Knowledge and Control*, London, Collier-Macmillan.

BERNSTEIN, B. (1974) 'Class and pedagogies: Visible and invisible', in BERNSTEIN, B. (1975) *Class, Codes and Control*, Vol. 3, London, Routledge and Kegan Paul.

BOYDELL, D. (1978) *The Primary Teacher in Action*, London, Open Books.

CHESTERTON, G.K. (1927) 'Lepanto' in POCOCK, G.N. (Ed.) *Later Modern Poetry*, London, Dent.

COHEN, L. and MANION, L. (1980) *Research Methods in Education*, London, Croom Helm.

CROLL, P. (1980) 'Replicating the observational data', in GALTON, M. and SIMON, B. (Eds) *Progress and Performance in the Primary Classroom*, London, Routledge and Kegan Paul.

DELAMONT, S. (1976) *Interaction in the Classroom*, London, Methuen.

DELAMONT, S. (1981) 'All too familiar? A decade of classroom research', *Educational Analysis*, 3, 1, pp. 69–84.

DENHAM, C. and LIEBERMAN, A. (Eds) (1980) *Time to Learn*, Washington, D.C., NIE (DHEW).

DENSCOMBE, M. (1980) 'Keeping 'em quiet': The significance of noise for the practical activity of teaching', in WOODS, P. (Ed.) *Teacher Strategies*, London, Croom Helm.

DENZIN, N. (1970) *The Research Act*, Chicago, Aldine.

EGGLESTON, J.F. *et al.* (1976) *Processes and Products of Science Teaching*, London, Macmillan.

GALTON, M. and DELAMONT, S. (1985) *Inside the Secondary Classroom*, London, Routledge and Kegan Paul.

GALTON, M. and SIMON, B. (Eds) (1980) *Progress and Performance in the Primary Classroom*, London, Routledge and Kegan Paul.

GALTON, M. and WILLCOCKS, J. (1983) *Moving from the Primary Classroom*, London, Routledge and Kegan Paul.

GALTON, M. *et al.* (1980) *Inside the Primary Classroom*, London, Routledge and Kegan Paul.

GRAVES, R. (1960) *The Greek Myths*, 2 vols, Harmondsworth, Penguin.

HAMMERSLEY, M. (1980) 'Classroom ethnography', *Educational Analysis*, 2, 2, pp. 47–74.

HAMMERSLEY, M. (1982) 'The sociology of classrooms', in HARTNETT, A. (Ed.) *The Social Sciences in Educational Studies*, London, Heinemann.

Maurice Galton and Sara Delamont

HAMMERSLEY, M. and ATKINSON, P. (1983) *Ethnography*, London, Tavistock.

HARGREAVES, D. (1967) *Social Relations in a Secondary School*, London, Routledge and Kegan Paul.

JACKSON, P.W. (1968) *Life in Classrooms*, New York, Holt, Rinehart and Winston.

JASMAN, A. (1980) 'Training observers in the use of systematic observation techniques', in GALTON, M. *et al.*, *Inside the Primary Classroom*, London, Routledge and Kegan Paul.

KRIEGER, S. (1979) 'Research and the construction of a text', in DENZIN, N. (Ed.) *Studies in Symbolic Interaction*, Vol. 2, New York, JAI Press.

LEACOCK, E.B. (1969) *Teaching and Learning in City Schools*, New York, Basic Books.

McCALL, G. and SIMMONS, J.L. (Eds) (1969) *Issues in Participant Observation*, Reading, Mass., Addison-Wesley.

McINTYRE, D. (1980) 'Systematic observation of classroom activities', *Educational Analysis*, 2, 2, pp. 3–30.

MEASOR, L. and WOODS, P. (1983) 'The interpretation of pupil myths', in HAMMERSLEY, M. (Ed.) *The Ethnography of Schooling*, Driffield, Nafferton.

MESSERSCHMIDT, D. (Ed.) (1982) *Anthropologists at Home in North America*, Cambridge, Cambridge University Press.

NASH, R. (1973) *Classrooms Observed*, London, Routledge and Kegan Paul.

PLATT, J. (1976) *Realities of Social Research*, London, Chatto and Windus for University of Sussex Press.

ROTH, J. (1966) 'Hired hand research', *American Sociologist*, 1, pp. 190–6.

SCHATZMAN, L. and STRAUSS, A. (1973) *Field Research*, Englewood Cliffs, N.J., Prentice-Hall.

SHARP, R. and GREEN, A.G. (1975) *Education and Social Control*, London, Routledge and Kegan Paul.

SIMON, B. and WILLCOCKS, J. (Eds) (1981) *Research and Practice in the Primary Classroom*, London, Routledge and Kegan Paul.

SMITH, L.M. (1982) 'Ethnography', in MITZEL, H. (Ed.) *The Encylopedia of Educational Research* (5th ed.), New York and London, Macmillan (4 vols).

SMITH, L.M. and GEOFFREY, W. (1968) *Complexities of an Urban Classroom*, New York, Holt, Rinehart and Winston.

SPRADLEY, J.P. (1979) *The Ethnographic Interview*, New York, Holt, Rinehart and Winston.

SPRADLEY, J.P. (1980) *Participant Observation*, New York, Holt, Rinehart and Winston.

STACEY, M. *et al.*, (1975) *Power, Persistence and Change*, London, Routledge and Kegan Paul.

STONES, E. (1978) 'Comment on paper by Donald McIntyre and Gordon MacLeod', in McALEESE, R. and HAMILTON, D. (Eds) *Understanding Classroom Life*, Slough, NFER.

STUBBS, M. and DELAMONT, S. (1976) (Eds) *Explorations in Classroom Observation*, Chichester, Wiley.

WAX, M. and WAX, R. (1971) 'Great tradition, little tradition and formal education', in WAX, M. *et al.*, (Eds) (1971) *Anthropological Perspectives on Education*, New York, Basic Books.

WOLCOTT, H.F. (1975) 'Criteria for an ethnographic approach to research in schools', *Human Organization*, 34, 2, pp. 111–27.

WOLCOTT, H.F. (1981) 'Confessions of a "trained" observer', in POPKE-T.S. and TABACHNICK, B.R. (Eds) *The Study of Schooling*, New York, Praeger.

WOODS, P. (Ed.) (1980) *Teacher Strategies*, London, Croom Helm.

WRAGG, E.C. (1975) 'The first generation of British interaction studies', in CHANAN, G. and DELAMONT, S. (Eds) *Frontiers of Classroom Research*, Slough, NFER.

10 Using Photographs in a Discipline of Words

Rob Walker and Janine Wiedel

The use of photographs is a well-established ethnographic practice, indeed the photographs and films made by early ethnographers have themselves become items of historical interest (see, for example, De Brigard, 1975). There are, however, few ethnographers of educational settings who have brought the use of film, and of visual material more generally, into the study of schools and classrooms (one of the most notable is Collier's study of Alaskan Elementary schools: Collier, 1973). Perhaps this is due to the fact that ethnographers of education tend not to treat the settings in which they work as culturally exotic or problematic, a view that is consistent with the fact that one of the few recent British studies to do so, namely Hamilton's work on the origins of classrooms as cultural inventions, has drawn him to make more use of visual material than other current studies.

While the use of photographs has a long history in ethnography, it is a history that is at times confused with the development of documentary traditions within photography itself. Becker (1975) and Stasz (1979) provide two of the few attempts to provide some bridge between the history of photography and the history of social science, drawing parallels between social documentary traditions in nineteenth century sociology and contemporary photography. Currently the connections between documentary photography (and film) and social science are more tenuous, though John Berger did address a British Sociological Association (BSA) annual conference on the subject of photography some years ago (Berger, 1978). In some respects this is surprising, for the issues that dominate documentary photography and photojournalism are very similar to those that dominate the fieldwork tradition in the social sciences: problems of objectivity, of access and confidentiality, of political and other commitments entering the debate between those striving for portrayal and those pursuing analysis, questions about control over access to audiences and manipulation of the relevant information channels by publishers and editors faced with the demands of the market. Such issues are not unfamiliar, yet cross-discussion seems virtually non-existent simply because of the different social structures, organizations and communities in which we work. So that when photographers and social scientists do collaborate (which is only rarely) the photographs are typically reduced to illustrations or treated as independent photographic essays. An instructive example is Dennis Marsden and Euan Duff's book, *Workless*, (1975) in which two men of considerable experience and repute in their own fields manage to construct a book in which they appear to hold each other's work at arm's length. The total lack of integration between photographs and text is apparently a remnant of archaic printing techniques. If ever a book called for a detailed methodological appendix it was this one, but the opportunity was lost, not once but twice, for when Penguin brought out an updated revision of the book they left the original photographs untouched on the grounds that these were less in need of updating than the text.

It is perhaps unfair to single out this example for in publishing terms follows the dominant tradition in the coffee-table book market, which is to juxtapose text and image rather than to work for integration, the collaboration between John Berger and Jean Mohr (see, for example, Mohr, 1978) marking a significant break in a convention established by Agee and Evans' classic study of poor white families in the thirties (1969).

It is not strictly the purpose of this paper to consider film and television, but it is worth noting that recent developments in filming equipment and technique, the use of which was pioneered in this country by Roger Graef, Nick Broomfield and others associated with the National Film School, and which has been popularized by the major television companies, has in many respects closed the gap between the concerns of ethnographers and of documentary filmmakers. Some of this work has involved close collaboration between film-makers and ethnographers (for example, the *Disappearing World* series), but when film-makers have turned to education, and particularly to schools (for example, Richard Denton's series *Public School* and *Kingswood* and Fredrick Wiseman's *High School*) they have generally chosen to deal directly with their subjects and to take the fieldwork role themselves. Denton, for example, lived on site for twelve months during the making of the Kingswood series and developed a set of relationships with people inside and outside the school quite comparable with those relationships reported by fieldwork social scientists. Graef's film, *School*, in his pioneering *Space between Words* series, did use the device of filming around the impact that the presence of a research psychologist had on one teacher and her class. But, given the separation between the worlds within which film-makers and social scientists work, we have generally failed to develop dialogues which make this experience available to the research community.

Behind these observations is a concern that, from the point of view of those of us working from a base within educational research or social science, we learn to think of visual information and visual records as something more than simply illustrative of literary themes. I am using the term 'literary' here in its wider sense to include social science theory, for it seems to me that social science has become dominated by the written word. Our concern has become the 'literature' and we frequently organize our own teaching around reading lists rather than around issues and concerns, with the result that we have squeezed out the role of imagery of a more direct visual kind. Even those of us who have taken a close interest in detailed study of small-scale human interactions have tended to do so in terms of transcripts — literized reductions of interaction which have been selectively chopped and framed to suit the demands imposed by the forms of publishing already available.

I make this comment immediately conscious that in offering the criticism I have no good alternative answers. While it is clear that research has gained considerably from communicating and cumulating in a literary form, it is difficult to see ways in which it might recapture what it has lost in ways that are intellectually and institutionally efficient. Yet it remains true that it has lost, and that those attempts that have been made to recover the visual imagination (Bateson and Mead, 1942, remains the outstanding example) have tended to fit uneasily within the mainstream of research and often to be left stranded by it. Perhaps this is why even an eminent figure in the fieldwork tradition of the social sciences who has also worked in and taught documentary photography and photojournalism, Howard Becker, has found himself apparently straddling two worlds rather than being seen to be integrating them.

I offer these introductory comments as background to a plea that those of us working in the fieldwork tradition in the social sciences and in education rethink the role of film, photography and video recording as techniques, and more generally that we consider the place of visual as well as literary imagination in our research. In part this is necessary, I believe, because much of the research we do restricts its audience and its impact by its wordiness, by its reliance on narrow technical languages and consequently by its distance from the worlds in which most people live, work and act. To find a place for the visual is not, I would argue, to develop yet another specialized and precious research concern, but to broaden access to our work.

'Pictures': A Collaborative Project

During the period 1977–79 Janine Wiedel, a photographer, and I attempted to carry out a collaborative research study in a London secondary school. It was a difficult study to coordinate given the scarcity of time and resources available, and we offer an account of it here in order to suggest possibilities rather than as an exemplary model for others to admire and to follow. It was a project that began with some of the high aspirations I have just outlined, and in particular with a concern to develop dialogue between the methods and process of documentary photography and fieldwork-based research in education. This is an important point to emphasize because it explains why we did not do a number of things that would have brought the two approaches together but would have minimized dialogue between them.

Before pursuing this point further it is necessary to spell out the nature and intent of the project concerned. The research task was to follow the experience of a group of first-year secondary school children through their timetable. We conceived of this as an applied research project in that we wanted to use observations and records of the various segments of the formal curriculum as a basis for the teachers and the school to consider their interrelation and coherence. We began, therefore, with a problem of educational practice rather than with a problem derived from theory, though clearly in a way that allowed the development of theoretical issues as the research proceeded.

The initial methodological problem was one of collecting evidence of children's experience in a range of timetabled subjects over a period of a year. There are many ways we might have done this but we decided to concentrate on classroom events and on the different ways in which teachers and children perceived pedagogic and curriculum variety. Again this left us with a number of options at the technical level, but for the reasons outlined above we saw this in part as a methodological experiment and chose to use a combination of visual and literary techniques within what might be described overall as a fieldwork role.

I should explain that both Janine and I had previous fieldwork experience. I had formal training in sociology and social anthropology and had made a number of educational case studies in research and evaluation. Janine had lived with a variety of nomadic groups on Baffin Island, in Iran and among Irish tinkers, in order to produce photographic exhibitions, essays and books. So while she had little formal social science training she had, as a photographer, learnt a good deal of the tacit and informal knowledge required of the fieldwork researcher.

One approach to the research would have been for the photographer to attempt to document interpretations made by the researcher; however, as we wanted to avoid assigning the photographs to a mere illustrative role, we decided to reverse the process. Janine and I made preliminary observations in the school together, having negotiated access with the school and with the teachers involved. We outlined to them a research design that involved Janine observing and photographing one first year class, initially in one department but subsequently throughout their timetable. Choosing one class meant that we could establish rapport fairly fast and get the children used to the idea of being photographed. At the end of the first observation period, which lasted two weeks, Janine began photographing the class during their maths lessons with the cooperation of the teacher.

Within two weeks we had these initial photographs printed and I took them back to the school where I used them both to interview the teacher, and later the children. Prior to this I checked with those who appeared in the pictures, where I could, whether they wanted to edit out any prints on the grounds that they felt they were in any way unfair or embarrassing to the point they did not want them discussed by the class. While people made characteristic responses to seeing pictures of themselves, no-one felt strongly enough to remove any prints, though this procedure did not entirely resolve the issue.

Having collected initial responses to the photographs, Janine and I edited them in the form of an exhibition in which the pictures and the responses to them were juxtaposed. This display was taken back to the class and then used as the basis for discussion by the maths department. Later it was used by the department as part of an evening meeting for parents. In these successive events we were not able to re-edit the display as much as we had intended simply because of the pressures of time, nor were we always able to observe the discussions as much as we would have liked. On the other hand, it was part of our intention to pass this process on to the teachers where we could; what we would have liked to monitor more closely was the process as it evolved.

The next stage in the project was to extend the study to other curriculum areas. Our assumption was that, having established a high profile in the school in the work we had done with the maths department, our intentions and role would be clear to others, and that this would provide a basis for an implicit contract with other teachers, so cutting the time we would need to invest in establishing rapport.

In this next phase of the project we repeated the process in other classes. Janine followed the class through their timetable with the agreement of the form tutor and the teachers concerned. Our assumption that, once the class was unconcerned about being photographed, then the teachers would be reassured was born out in practice. Certainly when I took the pictures into the school to interview the teachers (and later the children) they reported that Janine had been unobtrusive; indeed most teachers were amazed to see how many photographs had been taken in their classes. A good deal of this is explained by Janine's skill and experience, but is due in part to the fact that the children accepted her, and the fact that she was taking photographs as a normal and routine event.

It is probably helpful to give an example of the material that emerged, though before doing so it is important to point out that because of our starting point, the reasons we had for selecting from this material were complicated. In a straightforward research project the selection criteria are primarily in the hands of the researcher who draws on theoretical concerns in order to make sense of the data. The process of making sense is one that inevitably involves the loss of a good deal of information, information that in the light of other perspectives has both meaning and value. In this study there were two points at which major selection decisions were made within the constraints set by the design. One rested with Janine in the course of taking the photographs which formed the initial data base. The second emerged during the interview phase when people were invited to remove pictures in order to protect personal privacy, or at least to reduce their vulnerability by exposure, and in practice more significantly in what they chose to talk about.

In the initial taking of the photographs Janine drew on her experience as a photographer, which meant that in part aesthetic considerations were confounded with documentary concerns. She was looking to record what happened and trying to make good and interesting photographs. She also worked to a series of ideas that emerged from discussions we had both in observing within the school and in looking through the proof sheets as they emerged. For example, we found rapid sequences of photographs often more informative, and more useful in interviewing teachers and children, than single prints. Actually finding interesting sequences to record is a difficult art and one that often leads to false starts or missing images, so a typical contact sheet might have strings of up to twenty images which formed some kind of sequence interspersed with short sequences or single images. Another criterion for which we found an early need was to ensure that we had pictures which 'featured' each child in the class, otherwise some children felt left out, and indeed were when we came to ask them what they had been doing during the lesson. We also invoked a number of more characteristically 're-search' considerations. We were interested in the class as a social unit and the ways in which it interacted with different teachers in the context of different curriculum areas and different kinds of task. Did the class as a social group behave and act differently? Did the groupings themselves change? Did the children perceive of themselves differently from class to class? How did different teachers perceive of them as a class and as individuals? We did not pursue these questions in terms of an experimental design, or as rigorous research questions, but they formed a continuous agenda which Janine kept in mind when taking photographs, and which I raised as questions in interviewing.

As the research progressed other questions arose. Some of the teachers appeared to maintain very strong boundaries between inside the classroom and outside it. Inside they felt relaxed, in control and effective as teachers; around the more public spaces of the school this was not always the case. The school had a mixed intake and a large proportion of black children and children from other racial backgrounds. Teachers raised the identity problems faced by English-born children of immigrant families as an issue with classroom implications. There were, too, curriculum issues which raised questions about pedagogy and classroom organization.

All these questions provided a series of 'headings' for us as we collected the photographs and the interview responses. Any one of them might have formed the basis for the design of a more conventional research study, but this was an opportunity we were unable to take advantage of in the time we had available. All we could do was relate the issues, the concerns and the questions back to the school.

Rob Walker and Janine Wiedel

Maths: Ten Minutes at the Teacher's Desk in an Individualized Maths Class

This sequence of photographs shows the interactions around the teacher early in the school year. The commentary was added later using the teacher's and the children's responses to the photographs.

> *Teacher:* This was a bad day for me! I don't really like sitting at the front but prefer to move around the room. But this was the beginning of the year when they were still a bit unsure and so many of the children wanted to see me that I had to stay at my desk. I don't really like it because I feel pressurized. I prefer to be moving around the room because then *I* can set the pace. When they all start collecting round my desk I feel like shouting 'Go away!'

Teacher: Coral (in the middle) and Joyce are friends, Joyce often needs help with her work, but sometimes I think Coral pretends she doesn't understand just so that she can get my attention.

Teacher: The boy who has joined the group is Jonathan. He's a clever boy, but not in a swotty way, he's very sweet. He seems interested in Coral's test too.

Joyce: That's my book Miss is looking at. Coral is just looking into space.

Jonathan: Coral's stuck. I'm listening in case it's a card I haven't done and I might get it later. Coral's looking disgusted, so maybe she's got something wrong.

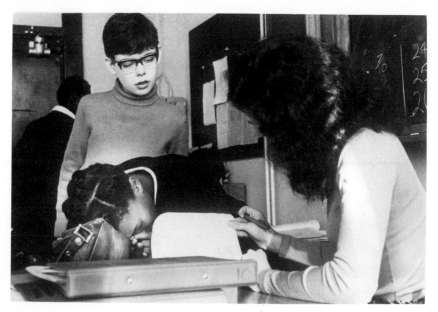

Teacher: Coral has obviously got something wrong and Jonathan is looking very wise!

Teacher: She's got something else wrong!

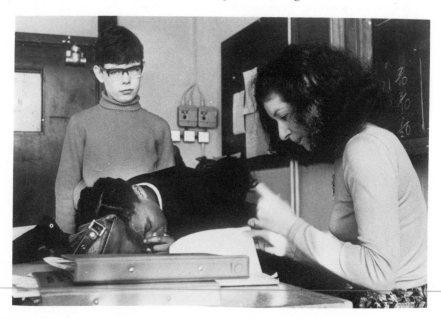

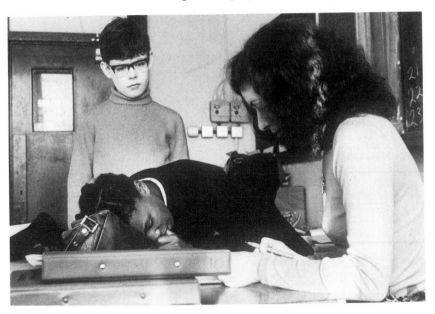

Joyce: She's sleeping!

Rob Walker and Janine Wiedel

Jonathan: Coral is doing a card on maps where you have to find the coordinates — you can see the squares on her book. I was waiting because I was stuck on prime numbers. You do all the cards and mark them yourself, then you do a test and the teacher marks that to make sure you've got it right and you're not cheating! I hadn't quite finished, I thought I understood it, but I wasn't sure so I wanted to ask the teacher.

Teacher: You see, when I'm not talking to her Coral reaches out for my necklace, maybe because she is interested in it, but also in a bid to get my attention back!

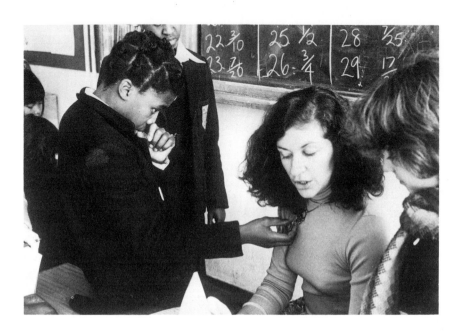

Joyce: She's playing with Miss' necklace. Miss told her to leave it alone and go back to her work.

Teacher: Oh dear! Jonathan is still waiting! So many others are waiting now and they are getting impatient. I hate them being round the front like this, and if it was anyone else but Coral I'd send them away. Jonathan looks so bored!

Jonathan: No, I'm not bored. Melanie's stuck on Magic Squares, and I haven't done that one yet. I'm looking like that because I'm reading the next page that Miss is turning over.

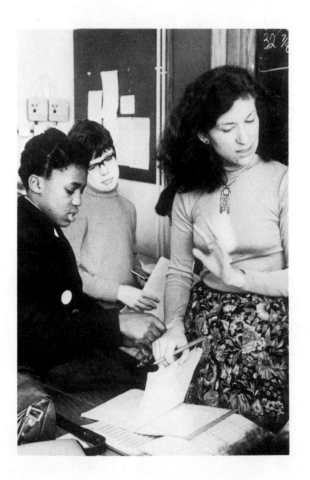

This sequence might be looked at in a number of ways. One that interested me concerned the interrelation of curriculum and pedagogy. Individualized learning schemes of this kind imply a particular view of efficient learning (SMILE, for those who do not know it is a version of the Kent Maths Project which programmes the children on different routes through a network of tasks set out on work cards). The general underlying assumption is that children learn best when working at their own pace on individual problems calibrated to meet their abilities and accomplishments. Such a scheme is specifically designed to meet the needs of mixed-ability classes, so that a boy like Jonathan need not be held back by the progress of 'slower' members of the class like Joyce; the teacher is also freed to work with Joyce while other children continue with their tasks. Jonathan's move to the queue and his long wait there is therefore of some significance, for the system is designed to prevent just this from happening. The teacher's initial response was that this constituted a fault or breakdown in the smooth running of the scheme. Seen from Jonathan's point of view this is not strictly the case. He likes watching the work of others, he finds it helpful to look at the cards others are working on, even if this does mean breaking out of his own sequence of tasks. That Jonathan was not just 'wasting time' in the queue was something of a revelation to the teacher, for the curriculum is set up in such a way that she was led to conclude that it was. Hence her surprise when she realized (in looking at picture 23) that she had misread Jonathan's expression — he was not bored, as she had surmised, but merely looking over the page.

Janine's interest in this sequence was rather different. She was interested in the interaction of the children and the teacher, and her focus was on Coral, whose moods seemed to shift so dramatically through this sequence. It was Coral's reaching out for the teacher's necklace which first caught the attention of the teacher, and of other teachers who looked through this sequence. Jane (the teacher in this sequence) told us:

> They often want to treat you as Mum. I'm not like that. I'm not that sort of teacher. Sometimes I think maybe I'm horrid to them! Not in a nasty way, but if they start putting their arms around me I tell them not to. They're always interested in personal things. They asked me what my husband gave me for Christmas. Well we don't really give each other presents at Christmas, but he had given me that necklace, so I said, 'Oh he gave me the necklace'. They thought that was nice,

and that he must be a good caring husband. They wanted to make sure he was treating me well!

They notice what you wear, even if it is an old skirt that you just haven't worn for a long time they'll notice it and ask you about it. When I first came here I'd worked in industry and I used to dress well — not like I do now! They always take an interest in what you are wearing, even the boys. I once wore this gold belt and one boy kept asking me about it and wanting to know if it was real gold!

Children this age are very interested in what you wear, especially the girls. They notice when you wear something different, even if it is something old, and the comments they make are always nice. They don't criticize or say they don't like things. They always say things like, 'I like your sweater Miss', or 'Isn't it a lovely colour.'

When they get a bit older they get more interested in their own things. Sometimes we take them away on trips and they'll spend ages deciding what clothes to take, and when they get there deciding what to wear. They'll have long discussions about, 'Shall we wear our plastics today!'

In the First Year they are still mostly in school uniform and carrying school bags. But this will change. We've already gone through the phase of pairing up boyfriends and girl-friends, and soon we'll get rifts between girls who have had tiffs over boys. As this happens the fashions start to change! First it is the bags and then the shoes, and then what they wear. Really small differences are very important to them. It's not just a question of wearing tennis shoes, they have to be a special make and style.

The head of the department (a man) added the following comment when he saw the sequence:

They're ever so interested in what you wear. I remember when I was on teaching practice here and I had a visit from my college tutor. She was sitting in the back of the class and part way through the lesson one of the girls went up to her and started playing with her jewellery and stroking her clothes — just like in this picture — almost absent mindedly.

This release of different perceptions illustrates well what Collier (1967) has called the 'can-opener' effect in using photographs. Even in terms of conventional ethnography, photographs can speed rap-

port, involve people in the research and release anecdotes and recol-
lections, so accelerating the sometimes lengthy process of building
fieldwork relationships and locating reliable informants. Interestingly
Jane had another researcher visiting her classes at the same time as
we were following this particular class. After looking through the
photographs, she said, 'I can see what you are doing. I can get
interested in it, and so can the kids. J [the other researcher] goes to
great lengths to explain to me what he is doing and why he is doing it,
but I don't really understand to the point where I can feel part of it,
or it seems part of me. Somehow it all seems to disappear into his
notebook and never come back.' Clearly there are dangers in
misleading Jane, for the photographs could equally be used in ways
that 'take the research away', but at least as a technique this approach
had the advantage of clarity and seeming transparent in intent.

Beyond the methodological level, questions of an epistemological kind are also raised by this approach. Research techniques that
release alternative perspectives inevitably raise questions about the
nature and location of truth. Using photographs sharpens these
questions because of the surface credibility of the literal image, as
Becker writes:

> ... whenever we interpret what we see in a photograph ...
> we raise the question of truth, because we suggest an answer
> to a question that might in fact have a different answer.
> Because the questions arouse strong interests and emotions,
> people may disagree about whether the answers are correct,
> often suggesting that they are not because the photographs
> are biased, subjective, or an unfair sampling. Many problems
> arise over ambiguity: a series of photographs suggests some-
> thing is true: we do not deny it but think that something else
> is also true ... there is no general answer to the question of
> whether a photograph is true: we can only say that the answer
> it gives to a particular question is more or less believable,
> keeping in mind that different questions may be asked of the
> same image. (Becker, 1980, p. 26)

In the project we have described, the implicit ambiguity of the
photographs became further complicated by the different questions
that preceded the photographic act. Janine had aesthetic and documentary motives immediately in mind, but these were channelled to
some degree by the discussions we had in advance which drew on
more orthodox fieldwork research themes and on the questions raised
by the teachers and the children. The fact that the photographs were

taken in the context of an unfolding fieldwork process further complicated the already complex set of intentions that lay behind each image.

In this sense the photographs are 'data' of a complex kind, in many ways the visual equivalent of the ethnographic fieldnote though, I would argue, with a surface validity and undeniability always denied the second-hand account. Despite the questions Becker raises about selectivity, photographs retain a documentary power always denied second-hand records, a power that I think derives in part from their relation to the nature of human memory.

Berger, in commenting on Susan Sontag's influential book, *On Photography* (1977), takes the point further (the quotes are from Sontag):

> ... unlike memory photographs do not in themselves preserve meaning. They offer appearances — with all the credibility and gravity we normally lend to appearances — prised away from their meaning. Meaning is the result of understanding functions. 'And functioning takes place in time, and must be explained in time. Only that which narrates can make us understand.' Photographs in themselves do not narrate. Photographs preserve instant appearances. Habit now protects us against the shock involved in such preservation. Compare the exposure time for a film with the life of a print made, and let us assume the print lasts only ten years: the ratio for an average modern photograph would be approximately 20,000,000,000: 1. Perhaps that can serve as a reminder of the violence of the fission whereby appearances are separated by the camera from their function. (Berger, 1980, p. 51)

Berger goes on to make the point he made in his address to the BSA in 1978, that there is an important distinction that needs to be made between two uses and intentions for photography. There is the *public* photograph which '... usually presents an event, a seized set of appearances, which has nothing to do with us, its readers, or with the original meaning of the event. It offers information, but information severed from all lived experience. If the public photograph contributes to a memory, it is to the memory of an unknowable and total stranger.... It records an instant sight about which this stranger has shouted: Look!' Berger contrasts the public photograph, which is essentially an alienated object, with the *private* photograph, which belongs to the realm of lived experience. 'The private photograph — the portrait of a mother, a picture of a daughter, a group photograph of one's own team — is appreciated and read in a context which is continuous with that from which the camera removed it. . . . such a photograph remains surrounded by the meaning from which it was severed. A mechanical device, the camera has been used as an instrument to contribute to a living memory. The photograph is a memento from a life being lived' (Berger, 1980, pp. 51–2).[1]

The project we have described here was directly influenced by this statement of Berger's. There are few forms of data gathering in social science that can be used in a way that allows the subject to retain a sense of ownership. Even the transcribed spoken word easily becomes, in the process of transcription, alienated and strange — the product and the property of the researcher rather than of the subject. The same is generally true (in my experience) of film and of videotape. The very nature of the technology confers ownership of images on those who 'take' them. Photographs are, however, more familiar and more continuous with everyday life. The process, while still a mystery to most of us in the technical sense, is a mystery we are prepared to risk and to suspend our disbelief when confronted with its products. I have written elsewhere about the need for educational research to find techniques and methods that allow people to 'own the facts of their lives' (Walker, 1980); photographs, used in the sense of Berger's notion of the 'private photograph' are to my mind the best technique available for developing research, and particularly educational research, along these lines.

Note

1 As I typed this the latest edition of Sara Delamont's book, *Interaction in the Classroom*, arrived on my desk, on the cover of which is one of Janine's photographs of Jane: a private photograph turned public!

References

AGEE, J. and EVANS, W. (1969) *Let Us Now Praise Famous Men*, London, Panther edition.

BATESON, G. and MEAD, M. (1942) *Balinese Character: A Photographic Analysis*, New York, New York Academy of Sciences Special Publication No. 2.

BECKER, H.S. (1975) 'Photography and sociology', *Afterimage*, 3, 1 and 2.

BECKER, H.S. (1980) 'Aesthetics and truth', *Culture and Society*, 17, 5, pp. 26–8.

BERGER, J. (1978) 'Ways of remembering', *Camerawork* 10, London.

BERGER, J. (1980) *About Looking*, London, Writers and Readers.

DE BRIGARD, E. (1975) 'The history of ethnographic film', in HOCKINGS, P. (Ed.) *Principles of Visual Ethnography*, The Hague, Mouton.

COLLIER, J. (1967) *Visual Anthropology: Photograph as a Research Method*, New York, Holt Rinehart and Winston.

COLLIER, J. (1973) *Alaskan Eskimo Education: A Film Analysis of Cultural Confrontation in the Schools*, New York, Holt, Rinehart and Winston.

HAMILTON, D. (1981) 'The classroom as a social invention', seminar given at the Centre for Applied Research in Education, University of East Anglia.

MARSDEN, D. and DUFF, E. (1975) *Workless*, Harmondsworth, Penguin.

MOHR, J. (1978) in *Camerawork* 10, London.

SONTAG, S. (1977) *On Photography*, New York, Farrar Strauss and Giroux.

STASZ, C. (1979) 'The early history of visual sociology', in WAGNER, J. (Ed.) *Images of Information: Still Photography in the Social Sciences*, Beverley Hills, Calif., Sage.

WALKER, R. (1978) 'Case study: Ethics, theory and procedures' in DOCKRELL, B. and HAMILTON, D. (Eds) *Rethinking Educational Research*, London, Hodder and Stoughton.

11   Opportunities and Difficulties of a Teacher-Ethnographer: A Personal Account

Andrew Pollard

This paper attempts to describe some of the opportunities and difficulties which I experienced as a full-time teacher doing an ethnographic study of my own school for a PhD (Pollard, 1981). The thesis was concerned to analyze the perspectives of teachers and children in the final year at an 8–12 middle school, in particular with regard to how they 'coped' with school. The research itself was, in a sense, a hobby. I embarked on it four years after starting teaching and, in that I depended for income and career on my teaching and on the institution being studied, the research always posed acute dilemmas regarding the allocation of time, energy and loyalty.

Getting Started

I had become involved in educational research in a rather indirect, but perhaps not untypical, way. My first real contact was when, partly as a means of by-passing a headteacher whom I perceived to be rather intransigent towards my career prospects, I embarked on an MEd course at Sheffield University. During this course I became particularly interested in classroom interaction and renewed my interest in interpretive sociologies which had begun during my first degree work at Leeds, in particular through courses on social theory run by Alan Dawe (Dawe, 1970). I also became fascinated by the research process and by the apparent insights into my daily practice in the classroom which it appeared to yield. I decided to continue such studies after finishing my MEd and so I registered for a PhD soon after starting in a new job at Moorside Middle School in 1976.

As I look back on it now, it seems surprising that I did not consider a form of 'action research'. I was aware of the Ford Teaching Project (Elliott, 1976) and Lawrence Stenhouse had just published his *Introduction to Curriculum Research and Development* (1975) with its powerful advocacy to teachers that they should research on their own classrooms as a means of professional and curriculum development. Happily the action research movement has grown in strength over the years since then (see Elliott's paper in this volume, Chapter 12), but at the time it did not provide for me the same sense of excitement that ethnography did. With its roots firmly in sociology, ethnography offered an incisive way of looking 'inside the school', of understanding its structures and processes as a whole and in a way which, it appeared, could have quite radical implications. Thus, as a product of the student movements of the late 1960s, I was particularly drawn to ethnography. In a way, too, it was a natural progression from the sociological 'action theory' (Silverman, 1970) and attention to 'subjective meanings' which I had studied at Leeds, through child-centred primary school teaching with its Plowdenesque philosophy based on 'understanding the child' and thus to ethnography with its concern to document and analyze perspectives. In any event I felt comfortable with the method and 'getting started' seemed to come fairly naturally.

The decision of where to locate an ethnographic case study is normally a matter of careful consideration and assessment with the advantages and disadvantages of various locations being carefully considered. In my own case the decision was relatively simple and reflected a particularly extreme form of the 'pragmatism' which Rock (1979) believes characterizes symbolic interactionism. Because of my circumstances my choice reduced to a straightforward decision between doing my research at the school at which I worked or abandoning my desire to do an ethnographic study altogether. In choosing the former I was aware of many disadvantages. The school was unusually large for a middle school and the almost balanced intake of native white children and children of Asian parentage seemed likely to make a particularly complex analysis necessary. Despite these factors, having a generally optimistic disposition, I decided to begin my study in my own school and to make the most I could of the opportunities which were available to me. I was on the staff of Moorside Middle School for two years, from September 1976 to August 1978.

A Teacher As Participant-Observer

The most important method which I intended to use was that of participant observation. Obviously I was a full participant because of my teaching position and a key question therefore concerned the degree and manner in which I could also fulfil the role of 'observer'. I was conscious of the fact that I had to maintain *both* roles in, as Hughes (1952) put it, 'an unending dialectic'. In particular I had to be careful to avoid 'going native'.

The phrase 'going native' essentially describes a state of mind in which, through a very close and emphatic identification with the subjects of the research, the demands of the research project itself fail to be met. In particular, having 'gone native' it is questionable to what extent a researcher could achieve the degree of detachment which is necessary to record, code and analyze data effectively. This of course is essential in ethnographic work. Indeed, if one follows the guidance of Glaser and Strauss (1967) in attempting to 'construct grounded theory', then the collection, coding and analysis of data *has* to proceed simultaneously, and clarity and awareness of methodological procedures and principles are crucial.

My particular circumstances were that I was appointed to the school as a scale two teacher responsible for remedial teaching in the third and fourth year units. This was my teacher-participant role. However, I came fresh from the year of full-time MEd studies and from the research project which had formed part of that work. Furthermore, I entered the school with the conscious intention of attempting to conduct a research programme in it. Thus, although I was a full-time teacher, and I hope a committed and conscientious one, I entered the school with a clear research perspective to balance my teacher role. An additional factor here again relates to my biography. My time at Leeds, and indeed my brother's influence before that, in a sense provided me with a basic consciousness of events and of social life which was further sustained every day through my marriage, my wife also having a sociological background. In many ways our joint sense of 'reality' (Berger and Kellner, 1971) was 'routinely sociological' so that in applying that thought to my place of work in 1976 I was only applying what was for us a relatively 'normal' type of perception and analysis and one which was partly built into our way of life. This made sustaining the necessary degree of observer's detachment far easier than might otherwise have been the case.

Throughout the study the researcher perspective was continually reinforced by coding and analysis which I undertook so that I was never really totally immersed in the school culture alone, without the counter-balance of the researcher perspective. This might have been more likely, had the data collection and analysis been discrete and sequential rather than simultaneous, or had my level of teaching competence been such that I unduly needed the support of the school culture to 'get through the day'. I think I was also helped in maintaining a degree of detachment by being one of only two 'Southerners' on the staff thus experiencing, to some degree, a cultural 'strangeness'. As any full participant-observer must, I also actively cultivated a degree of skill in retaining detachment in my 'head' whilst protecting involvement in my 'presentation of self'. My field note-books were a great help in this.

Although I was conscious of the need to maintain a researcher/ observer perspective despite my full participation, I was also aware of the considerable benefits which that participation gave me. For instance, before the research began I formally sought and obtained the permission of Mr Smith, the headteacher, for a study to take place. This permission was given without hesitation and the key problem of my access was solved with no difficulties whatsoever, I think primarily because of my teacher role. I was also fortunate here in that I had known Mr Smith for some years through union activities, since I had taught at a nearby school previously. We always seemed to have a good understanding of each other's perspectives and during the period of the research this was kept alive during discussions over dinner, because we happened to be frequently on the duty rota together. Throughout the study he was fully supportive. For instance, he assisted me in obtaining support for my work from the local education authority.

My friendship with Mr Smith was also a great help in establishing a good relationship with other staff. When I first went to the school I think I was regarded as being a little unusual, having previously taught infants and having just completed an MEd. Although this was partly offset by the fact that I had lived and worked in the area for three years previously, it was my relationship with Mr Smith which provided me with the most significant degree of 'sponsorship' among the staff. This, in combination with the period during which my teaching competence was accepted, was enough to enable me to establish friendly and non-threatening relationships with the staff quite quickly.

The benefits of the participant role that I had adopted were not, however, just to do with access. As Rock (1979) has written, the whole point of participant observation as a methodology is that it: '... uses the self of the sociologist as a tool to explore the social process.... Its justification stems from the definition of knowledge as an ongoing practical activity and from the argument that sociologists cannot know by introspection or surmise' (Rock, 1979, p. 178). In Polanyi's (1958) terms, by participation in the social process, it should have been possible for me to accumulate not only the 'explicit knowledge' and 'focal awareness' of events which any observer could obtain but also the 'tacit knowledge' and 'subsidiary awareness' which could only come from direct experience. This is an important point and one which has been interestingly explored by Hitchcock (1979). He argues that 'doing ethnography' should be '... viewed as a series of accomplishments involving active work on the part of the researcher ...' and that in his own research he was '... learning as a result of [his own] experiences in the field, how to get by, make out, and do relevant aspects of the social organisation' (Hitchcock, 1979). As a full participant I had to be able to *do* the social organization of Moorside Middle School, and I did my best to see this as a source of opportunity and advantage over less immersed research roles.

During the time in which I was at the school I carried out my role as a teacher to the best of my ability. It was, after all, my profession and it would have been unfair to the children to have done otherwise. As I suggested above, this involvement was in no way wasted from the research point of view because it led to the accumulation of knowledge and awareness which, although often hard to verbalize, was a great asset in analysis and in 'filling in' accounts and in establishing relationships. Another way of putting this would be to say that through my participation I learned 'the code' (Wieder, 1974) with all its nuances and subtlety. After all, I was myself 'coping with deviance' within the very same institution and within very similar patterns of constraint and resource as the teachers whom I studied. This undoubtedly *saved* a lot of time when establishing rapport and also gave a type of 'sureness' to the analysis.

I do not regard the acknowledgement of this use of a naturally developed 'subsidiary awareness' as an admission of having 'gone native' — to be conscious of the origin of such knowledge is, in my view, reasonable guard against that. The point is that, by means of participation, knowledge and understanding were accumulated which could not have come in any other way. Meanwhile, such involvement continually renewed my 'credit' with the staff. I was not simply in the role of 'taking' from the school with an air of detached ivory-tower research authority, I was also 'giving to' and of course 'needing' the school, which provided a far more natural balance of rights and obligation on which to build a relationship of trust than a pure observer role could have done. I think this fact is reflected quite regularly in the quality and frankness of the data which I was able to collect. There were, however, considerable technical difficulties regarding my researcher role.

One of the main problems of attempting to do research at the same time as being employed full-time concerns *time*. For me there were two major difficulties. First, I had the problem that although I would have had very easy access to classrooms for observations I did not have the opportunity to exploit this potential since I was myself teaching and was unable to negotiate any significant periods of time off. This was the reason for the scarcity in the eventual thesis of classroom observational data and analysis, and was the origin of a considerable methodological weakness in that I was forced to depend far more than I would have liked on interview data for some parts of the analysis. Of course I was able to reflect on my own ongoing classroom experiences and I would be prepared to argue that such experiential data have a unique quality, but nevertheless my sources of data were restricted.

A second respect in which time was a major constraint related to the speed at which I could collect data. I collected data of a general nature in notebooks all the time and this was not much problem in the two years in which I was at the school. My fieldnotes provided the basis of an analysis of social values, of the school organization and of teacher interests-at-hand. However, when I began to interview the children hoping to cover a whole year group, I eventually ran out of time. My interviews were conducted during dinner-times, which were one and a half hours long, this being the only non-teaching time available to me. In the first academic year in which I was at the school I ran various pilot schemes and began to investigate the second year children with a view to being able to build into the study a longitudinal element as they progressed through the school. During this period I was experimenting with various approaches to the research, doing a lot of reading and generally 'floundering around'. My fieldnotes were being collected routinely but I was also accumulating significant numbers of 'theoretical' and 'methodological memos' which did not then have real coherence. I was particularly undecided about how to collect data on child perspectives and on which children to focus.

By the time I had resolved these issues it was obvious that, if I was to study a complete year group, data collection would have to begin systematically in the following September (1977). I decided to do this and to interview all the white children first, followed by the Asian children. This priority was decided for two reasons. First, because the white children showed particular interest in my activities (a necessity for my interviewing strategy), and secondly, because I judged the problem of the teacher-as-researcher role to be easier to resolve with the white children than with the Asians because of my greater awareness of their cultural forms. I saw no theoretical problems associated with this priority since the focus of the study was on generating models of teacher-pupil action in general, rather than on the substantive area of multiracial education itself. My intention was to interview the Asian children in the same way as I did the white children and to analyze the data using the constant comparative method (Glaser and Strauss, 1967) to further refine my models. In fact I did not get that far because the time resource of my lunch times simply was not long enough to complete the interview work. I did interview several Asian groups, but in nothing like the numbers which I would have liked and not enough to provide me with enough data for an entirely reliable analysis even when set alongside data from fieldnotes, essays, documents and observations of behaviour in informal settings. The Asian children and the whole issue of their particular perspectives and coping strategies were not therefore analyzed at any length in the thesis. I did feel that the data which I was able to obtain, particularly through a screening device of written essays, were generally supportive of my basic analysis although obviously it is likely that, had a full analysis been made, new categories and concepts relating to the particular difficulties of Asian children in schools would have been generated. At one stage I considered correcting this imbalance during a second year of data collection from the next fourth year group of Asian children, which, although having difficulties of its own, would have been better than nothing. In the end this plan was overtaken by events when I was promoted to a new teaching post at another school. This last event illustrates the fact that in my own case the constraints on time were crucially overlain by the fact that teaching was my chosen profession and research simply my chosen interest. This is a significantly different position from that of most participant observers whose participation forms part of a research strategy alone. For me, the participation was real — it was through teaching that I earned my income and saw my career development. The fact that my participation was also used as a research strategy was a pragmatic necessity.

This fact of course had the result of posing daily dilemmas

regarding the deployment of my finite resources of time and energy, and my experience at the time was very much one of struggling to reconcile and cope with the demands of both spheres of my activity. For instance, ... should one — on returning from the staffroom at playtime — make fieldnotes or start the next lesson? In fact I often ended up doing a bit of both, but throughout the period of the research it remained the case that much of my interest and enthusiasm was in the research, the demands of which were thus sustained. As Woods (this volume, Chapter 3) has argued, a great deal of creativity is involved in research work and, when a picture of social life is unfolding, it can be a very great attraction and source of fulfilment. In fact I felt that I could discharge my responsibilities towards the children whom I taught without too much difficulty and I was also involved in a number of other developments within the school. That I had succeeded professionally to a reasonable degree was in a sense confirmed by my move — an event which also reasserted the claims of career development and put the 'hobby' back in its place.

Collecting Data from the Staff: An Ethical Problem

The management of my role with the staff was not always easy and indeed it posed some ethical problems which were perhaps even more extreme than those discussed by Burgess in this volume (Chapter 8). I had begun to collect data about the school, its policies and practices, almost as soon as I began teaching there. These data were recorded as events occurred naturally both in school settings and outside school. For instance, several teachers with whom I became particularly friendly talked about school policies and events when we met socially and this was very helpful to me. One of the female teachers with whom I cooperated in my day-to-day teaching was extremely knowledgeable about attitudes, aspirations and manoeuvrings among the staff, particularly the other female staff with whom I felt I might have had difficulty in collecting data in depth.

Regarding this aspect of the research I was not fully frank in the sense that although the staff all knew that I was conducting research, that I had Mr Smith's support, and that I was interested in their views, they were not aware of the specific way in which their perspectives were being recorded in my notebooks or of the interpretation and analysis to which that data would later be subjected. Of course it is true that, by the nature of the research design and method, I also had no clear idea of the analysis which would result. Nevertheless, it was my deliberate intention to make my participant role prominent at this stage and to collect unforced data from natural settings such as the staffroom. After a period in which the staff were conscious that I was 'doing my research', it appeared to be largely forgotten or to be assumed that, because I spent a lot of time talking to children, I was not investigating elsewhere. I did nothing to dispel this assumption.

Such semi-covert research, of course, raises ethical questions. The teachers whose views I recorded were, and in some cases remain, personal friends. I was a teacher with them, sharing their experiences and their frustrations. As a teacher I needed their friendship just as most teachers tend to feel a need to be part of their staffroom community. However, my role as researcher with, as Barnes (1979) suggests, responsibilities to fellow researchers and the wider society as well as to my informants, created a distinction between us of which perhaps only I was fully aware. Thus, although I was collecting data as events occurred throughout the school, prior to my more formal interviews of staff, I was seen by them almost exclusively as a teacher with them, and only as a researching 'observer' of the children. I felt the ambiguity in my role at this point but decided to try to resolve the issue at a later stage by reporting back and clarifying my position then. This was a pragmatic solution to a difficult dilemma which involved not only the question of ethics but also that of the quality or 'naturalness' of data collected.

Towards the final stages of data collection I moved to a more clear-cut 'researcher' role regarding the staff. A meeting of the headteacher, deputy head, senior mistress and staff was held at which my analysis of child perspectives and a typology of forms of censure and deviance were reported back to the teachers for their comments (see Pollard, 1979). I was delighted that the responses were positive and supportive. The staff were also made aware of the broad shape of the thesis and the reasons why I required data on their perspectives and teaching styles. They were shown an embryo model of coping strategies (which eventually resulted in Pollard, 1982) and told about the type of data which I had been able to collect as a participant. They were then asked to take part in a series of more formal interviews to fill in particular details which I had been unable to collect in the more natural unforced settings during the previous two years of participant observation. This they agreed to do. The only area of concern which was brought up at this stage was: 'What will Mr Smith say when he hears about this ... you know ... what we really think?' I was able to reassure the teachers on the basis of two extremely full and frank

interviews with Mr Smith. In one of these I had put to him my
concern over the ethical issue and over how to handle anything which
might be seen as being critical of him or of the school. He replied
with his admirable directness:

> Don't worry about any of that ... it'll all be anonymous
> anyway and even if it comes out I don't mind. I know
> everybody doesn't agree with me on everything. It'd be a
> funny place if they did wouldn't it? No ... you go on, lad,
> get on with it.

I did precisely as Mr Smith suggested, but I did so with some concern
for, as Becker (1964) pointed out, if one is studying an internally
differentiated organization then there is little chance of achieving a
consensual agreement with the analysis which is presented back, and
only the researcher himself can make the final judgments about the
balance of 'scientific gain' and 'suffering' which might arise. I made
judgments to report fairly frankly based mainly on my knowledge of
the people involved, and in particular I put a lot of trust in Mr Smith's
tolerance.

Having completed the final stage of data collection from staff, I
felt happier on the ethical issue since the degree of covertness had
been discarded, and I felt that by tackling the data collection in two
parts with a feedback session between them I had been able to
maximize the advantage of being a teacher/researcher as far as I could.

Collecting Data from the Children: An Identity Problem

My advantages of access regarding the staff could have been directly
reversed regarding the children. As a teacher during school-time I felt
it to be of crucial importance to attempt as far as possible to establish
a non-evaluative, 'researcher' role when out of school time and
collecting data. In fact, much to my surprise, I found this problem
less difficult than I had anticipated. I had taught all the children in the
year group studied during the previous year and perhaps benefited
from them looking back on that year's experience as having passed,
and by their relating with me as 'people-who-know-each-other-and-
have-experienced-the-same-experiences' and also as having 'passed
on' and 'gone up' beyond my jurisdiction. During that year I had
been mainly attached to the third year unit and by the end of it had
developed a knowledge of and working relationship with most of the
children who in 1977/78 were to become fourth years.

Of course the 'teacher' role is one of the few natural roles open to an adult wishing to do a participant-observation study in a school; and although it is not a participant role vis-à-vis children by 'identification', it certainly is participatory by 'interaction'. I decided that I could positively use the shared experience and rapport which I had built up previously to the advantage of the research, if I was sufficiently careful about the obvious difficulties of my role as teacher and authority figure intruding upon my aspiration to be seen as a natural, non-threat, trustworthy researcher. I realized quite early on that the use of dinner-times for collecting data could be useful not only because I had no other responsibilities but more importantly because that time carried with it relatively open-ended expectations regarding the teacher-role on the part of the children. Chatting with the teachers, joining in with extra-curricular activities, 'doing jobs', and so on, were routine for that time at Moorside and I felt that I could develop expectations which would be favourable to the research process from within those broader conventions already existing.

I also adopted what is, I think, a rather unusual interviewing strategy by involving some subjects of the research in the collection of data on others. Beginning in the first year of the study I had spent regular playtimes with the children, joining in many of their activities and talking informally. For instance, I developed an ability and reputation at marbles, which was a 'craze' at the time. At the same time I began to identify children whom I judged to be amenable to participation in the study, who reflected the range of types and friendship groups existing, and who were fairly popular within those groups. In this I was assisted by sociometric data when it became available. In September 1977 these children were invited to form a dinner-time interviewing team to help me, as I put it, 'find out what all the children think about school'. This group very quickly coined the name 'The Moorside Investigation Department' (MID) for themselves and generated a sense of self-importance. Over the next year the membership of MID changed gradually but I always attempted to balance it by having members of a range of groups. Normally about six children were involved at any one time and the total number of children involved during the year was thirteen. This small group was very interested. In particular they seemed to enjoy being 'investigators' which fitted into a theme of the child culture then existing, they enjoyed using the recording equipment which they did not normally have access to, they enjoyed being in the role of interviewer and questioning other children and they seemed to enjoy the fact that they were working *with* an adult. My intention in setting up a *child* interviewing team was to break through the anticipated reticence of children towards me as a teacher. I spent a lot of time with the MID members discussing the type of things I was interested in and establishing the idea of immunity to teacher-prosecution and of confidentiality. We then began a procedure of inviting groups of children — in twos, threes or fours to give confidence — to be interviewed by a MID member in a building which was unused at dinner-times. Sometimes the interviewers would interview their own friends, sometimes they would interview children whom they did not know well. Initially, I did not try to control this but left it very much to the children. Interviews were recorded onto cassettes which I analyzed each evening.

For the first few weeks I left the children to get on alone and did not join in any interviews. During this time I think three important things happened. First, the year group as a whole became aware of what we were doing and many of them evidently felt that joining in might sometimes be more interesting than playing out. This was particularly so in cold weather. Secondly, the children in MID projected a sense of secrecy and played up the principles of confidentiality and immunity in ways which were excellent for my purposes. The project also began to echo some of the characteristics of the 'secret societies' which were popular among the children at the time and yet it did not stand out unduly since it could be seen as a 'normal' dinner-time 'activity' or 'club' similar to others which were organized by other staff at the same time. It was also helped by the fact that the MID members were popular among their friendship groups and by the fact that word gradually spread round through the children's own networks from the interviews that were actually taking place. Confidentiality and immunity were also seen to be maintained and I think the children's confidence grew. Thirdly, the MID interviewers obtained some valuable experience at interviewing.

Of course, the quality of these initial interviews was very patchy for my purposes because of the interviewer's weak knowledge of theoretical relevance. In fact I gave the children a minimum of guidance each day, such as 'see if you can find out which teachers they like best', my requests being based on my unfolding analysis following the rubric of 'theoretical sampling'. Obviously the discussions ranged very widely around such starting points although the theme of 'finding out what they think about school' was one which I constantly reinforced and encouraged the interviewers to bear in mind. Of course many interesting opportunities for data collection were nonetheless lost. However, the advantages of the procedure were enormous for me because a workable degree of trust was established. The interviewers were given a lot of scope and responded by identifying very positively with the project and thus sponsoring it among their peers. They also became very informative themselves. Having waited for these favourable developments to occur, I then felt able to routinely join interviews at mid-points. Thus child-child interaction would initially break the ice over key issues and bring them into the open, at which point I found I could usually join the discussion and begin to explore any particularly interesting accounts and perspectives without causing the interviewees to dry up. This remained the procedure for most of the period of data collection. In total ninety children were interviewed (seventy-five white children and fifteen Asian). Of the eighty white children in the fourth year, four were interviewed once, twenty-eight twice, thirty-three three times and ten more than three times.

Almost all of the interviews were based on groups of children. Woods (1979) used a similar strategy and explained its advantages as follows:

> ... The company of like-minded fellows helped to put the children at their ease. The bond between them and the way it was allowed to surface shifted the power balance in the discussion in their direction. As long as my interventions were not too intrusive, it might facilitate the establishment of norms, and I might become privy to their culture, albeit in a rather rigged way. Other advantages were that they acted as checks, balances and prompts to each other. Inaccuracies were corrected, incidents and reactions recalled and analysed. Many of the conversations became ... part of their experience rather than a commentary on it. (Woods, 1979, p. 265)

My use of child interviewers represents an extension of Wood's approach and I think had the degree of symbolic significance which was necessary to overcome my teacher role in the eyes of the children. The groups of friends who were invited to talk were invited by other children, children operated the cassette recorders, children set the scene and children initiated the discussions. The message being conveyed was that going to be interviewed was 'safe' and 'could be fun'. This trust became increasingly secure during the year and my degree of intervention grew with it.

Apart from overcoming my difficulty of gaining the trust of the children, the discussions were very important sources of data in themselves. Sometimes the children interviewing and the children being interviewed differed in their views and would become engaged in animated conversation, thus revealing their respective perspectives far better than I could have hoped for had I been conducting the interviews alone. I had to be careful to evaluate the opinions voiced to avoid accepting exaggerated statements at face-value and I also had to watch for, and balance, the impact of particularly dominant individuals in seeking to understand the perspective of their group. In making these judgments I think my previous experience with and knowledge of the children, accumulated as a teacher in their third year, was particularly useful.

The ethical problems of this research strategy were not as difficult to resolve as those regarding the teachers since the children were both more anonymous in the analysis and less likely to be affected by it. The most awkward problem arose when I heard about things which in a teacher-role I would have been likely to act upon. One particular situation arose when I was told about 'nicking sweets' and the theft of a five-pound note from a local shop. This was a test-case for my credibility and I did nothing, thus perhaps condoning the activity. This, apart from the rights and wrongs of the case, would have been extremely awkward to explain to the headteacher had my knowledge of the culprit come to light and it might have threatened my relationship with the staff. Such dilemmas were an inevitable product of my teacher-researcher role.

The results of the analysis were not discussed with the children at the same analytical level as with the staff but the grounded base of such theorizing was constantly referred to them. I would offer them the role of 'expert' and say, 'now, this is what I think we've found out ... have I got it right?' Comments and thus more data would result. Overall I found the working relationship which I developed with the MID children very rewarding both from the research point of view and personally, and I felt it was about as near as I could get to overcoming the major disadvantage of my participatory teacher role.

Coping with Participatory Research

One way of attempting to describe the difficulties and real experience of attempting research 'from the inside' is to characterize it as an attempt to 'cope' in two spheres simultaneously and, following my own analysis of coping (Pollard, 1982), I would suggest that one of the crucial factors here concerns biography and the type of person making the attempt. This clearly links with the argument put by Burgess that 'research is infused with assumptions about the social world and is influenced by the researcher' and is 'no longer viewed as a linear model but as a social process' (Burgess, 1984; p. 2). I find it hard to comment in detail on how 'the type of person I am' affected the research, although I am sure it did; indeed, it was my deliberate intention to use my 'self' as a tool in the research process. I have already identified the consciousness-raising impact of my first degree and the maintenance of this consciousness through my marriage. I can also identify my earlier upbringing and socialization within a comfortable, middle-class family of West Country entrepreneurs which gave me a severe dose of the Protestant ethic which undoubtedly helped me to face the work-load involved. I suspect that what I like to think of as a fairly easy-going personality may have been even more crucial in that it enabled me to establish rapport with the people involved in the study quite quickly, but when we get into reflexive issues such as this I feel in need of other opinions. The interpersonal relationships between researchers and the researched would make a fascinating topic for study in itself. There are so many seemingly random but crucially important factors in research work. In my own case again, how does one assess the degree of knowledge and support of my wife? . . . or the fact that because our young son slept badly during the evenings we did not go out much so that I got a lot of research work done? . . . or the fact that I got a considerable amount of encouragement from academics with whom I made contact which had a huge impact on my motivation? . . . or the fact that my tutor and I got on really well?

This discussion may be seen as somewhat self-indulgent, and it is certainly not the type of analysis which is routinely included in methodological accounts. However, I think it helps in understanding how my research came to be completed and written, for certainly in my own case I do not think I would have completed the task without the factors considered above. The relationship between the writer and what is written is in reality very close and it is only when a report takes on a reified form that a methodological account which excludes biography and other unique factors appears to be acceptable. We then all assiduously read the preface, the introduction and collect academic gossip in order to discover the subsidiary and 'real' factors involved. In my own case the unusual nature of my study made the discussion of such factors particularly essential in a methodological account and I hope it goes some way to explaining the 'personal infrastructure' which was important to my work.

Conclusions

At various points in this paper I have indicated what I see as advantages of a fully participant teacher research role and I have also tried to explain frankly the serious disadvantages which I found. Most of the advantages stem from the naturalness of the solution to the problem of access and I have particularly identified the ease of establishing rapport and trust and the opportunity to acquire 'subsidiary awareness' and 'tacit knowledge'. One would expect these factors to affect both the quality of data and the accuracy of interpretation. Most of the disadvantages of the fully participant role stem from the degree of commitment to that role which it is necessary to give in order to sustain it, and here I have particularly identified the scarcity of and constraints on time. My experience in attempting ethnographic research as a full-time teacher has thus been one of finding considerable difficulties and dilemmas. My attempts to resolve them may not have always been the right ones and there was always the danger of striving in two spheres of activity and succeeding in neither. On the other hand, I always reasoned that whilst I was enoying doing the research there was every reason to carry on trying to combine it with my teaching. My conclusion then is a personal one — I found that the research process as a full participant was often tiring, frustrating and difficult, and yet it was also fascinating and very rewarding to identify patterns in the data and to hesitatingly, step-by-step, attempt to construct a deeper understanding of the events and social relationships in which I daily participated.

References

BARNES, J.A. (1979) *Who Should Know What?* Harmondsworth, Penguin.

BECKER, H.S. (1964) 'Problems in the publication of field studies', in VIDICH, A.J. *et al.*, *Reflections on Community Studies*, New York, Wiley.

BERGER, P.L. and KELLNER, J. (1971) 'Marriage and the construction of reality', in COSIN, B.R. *et al.*, (Eds) *School and Society*, London, Routledge and Kegan Paul.

BURGESS, R.G. (1984) 'Introduction', in R.G. BURGESS (Ed.) *The Research Process in Educational Settings: Ten Case Studies*, Lewes, Falmer Press.

DAWE, A. (1970) 'The two sociologies' *British Journal of Sociology*, 21, 2, pp. 207–18.

ELLIOTT, J. (1976) *The Ford Teaching Project*, Cambridge, Cambridge Institute of Education.

GLASER, B. and STRAUSS, A.L. (1967) *The Discovery of Grounded Theory*, Chicago, Aldine.

HITCHCOCK, G. (1979) 'Fieldwork as a practical activity: The fieldworker's experience as a source of data in an organisational setting', paper given at the Ethnography of Schooling Conference, St Hilda's College, Oxford, September.

HUGHES, E. (1952) *Cases on Fieldwork*, Chicago, University of Chicago Press.

POLANYI, M. (1958) *Personal Knowledge*, London, Routledge and Kegan Paul.

POLLARD, A. (1979) 'Negotiating deviance and "getting done" in primary school classrooms', in BARTON, L. and MEIGHAN, R. (Eds) *Schools, Pupils and Deviance*, Driffield, Nafferton.

POLLARD, A. (1980) 'Teacher interests and changing situations of survival threat in primary school classrooms', in WOODS, P. (Ed.) *Teacher Strategies*, London, Croom Helm.

POLLARD, A. (1981) 'Coping with deviance: School processes and their implications for social reproduction', unpublished phD thesis, University of Sheffield.

POLLARD, A. (1982) 'A model of classroom coping strategies', *British Journal of Sociology of Education*, 3, 1, pp. 19–38.

POLLARD, A. (forthcoming) *The Social World of the Primary School*, London, Holt, Rinehart and Winston.

ROCK, P. (1979) *The Making of Symbolic Interactionism*, London, Macmillan.

STENHOUSE, L. (1975) *An Introduction to Curriculum Research and Development*, London, Heinemann.

WIEDER, D.L. (1974) 'Telling the code', in TURNER, R. (Ed.) *Ethnomethodology*, Harmondsworth, Penguin.

WOODS, P. (1979) *The Divided School*, London, Routledge and Kegan Paul.

12   Facilitating Action-Research in Schools: Some Dilemmas

John Elliott

The Organization of the TIQL Project

The 'Teacher-Pupil Interaction and the Quality of Learning' project (TIQL) was a two-year (March 1981–March 1983) teacher-based action research project into the problems of teaching for understanding. Organizationally it was complex. There was an *inner network* of nine schools: five secondary schools, one sixth form college, one middle school, one primary school and one infant school. Within each school there were teams of teachers varying in size from eight to two. Each team had an in-school coordinator who was a senior member of staff responsible for coordinating the teachers' research in the school and liaising between the team and the 'senior management'. In negotiating school involvement we sought coordinators (or some other member of the team) who had an understanding and experience of action research strategies and methods, developed through their involvement in research-based award bearing courses at the Cambridge Institute of Education. The coordinators were also the main link between the school and the central team based at the Institute.

Within the central team, I, as director, had responsibility for the overall direction of the programme. Dave Ebbutt, research fellow, had responsibility for its day-to-day coordination. Seven people acted as external consultants to teachers in schools: Jennifer Nias, Mary Hope, Marion Dadds (Institute tutorial staff), John Haysom, David Prideaux (visiting scholars), Dave Ebbutt and myself. This central team of seven were assisted by a full-time secretary, Jean Southwell. In addition, two teachers undertaking the Institute's Advanced Diploma course were linked to the programme. Each team member was attached to a participating school for the purpose of helping the staff to collect and analyze data around the theme of 'teaching for understanding'.

The central team met monthly, and the school coordinators, plus any members of their teams who wished to come, met twice termly. Nominated representatives from participating local authorities were invited to attend both types of meeting. Their role was to represent their respective LEAs in their dealings with the programme.

At the central team meetings progress and problems in individual schools, and in the work of the project as a whole, were reviewed from the point of view of the consultants. At the inter-team meetings progress and problems were reviewed from the point of view of the school coordinators and their teams. In addition, the director and coordinator consulted the members of both meetings concerning future policies and practices.

Facilitation As a Dilemma Resolving Activity

Ian Lewis, a visiting scholar from the University of York, circulated his reactions to a central team meeting held during the first operational term of the programme on 28 May 1981. He spoke of underlying tensions he perceived at the meeting:

> ... CIE members have to operate in a situation in which they are subject to conflicting pressures. On the one hand the outside world, presuming a traditional research role of authority and control; on the other the logic of the project, which entails a novel relationship with teachers.
>
> The situation is in principle difficult because it is novel — in breaking new ground in giving teachers responsibility and the opportunity to generate and implement their own research in their own terms — because it is potentially open to significant criticism from influential outsiders.
>
> These difficulties are further compounded because every participant will have personal reasons — in addition to project allegiance — to support involvement. For many of the teachers, too, there will be the additional complication of inexperience.
>
> To maintain the underlying project ideology — of allowing control and direction to lie essentially with the teachers, and preserving a non-directive enabling relationship for the CIE members — is something which requires, I

believe, a constant and conscious re-affirmation. Sensitivity to potential issues which might seek to promote — whether deliberately or otherwise — teacher-dependence will be difficult to sustain, but essential if the project is to remain true to its guiding principle. Recognition of issues which are of merely superficial concern, but which act as a focus for the airing of the different ideological stances on the project, is but one of the ways in which team members can continue to remind themselves of the difficulties they face.

Well before the end of that first term Ian Lewis returned to the University of York. It is only now — eight months later — that I am able to fully appreciate the prophetic significance of his 'Note'. In September 1981 another visiting scholar attended our team meetings, Professor John Haysom from Canada. On 5 November he penned the following memorandum to me.

MEMORANDUM   5 November 1981

To: John Elliott
From: John Haysom

MAPPING THE EVOLUTION OF THE TIQL PROJECT:
Monitoring the conflict of ideas as to how the Project should proceed

1. November 5 1981: At the time of writing this memo I have been at the Cambridge Institute for about two months, have attended two team meetings and one inner network meeting. My major impression of the Project is that it is certainly very much on the move (see for example the minutes of the team meeting of 20 October) and yet it is very open ended.

2. Although the overall purpose of the Project is reasonably clear (see for example the documents and working papers), the ways of achieving this purpose have been left uncharted. There is no critical path schedule on the wall of the Project Office. (Are there indeed any target dates for completion of component tasks?)

3. The team meetings, in contrast to many similar progress meetings that I have attended, seem not only to contain

the ingredient of reporting what has happened since the last, but also the ingredient of formulating, perhaps for the first time, what we should do next. In other words the team members are invited to be responsive to what has happened and to forge the direction the Project should take.

4. The forging of direction is seen clearly where there are conflicting ideas. These are not suppressed. Moreover I remember John Elliott saying that he welcomed conflicting opinions in the team meeting of 20 October. This forging of direction is evident in sections 3 and 4 of the Minutes of this team meeting.

5. The forging of direction as evident in the conflict of opinions was also apparent in the inner network meeting (19 October 1981). At one point the subject under discussion was, who is the Project for?

6. I mentioned these ideas about monitoring the course of the Project by studying the conflict of ideas to John Elliott, and his initial reaction was to support it. He suggested that he and Dave Ebbutt could review the time period past-present and that I could record future conflict in the team meetings and inner network meetings.

7. If this is agreed to, I will begin data collection by transcribing relevant extracts from team meetings and inner network meetings.

John Haysom

His view that 'the forging of direction is seen clearly where there are conflicting ideas', that decisions about overall direction are made in response to manifest conflict, suggested a method for monitoring the progress of our project. What I did not appreciate at the time was the extent to which his remarks echoed those made by Lewis over five months earlier (see particularly the final sentence in the excerpt from his Note above).

Shortly after Haysom's memorandum I received a fascinating paper from Richard Winter (1982) outlining a data analysis method he had developed for his own action research in the area of teacher education. He argued that in struggling to make sense of his own actions as a teacher educator he discovered that they constituted responses to perceived dilemmas. Winter pointed out that although a number of methods for data collection had been developed by educational action researchers, there was a paucity of ideas about methods of data analysis. His point struck home. Brian Wakeman, one of the project's school-based coordinators, had also been arguing this. He was facing the problem of helping the teachers in his team to analyze the data they had collected and felt the external consultants should be able to cite some methods for doing this.

The idea then of doing a dilemma analysis of overall project decision-making began to take shape in the Autumn Term 1981. Although our central team meetings could be described as a process of dilemma analysis — we shared progress reports from individual consultants, diagnosed current problems and issues, and deliberated about strategies for resolving them — I felt a need for a less piece-meal and more general view of the direction we were going in before it was too late to change it. I see what follows very much as a piece of second-order educational action research. In other words, it focusses not on the educational actions which participating teachers are deliberating about in classrooms, but on the actions of those responsible for facilitating teacher deliberation.

The analysis which follows is structured around certain key dilemmas that I have analyzed from project documents, having scanned through them during the course of an afternoon. The documents drawn on include:

1 Minutes of Central Team Meetings;
2 Minutes of Inter-School Meetings;
3 Director's Memos distributed to school teams in order to clarify some aspect of the project;
4 School Coordinators' progress reports;
5 Reports and notes of progress written by external consultants and LEA advisers;
6 Papers on action research processes and methods written by myself or the project's coordinator, Dave Ebbutt.

The procedure I have adopted in presenting my analysis of a dilemma is as follows:

a describe the dilemma and cite evidence in support of one's description;
b describe and explain the response made to the dilemma and cite evidence which supports the account;
c examine the implications of the response for the practice we are attempting to facilitate; namely, educational action research.

Finally, a short account of the nature of a dilemma is in order before proceeding. A dilemma is a situation which appears to require two equally desirable but mutually inconsistent courses of action. The equal desirability stems from the perception that each course of action would fulfil certain ethical requirements in the situation, and the inconsistency stems from the perception that each requirement can only be met by denying the other. Dilemmas are essentially moral problems, and as such can be contrasted with technical problems. With respect to the latter, an agent is also faced with a decision between alternatives, but what change is required is clear and unambiguous. The technical problem is how to bring about a certain state of affairs by the most efficient and effective means. Whereas technical problems can be resolved simply by discovering the effective means, it is not so easy to see how dilemmas can be resolved. In some cases the 'solution' involves a reconceptualization of the nature of the problem situation. Here one's concept of the situation shifts so that it no longer appears ambiguous. In other cases no satisfactory solution is discovered; the dilemma persists and one is forced to opt for a course of action which satisfies one value but denies another. However, one may limit the extent to which one pursues a particular course of action for the sake of the values it denies. Thus a judge may temper his administration of 'justice' with a little 'mercy'.

Dilemma 1: Who Defines the Focus of the Research: The Teachers or the Central Team?

On 5 May 1981 school team coordinators came together to present their teams' research plans to each other. The external consultants, in their negotiations with potential teams during the Autumn 1980 and Spring 1981 terms, had suggested that within the overall theme of 'teaching for understanding' the teams and teachers involved should produce their own 'research designs'. At our team meeting on 29 January 1981 we decided to recommend that coordinators hold three meetings in their schools during the Easter Term 'to clarify their plan of action'. The coordinators would then present their plans on 5 May at the Institute (at the beginning of the first 'operational' term of the project). It was also decided to send a package of support materials for the planning exercise to each coordinator.[1]

    The purposes underlying the package were:

1   to clarify what the project was about;
2   to clarify the methodological principles governing the action research process;
3   to facilitate team planning in schools with respect to:
    a the identification of specific problems of 'teaching for understanding';
    b the organization of the action research process and the selection of appropriate strategies and methods for collecting and analyzing data.

The director and central team therefore took initial responsibility for specifying the general principles governing the selection of both the content and methods of inquiry. But we felt that decisions about specific content and methods in the light of these principles should be the responsibility of teachers. The central team saw itself in this latter respect as facilitating teachers' decisions rather than prescribing what they ought to do.

On 5 May the 'plans' presented by the team coordinators revealed the following characteristics. They were extremely diverse and often relative to the idiosyncratic concerns of individual teachers. Only three teams described a common problem for investigation. Also, in many cases the problem areas cited were not explicitly linked. However, most of the teachers had described problems which they experienced as significant. I was confident that as the process of action research developed the concerns of the teachers would become explicitly linked with those of the central team (without the latter having to force such a linkage), and that individual teachers would increasingly be able to link their concerns with each other's, both within school teams and more generally. However, such confidence was by no means shared by all the members of the central team.

My perceptions of the meeting were not shared by some of the observers present. One LEA Adviser remarked on leaving that we were going to have a job in getting something coherent to emerge from the diversity of concerns expressed and their apparent disconnection from the overall theme of the project. The director of the Schools Council programme which was sponsoring us expressed anxiety· during the meeting about a lack of relationship between the project's espoused focus — that it had been commissioned by the Council to do — and the teachers' proposals. In particular, he was worried about the lack of reference to 'examinations and assessment'.

The issue about 'diversity' of problem definitions and their apparent 'disconnection' from what the project was about is captured in the following extract from a report on the conference by Jean Southwell (project secretary).

> *Divergence of Themes*
> It was felt that there was a considerable divergence in the research proposals. The Programme Director, Don Cooper, expressed concern that there was so little on assessment, but John Elliott said that the project was looking at ways in which the quality of learning can be improved in the classroom....
> ... He felt that one of the major obstacles to learning for understanding is the sort of assessment system used in many schools. If people find constraints on the development of understanding, then they should look closely at the assessment situation as it is operating.
> One LEA representative asked if the team envisaged any generalisations. John Elliott felt that common themes would emerge from the disparity. It was suggested that at future conferences several schools should submit papers to be read in advance and that common themes could be discussed on the day of the conference. 'Start with individual studies and discover cross-linkages across the studies' [argued John Elliott]. (Working Paper No. 4)

The diversity of problem definitions appeared to be linked in some people's minds with their perceived disconnection from the central team's idea of what the project was about — namely 'teaching for understanding'. Greater attention to the latter, it was felt, would have resulted in a more coherent and related set of 'problem definitions'. From the point of view of the Schools Council programme director, Don Cooper, and some LEA Advisers present, the central team should have been less permissive over what was to count as a valid issue/topic for investigation within the overall theme we had specified. After all, it could be argued, the Council was sponsoring the project to the tune of £45,000 and there was an important issue of accountability involved. Did not it have the right to insist that the research be carried out along the lines of the proposal which it had funded?

Don Cooper was surely right in reminding the meeting of the project's accountability. Harry Thompson (1981), a project observer at the initial stages, interviewed him after the conference:

He felt that some team reports were clearly too divergent from the focus of the Project. He was concerned that his intervention at the conference, in commenting on this, might have worried the teachers but felt the need from the Schools Council's point of view to play a monitoring role. He would like the LEA Advisers to play a more active role — to be 'partners in the research'. (Working Paper No. 4)

There was an evident disparity of view between Don, LEA officials, certain members of the central team, and me, on how relevant the teachers' 'problem definitions' were. This disparity appeared to stem from rather different interpretations of written statements concerning what the project was about. There were different views on what problems were relevant to the general idea of *'teaching for understanding'*. But this was exacerbated by the fact that Don seemed to think that I had defined the major problem teachers faced in pursuing this idea: namely, the examination and assessment requirements teachers had to meet.

The introduction to the original proposal did suggest that one of the major problems in 'teaching for understanding' lay in a potential dilemma between implementing this teaching approach and one which met the requirement to maximize examination success. Under 'Aims' the proposal (1979) stated:

The proposed project will aim to:
1 help teachers monitor the extent to which the higher level understanding tasks they plan for pupils — either as individuals, teams, or departments — qualitatively differ from those which pupils actually come to work on in classroom settings;
2 help teachers to identify —
  a the strategies pupils and teachers employ to renegotiate their learning tasks;
  b the contextual/organisational factors which constrain and enable teaching for understanding, e.g. decisions about syllabuses, modes of assessment, time-tabling and pupils grouping arrangements, the system of positive and negative sanctions which influence pupil motivation;
3 help teachers and schools develop organisational, curricular, and teaching strategies for resolving the dilemma between 'teaching for assessment' and 'teaching for understanding'.

The first two aims simply state the kinds of task involved in any action research into the problems of implementing a general educational idea in classrooms, that is, identifying any gaps which exist between intentions stated in plans and those which exist in practice, how the latter are renegotiated through classroom interactions, and the contextual conditions which constrain or enable a teacher in his or her attempts to implement their aims. With respect to the last, 'the mode of assessment' is cited as a possibly significant contextual factor but its significance is not asserted. But in the third aim it is cited as a specific problem in teaching for understanding. Thus, in addition to citing 'a general idea' and the kinds of research tasks teachers would need to accomplish in order to understand the problems of implementing it in practice, we did anticipate a specific problem they would face.

Our negotiations with potential schools and teachers were based on a shorter three-page 'summary' of the original proposal I had drafted to the Schools Council (Elliott *et al.*, 1981). It was signed by members of the central team and counter-signed by Don Cooper. On the very first page the document states: 'Working with external consultants the teams will investigate and attempt to resolve the apparent dilemma between: teaching for understanding and teaching for assessment.' It then went on to cite *Aspects of Secondary Education* (DES, 1979) in support of the view that the pressure to ensure examination success constitutes a major problem for those teachers who aspire to 'teach for understanding'. However, later in the document there is another statement of what the project was about:

(1) Collecting and analysing evidence about the problems of implementing 'understanding' tasks in classroom settings. This will involve the study of organisational as well as classroom factors e.g. timetabling patterns.
(2) Developing and testing strategies for resolving the problems identified at both the classroom and school organisation levels.

In both documents there appears to have been an ambiguity about the focus of the project. On the one hand, it expressed a desire to leave 'problem identification' open as part of the action research process, and simply specified the general area in which problems were to be identified, and the kinds of research task involved. On the other hand, it identified and defined a particular problem as a major focus for the teachers involved.

Don Cooper had justification for his claim that the teachers were not apparently focussing on what the project had been funded to focus on. The project could indeed be interpreted as focussing on the specific issue of 'teaching for understanding vs. teaching for assessment'. In my response to him at the meeting I argued that he had misinterpreted the proposal. The focus, I claimed, was the more general and open one of 'teaching for understanding'. Whether examination/assessment requirements posed a problem in this respect was something to be examined alongside other possible constraints, and not asserted in advance of the research. I argued that I could easily justify the initial 'problem definitions' teachers brought to the meeting in terms of the proposal. However, in retrospect this appears to have been a piece of 'bravado' fabricated by me for the sake of the teachers present.

From a fairly early stage in our negotiations it was clear that many teachers were not prepared to accept someone else's 'problem definitions' as a condition of their participation. They wanted to be reassured that they were not being required to do something for 'the Cambridge Institute' or 'the Schools Council'; that they would be able to focus on problems of real concern to them. Since we believed that this requirement was part of the logic of action research, we went out of our way to reassure teachers on this point. Action research addressed itself to the practical problems practitioners experienced and to the strategies they could employ to resolve them. We also claimed that this approach was entirely consistent with the ideas of the 'new' Schools Council programmes. They were established to respond to needs identified by practitioners at 'the grassroots'.

However, while reassuring teachers on this point, we also made it clear that the project would be concerned with 'teaching for understanding' and that they would be expected to focus on problems that could be linked with this general idea. If they could not in all conscience make this link, then they should feel free to opt out of the project. We 'gave' this freedom throughout the planning term at the beginning of 1981, arguing that any teacher could withdraw without any 'hard feelings' right up to the point at which the work would get underway in the Summer Term of 1981. After that we expected them to commit themselves to the enterprise.

We also left it up to the teachers to judge the extent to which their initial 'problem definitions' reflected a general concern with the idea of 'teaching for understanding'. Any attempt on our part to prescribe what was relevant and irrelevant to the idea would have contradicted the logic of action research. (I will explain why later.)

The stance we adopted in our initial discussions with teachers respected the logic of action research, but this was only ambiguously reflected in our written accounts of the project. By the time the May 1981 conference came I had forgotten the element which contradicted it, but which had evidently been picked up by the programme director. I felt that quite a few of the teachers present found my response to his intervention reassuring. Harry Thompson reported on the basis of post-conference interviews with teachers that:

> One of the most frequently recurring comments made by the teachers was that they found the conference very reassuring. They had come feeling very insecure, that their efforts were inadequate compared to what other schools had done, that they were poorly prepared and that they had possibly misinterpreted the main focus of the research. By the end of the conference most of the teachers felt considerably more confident about their work and the contribution they could make. (Working Paper No. 4)

Although I interpreted this as evidence that teachers found my contribution reassuring, the programme director later argued that it could equally support his impression that some teachers found him reassuring. A colleague interpreted Thompson's remarks simply to mean that teachers were reassured by listening to each other.

Although my central team colleagues pointed out in a subsequent meeting that the proposal was more ambiguous about the major focus than I claimed at the conference, another response to Don's intervention indicated that I was at least subconsciously aware of being caught in a dilemma. As far as I can recall it went something like this: 'I am accountable to the Council for whether what is done conforms to the proposal, not the teachers. They ought to focus on the problems they have identified and not worry about your expectations. I'll worry about those.' In saying this, I was both respecting the logic of action research by asserting the teachers' right to proceed from their own 'problem definitions', while at the same time tacitly admitting that this involved some deviation from the proposal the Council had funded. However, this was something I, rather than the teachers, should be held to account for.

If the teachers had written and negotiated this action research proposal directly with the Schools Council[2] there would have been no contradiction between respecting the concerns of teachers and responsibility to the sponsor, since the sponsor would have funded action research into a specific problem/issue which clearly reflected teachers' concerns. The contradiction occurs when an external facilitator defines a specific problem as the focus, gets funding, and then attempts to negotiate that focus with a group of teachers. In citing a specific problem area in our proposal for funding prior to extensive discussions with teachers, I created a dilemma for myself and my colleagues in the central team. On the one hand, we saw our role as a *facilitating* one, yet on the other, I had made the project team accountable to the Council for ensuring that teachers addressed the specific issue of 'examinations/assessment'. My way out of this particular dilemma was to opt for *facilitation* rather than *control*. At the May conference I attempted to eliminate the ambiguity in the existing accounts of what the project was about, while pretending even to myself that it did not exist. The new statement (Elliott, 1981b) was later written down and circulated to the school coordinators, LEA representatives, and Don Cooper.

Memo No 3

The Research Task for Teacher Groups in Project Schools
This is a slightly reformulated version of a statement I made at the last meeting for co-ordinators and teachers in the Project's Inner Network.

As I see it the research task of the Project can be formulated in terms of four key questions.

(1) With respect to the tasks we are setting in classrooms, and the ways we interact with pupils in relation to these tasks, are we giving pupils opportunities to develop their understanding of the subject?

(2) What specific problems/constraints do we face in teaching for understanding? To what extent do the assessment/examination procedures we employ for evaluating pupil learning constitute constraints?

(3) How and why do the problems/constraints we have identified come about?

(4) In the light of (3) what action steps can be effectively taken to resolve the problems we have identified?

This re-statement merely suggests that examination/assessment procedures are a dimension worth exploring when seeking to identify issues/problems for investigation. Nevertheless, the very fact that it is the only dimension cited as a possible problem in teaching for understanding, constitutes a gesture towards *control* over teachers' problem definitions. Respect for the autonomy of teachers' judgments was tempered with a degree of *control*.

Why did the examination/assessment issue get cited in the original proposal? The answer is two-fold. First, it increased the likelihood of securing funds, in as much as it linked the idea of 'teaching for understanding' with a major policy issue posed by HMI in their national survey of secondary schools (DES, 1979). HMI claimed that teachers failed to teach for in-depth understanding of their subjects by over-emphasizing the importance of getting pupils through public examinations. Secondly, the fact that HMI had drawn the public's attention to an issue about the quality of teaching provided an opportunity to put teacher-based action research 'on the map' as it were. However, the problem lay in the fact that it was the facilitators', and not the teachers', thinking that informed the citation of the assessment/examinations issue. According to one of my central team colleagues, the initial meeting was not reassuring at all for one school team present.

> They found this meeting *disturbing* not reassuring because they thought TIQL was about assessment/understanding and had planned work along these lines. They could not, by contrast, come to terms with the looser definition propounded at this meeting. Also, the ambiguity displayed at this meeting and your reformulation did not make the teachers at this school feel autonomous. It made them lose confidence in the professional judgement of ourselves at CIE.

Dilemma 2: Who Defines the Pedagogical Aims of the Project: Teachers or Facilitators?

Some pressure emerged, from both project observers and some of the teachers involved, for us to define 'understanding' as an aim much more precisely. One school team eventually dropped out, partly because its members felt: 'The initial aims were not clearly stated — this encouraged involvement from people who showed only a superficial understanding' (letter from school coordinator to John Elliott, 9 December 1981). Earlier, in November 1981, an LEA Inspector wrote to me airing a number of her concerns about the progress of the project. One was this:

> ... the 'research' element seems to me to be pretty nebulous,

and not sharpening up as by this stage I had hoped it would be. I understand that 'action research' and 'research' are not synonymous, and that the former is a great deal slower to crystallise. At the same time, the time scale of the project does suggest to me that the questions need now to be posed more specifically, if identifiable outcomes are to emerge. (I think I expect you to disagree with this, on the grounds that we are concerned with process rather than result!) On the other hand, process is surely inextricably interwoven with out-come? If outcomes are irrelevant, what price process?

The Inspector had already argued at a team meeting that: '. . . a more directive framework might give more initiative to proceed' (Minutes, 29 September 1981). I interpreted these concerns about direction as indicative of a feeling that we ought to clarify what we meant by 'teaching for understanding', since the teachers felt uncertain about what this involved in practice. It was assumed that so long as teachers were unclear about it, the slower the progress they would make in identifying relevant issues and getting their research under way. In other words, clarity about pedagogical aims was needed before teachers could proceed with the action research. How can teachers reflect about the extent to which they are achieving their aims if they are not clear what they are? Members of the central team also experienced some pressure from teachers to give them direction with respect to the stated pedagogical aim of the project. On the other hand, some of us believed that greater clarity about pedagogical aims proceeds interactively with the study of pedagogical means. In my reply to the Inspector's November letter, I argued 'that "aims" in education are best clarified by looking at practice and not in advance of it' (John Elliott, 3 December 1982).

The difference of viewpoint here may depend upon whether one sees teaching as a technical or an ethical activity (see Aristotle's *Ethics* for the distinction between the 'technical' and 'ethical'). When it is construed as a technical activity, it is assumed that pedagogical aims can always be operationally defined as extrinsic and quantifiable outcomes of a process. They would constitute intended learning outcomes operationally defined in terms of specific and measurable changes in pupil behaviour. Certainly some teachers began to embark on their research with a technical interpretation of the action research task: namely, to study and resolve problems of *producing* 'under-standing' in pupils. For such teachers, help in producing operational definitions of 'understanding' in their subject areas in the form of specific and measurable learning outcomes, might have constituted a reasonable expectation of the external consultant's role.

When teaching is construed as an ethical activity pedagogical aims cannot be operationally defined. They embody abstract conceptions of ends which are intrinsic qualities rather than extrinsic products of the processes *in* which they are realized. Ethical conceptions of pedagogical aims specify general educational values to be *realized in* the process of teaching and learning rather than its outcome for the learner. Qua educators, I would argue that teachers have a responsibility for the quality of the provision they make for learning, for establishing certain conditions which *enable* rather than *produce* understanding. Whether pupils learn what they are *enabled to learn* by their teachers is their responsibility. In contrast, the idea of *producing understanding* suggests a passive process over which learners exercise little control.

When pedagogical aims are viewed as ethical rather than technical ends, then a different interpretation is placed on the general idea of 'teaching for understanding'. From a technical perspective the end of teaching is 'understanding'. However, from an ethical perspective the end of teaching is 'teaching for understanding'. The latter does not refer to extrinsic end-states in the learner, but to intrinsic qualities to be realized in the process of teaching itself, in the tasks teachers set pupils and in the way they interact with them as they try to accomplish these tasks.

I would claim that the idea of 'teaching for understanding' is entailed by *educational action research*. The latter has as its general focus *educational action*, and what makes an action *educational* is not the production of extrinsic end-states but the intrinsic qualities expressed in the manner of its performance. Thus educational action research is a mode of practical deliberation about the ethical quality of the teacher's provision for learning rather than his or her technical productivity. The general idea of 'teaching for understanding' simply specifies a quality of educational action, and as such guides, rather than directs, teachers' deliberations about how to improve the *educational quality* of their teaching. Decisions about teaching strategies which arise from such deliberations must necessarily be matters of personal judgment concerning what are negative and positive instances of *educational* action. This is why problem definition in educational action research should not be controlled by an external agency.

The process would be something like this:

1 In the light of the idea of 'teaching for understanding' teachers focus on certain aspects of their pedagogy which they assume to be problematic.

2 As they reflect upon these aspects they will ask, 'Do these constitute negative or positive instances?' of the idea. This will involve an interactive mode of reflection which examines the instance in the light of the idea and the idea in the light of the instance.

3 This joint reflection about means and ends together leads to a sharpened conception of the pedagogical aim, which in turn illuminates other problematic areas of practice and so on ad infinitum.

In educational action research the teacher is constantly changing his or her view of pedagogical problems in the light of changing conceptions of pedagogical aims, and changing the latter in the light of the former. Whereas from a technical perspective a pedagogical theory of ends is developed independently of, and often prior to, the study of practice, in educational action research it is developed interactively with it.

Having stated this position, I still feel that there is some justification to the view expressed by project observers: namely, that as facilitators we had some obligation to help teachers clarify the pedagogical aim of the project. After all, we specified the idea in the first place. Surely, then, we were under some obligation to spell out the meanings we ascribed to it? I would certainly accept the implication of my previously stated claim that educational action research entails 'teaching for understanding' as 'a general idea' which orientates reflection. The implication is this. Facilitators of educational action research can only execute this role on the basis of some understanding and experience of what educational action involves. They should therefore give practitioners access to their understanding of the nature of educational action. If educational action is believed to involve 'teaching for understanding' as its pedagogical aim, then they should not only state this belief but also explain and justify it. In other words, they should spell out their understanding of the idea. Surely, this is necessary even at the negotiation stage if potential participants are to make an informed and responsible response?

There appears therefore to be a dilemma for facilitators of educational action research which stems from its apparently paradoxical logic. Since educational action research implies the pedagogical aim of 'teaching for understanding', the facilitator's grasp of the logic of the process must entail an understanding of the guiding idea. On the other hand, if one specifies what this understanding is, does not one prevent participants from exercising their personal judgment about what are to count as negative and positive instances of the idea?

Looking back over our central team meetings, we appear to have been in a continuous quandary over whether, when, and how we should introduce externally derived understandings of the pedagogical aim of the project to teachers. Thus while adopting the position that teachers would clarify the aim for themselves through studying their pedagogical methods, we also expressed continuous concern about whether or not to introduce both our own understandings and 'typologies of learning and understanding' developed by other researchers.

Involvement of Philosophers

John Elliott would like to see what a group of philosophers would make of what goes on in the classroom.

Suggests 3 or 4 meetings over duration of the project.

John Elliott to write to the following, inviting them to key into the project: [Names of some philosophers of education followed]. (Minutes of Team Meeting, 12 February 1981)

The idea was that a group of professional philosophers of education would examine the aims being pursued by teachers in the classroom in the light of the idea of 'teaching for understanding'. I did not write to the group nominated, but 'shelved' the idea, feeling that the involvement of professional philosphers at an early stage before teachers had had an opportunity to reflect about the aim themselves, might create an authority-dependence which would restrict their own thinking.

The first major discussion of the project's pedagogical aim, half-way through the second term of the research, reflected a happy coincidence of two sets of concerns. First, the project team was concerned that teachers should begin to arrive at some shared understandings of the pedagogical aim. Secondly, the teachers were beginning to feel that they needed to clarify it in their own minds. Our placing it on the agenda at this point was therefore timely. If the teachers had expressed less concern about the nature of understanding, the agenda decision might have promoted the feeling that we were foisting issues of clarification onto them.

At the next central team meeting the issue of facilitating teachers' thinking about the pedagogical aim of the project was taken up again by me:

John Elliott offered to write an introduction [to the transcript on understanding] to put the report in context and explain why the project had not previously defined 'understanding'. It was also suggested that at a later date this transcript could be linked with other data on 'understanding'. (Minutes, 17 November 1981)

What I did over the following weeks was to attempt to explicate the different views of 'learning' and 'understanding' embedded in the teachers' discussion, to pose issues for further reflection, and to link these issues with relevant theoretical literature. This paper (Working Paper No. 7, Elliott, 1982) was then attached to the transcript and circulated to all the school teams. Again I was trying to 'match' the external input of ideas to teachers' own thinking as it emerged, so that the latter could productively interact with the former without being negated by it.

Subsequently what happened was that individual teachers made use of various 'theories' and 'typologies' to refine their own thinking about the aims of the project. Some of these were provided by their external consultants, while others were discovered by individuals independently through their own reading. During Spring Term 1982 a number of research reports produced by individual teachers were circulated around the inner network and presented at meetings. They frequently cited theories and typologies of learning and understanding. We had evidence that other teachers were drawing on them as a basis for analyzing data from their own classrooms. By initially trying to match external input with the emergent thinking of individuals, and then making their use of this input more widely available; we tried to facilitate the process of aim clarification without imposing our definitions on teachers.

What has been portrayed above is the problem of facilitating the process of generating grounded theory (see Glaser and Strauss, 1967; Schatzman and Strauss, 1973). Although the facilitator must avoid controlling the teacher's interpretation of the data through theoretical input, he or she must not be naive enough to assume that new ways of conceptualizing situations and issues will automatically emerge from the reflections of individuals who have little access to theories other than their own. One of the facilitator's roles is to mediate theoretical resources in a way which enhances rather than constrains teachers' capacities to develop their own theoretical understandings.

So long as the introduction of external ideas constitutes a support rather than a substitute for teachers' own thinking, it can speed up the process of aims clarification and consequently the process of problem identification, analysis, and the formulation of strategic action. Given this supportive rather than controlling context, the introduction of external ideas also gives teachers greater opportunities for making original contributions to the development of pedagogical theory.

The more a teacher generates his or her own theories via a critique of existing ideas, the more original they are likely to be. The teacher who develops his or her theories solely from reflection upon experience, in ignorance of the past and present deliberations of others, will simply 'reinvent the wheel' rather than push beyond the existing state of professional knowledge. Although it could be argued that this is sufficient for the professional development of individual teachers, it is not, as I shall argue later, sufficient for the development of the teaching profession generally through action research.

Dilemma 3: Process versus Product

... John Elliott explained that he saw the main aim of the project as generating, through teacher research, a relatively coherent set of ideas about the problems of teaching for understanding in classrooms. These ideas would be grounded in evidence and presented in a form which would help other teachers to test them against their experience. One consultant expressed a fear that the teachers would feel they had to produce a product for the consultants, and said they would be satisfied if the project simply resulted in staff development. John Elliott replied that he thought that staff development was an important outcome but not the primary aim of the project as a whole, the primary aim being to prove that teachers can make an important contribution to public knowledge about problems and issues in teaching. However, John Elliott agreed that the achievement of that aim necessitated staff development, which should be the primary concern for team co-ordinators. (Minutes of Team Meeting, 20 October 1981)

This internal discussion about the importance of process versus product followed an inter-schools meeting on the previous day in which I had tried to argue that the requirements of action research went beyond 'mere' self-evaluation activity.

John Elliott felt strongly that the main aim of the project

was research, not simply self-evaluation. He pointed out that if the teams are doing research, rather than merely self-evaluation, then one characteristic of teachers doing research is that they should be prepared to make their work publicly accessible to other teachers.

One co-ordinator expressed a fear that the idea of a public product would make some teachers feel threatened. John Elliott replied that the product could be a product of shared rather than individual thinking, but he stressed that the research has to be captured in some way in written form.

One of the consultants again said that they did not want teachers to feel they had to produce research 'for' the consultants. John Elliott argued that he didn't want that, but that even the development of individual self-awareness depended on the capacity of teachers to share and discuss their ideas with other people. (Minutes of Inner Network Meeting, 19 October 1981)

These excerpts express the dilemma I experienced. One school coordinator in particular stressed that the value of the project lay in the process of self-evaluation which it had fostered and not in the production of written accounts of 'findings'. The former had evolved in some schools as a 'private' and 'solitary' activity with little sharing of information and insights between individuals. The only people who shared the 'realities of classroom life' with individual teachers and their pupils were the external consultants, who knew more, in some cases, about the extent to which teachers were reflecting about their practices than their colleagues or team coordinator did.

This view of self-evaluation as essentially a 'private' and 'solitary' activity probably derives from the traditional isolation of teachers, a situation which has received ideological legitimation through the idea of professional autonomy. But the view was also reinforced to some extent by the role the external consultants adopted from the beginning of the project. This can be described as follows:

1   They only visit teacher's classrooms on request.
2   They observe and record lessons and interview pupils but allow the teachers to determine their own information needs; what the consultant's observations and interviews should focus on.
3   They avoid persecuting teachers with their own insights but pose questions and critical issues arising out of the data for further reflection and discussion.

4   They give teachers ownership of data and control over how it is used and to whom it is released. Recordings are normally left with teachers rather than placed 'on file' back at the office as a resource for outsider research.

This role relationship, between individual teachers and the external consultants, was perceived by teachers to be of personal value in helping them to reflect individually about their practice in a relatively non-threatening context.

However, I saw this 'solitary' mode of self-evaluation merely as an initial stage of a process which would eventually involve a sharing of information and insights across classrooms, the identification of common themes and issues, and the development of some shared practical knowledge about how to realize the aim of 'teaching for understanding'. Thus the process moved from individual to collaborative reflection on common issues and themes, and from the development of individual to shared insights. I could not see how this process could develop without teachers writing up and sharing accounts of their practice with each other. Such 'products' were not so much conceived as terminal end-points, but as part and parcel of an ongoing process. However, within the time limit on the duration of project support I did want a written product reflecting the common experience and insights which had evolved through the project; for other teachers to use as a resource when reflecting about their teaching.

What I was really aiming at in this project was the development of a fairly coherent set of insights into issues of 'teaching for understanding' produced by practitioners rather than external professional researchers. The audience for this 'product' was not the central team of consultants, which was how my emphasis on it was sometimes interpreted, by other members of the teaching profession. But it could be argued that this requirement transcends the needs of the individual teachers involved, and only confirms the original suspicion that the project involved doing something for others rather than oneself.

There was a tendency for some secondary teachers to resist moving beyond the stage of private and solitary reflection. (It was less evident in our primary and infant school teams). This resistance was articulated in terms of 'doing something for oneself' as against 'doing something for others'. Some school coordinators and colleagues in the central team were understandably reluctant to risk what had already been achieved at the level of individual self-evaluation by pressurizing for written products. They were reluctant to make more demands on teachers' time in terms of an effort, which although valuable to others was not relevant to the professional development of the individuals involved. Moreover, as one coordinator pointed out, teachers felt threatened at having to report information and insights about their classrooms to colleagues and coordinators (who were often members of senior management).

How was this dilemma between sustaining self-evaluation for staff development and producing a coherent end-product 'resolved'? Not wishing the coordinators to feel they were being pushed into endangering the staff development process, which was the major value some of them found in the project, I agreed that they should be primarily concerned with safeguarding this process rather than trying to get their teachers to write things up. What then happened was that the team of external consultants increasingly took responsibility in some schools for helping individual teachers to produce written accounts and share their insights with others.

The external consultants found that a major obstacle was a lack of conviction on the part of many teachers that the private insights they had gained through self-evaluation had any public value. They lacked any confidence that their personal insights would be of use to other teachers. The external consultant's role, knowing something of the nature of these insights, was to convince individuals that they did have something worth saying to others. This was done by spending time listening to their ideas, sometimes tape-recording and transcribing their comments, and then working out with them a suitable format for written presentation. By giving teachers a form of recognition for the insights they produced and by expressing a degree of confidence in their value, which the teachers themselves often lacked, the external consultants were increasingly able to get them to produce written accounts for circulation to, and discussion with, colleagues.

During the third term of the project (Easter 1982) over a dozen teachers contributed papers which were discussed at the twice termly inter-school meetings. In some schools a sharing of ideas within teams emerged. Three schools located near to each other met regularly together quite independently of the external consultants. However, for most of the teachers involved it was the externally convened inter-school meetings where insights were shared, and common themes and issues generated. More and more teachers were linking research into their own classroom practice with that of other teachers. One of the pleasing aspects of this process was the way secondary and primary teachers, and teachers of different subjects in secondary schools, were increasingly making linkages between each other's work. Eventually twenty-three case studies emerged from individuals. These were then subjected to comparative analysis in the light of particular issues at a residential weekend conference. The outcome was a list of hypotheses. In the final phase of the project a number of teachers selected hypotheses from this list and grounded them in the case studies in the form of written research reports. These reports are included in a volume entitled *Issues in Teaching for Understanding*.

The project moved beyond private self-evaluation into an action research mode. However, the way we resolved the dilemma between the process of 'staff development' and the production of written accounts was not entirely satisfactory from the standpoint of institutionalizing action research in schools. The latter process was in many cases heavily dependent on the central consultancy team for coordinating the process of writing up and sharing accounts. We obtained a fairly coherent 'product' by holding a weekend conference in which teachers refined and wrote up the common understandings they had developed. This may well prove useful to teachers generally, but there was a danger that when the central team 'closed down' in March 1983 there would be few structures remaining to sustain processes of collaborative reflection. The reason for making the school-based coordinators, most of whom had previous experience of action research methods, the back-bone of the project was to secure the institutionalization of collaborative reflection within schools. Although this still poses the problem of establishing structures for communication between schools which are independent of specially funded projects, it would at least have constituted a significant breakthrough with respect to the institutionalization of action research within the educational system.

Although I was not able to articulate this fully at the time, there is no contradiction between the professional development of individual teachers through self-evaluation and the production of a common body of insights about teaching. I would argue that the professional development of individual teachers involves a process of corporate rather than private reflection. One can go so far on the basis of the latter but it can only be an initial stage to establish confidence in a non-threatening environment. Without access to a common culture — a shared body of professional knowledge — the individual teacher's opportunities to develop his or her practice are very limited. The absence of a strong professional culture, sustained by the individualistic manner in which teachers are inducted (see Lortie, 1975), weakens their claim to be called professionals. In sharing insights and thereby developing a body of common professional understandings, individual teachers are not doing something for others rather than themselves. In contributing to the development of a common culture through action research, each individual gains access to a stock of knowledge he or she could not generate alone.

In my view, the institutionalization of collaborative reflection about the practice of teaching (action research) within the educational system is a necessary condition for the development of teaching as a profession. If teachers continue to relegate their own insights to the status of private rather than public knowledge, and cling to the view that the latter is the domain of specialist researchers, they will never build that common stock of practical wisdom which is the mark of a professional group.

Concluding Remarks

Facilitators of teacher-based action research need to be constantly deliberating about their own practice and its relationship to the nature of the activity they are trying to facilitate. If they do not engage in this kind of *second-order action research* they will succumb to pressures to control teachers' thinking, and thereby distort rather than enable the processes of *first-order action research*.

Although this paper may constitute a bad example of second-order action research, it has helped me to reflect more systematically about the practical dilemmas I have faced as a facilitator and be clearer about the lines of action which are required in the future. But since means and ends are objects of joint reflection in action research, I have also been able to clarify my own understanding of what the aim of 'facilitating educational action research' involved with respect to establishing certain enabling conditions. These can be represented in terms of the following principles:

1 Allow teachers to define the specific problems and issues for investigation within the framework of a shared pedagogical aim.
2 Help teachers to clarify their pedagogical aim by focussing attention on their practice. Do not encourage a tendency to treat ends and means independently and in separation from each other; for example, by rigid pre-specification of aims.

3 Match theoretical inputs to the problems and issues as they emerge from teachers' reflections about their concrete problems.

4 Provide opportunities for teachers to render accounts of their reflections to others, and thereby to discover linkages across individual experience.

5 Provide opportunities for teachers to deepen their own understanding of issues through discussion with each other.

6 Provide opportunities for the reporting of common understandings, developed through collaborative reflection, to the profession at large.

Notes

1 This package would include:
  a an introductory letter from Dave Ebbutt outlining its contents;
  b a brief account of what the project was about written by me (see Elliott *et al.*, 1981);
  c press cuttings about issues of 'teaching for understanding' in schools (to demonstrate that it was not simply the central team who felt there were issues to be raised in this respect) (see Ebbutt, 1981);
  d a working paper (see Elliott, 1981a) entitled 'Action-Research: A Framework for Self-Evaluation in Schools'. It outlined principles governing the conduct of action research and some suggestions about strategies and methods for collecting and analyzing data. (Now, in a slightly revised format, it constitutes Part 2 of Elliott, 1981a.)
  e a short working paper (see Ebbutt, 1981) providing some 'answers' to questions we anticipated teachers asking at the planning stage. They were:
    i   What sort of research will we be engaged in?
    ii   What are we focussing in on?
    iii We are all already aware of the problem; surely the good intuitive teacher does all this anyway?
    iv   What means can I use to gather evidence/data about the 'problem'?
    v   What is the basic unit of organization for the research team?
    vi   How many classes will form my research 'sample'?
    vii How much time will I need to devote to the research?
    viii What support can personnel from the Cambridge Institute give to teachers carrying out the research?
    ix   How many people will comprise a team?
    x   Should the research team be made up of teachers from a single department/subject area?
    xi   How much writing will be required for each case study?
    xii What about meeting other teachers from other project schools?

xiii What if I anticipate the possibility of applying for promotion elsewhere during the duration of the research?

xiv When is the latest date at which we can 'back out' of the research?

xv What is the next stage in the planning of the research?

xvi Which questions and suggestions that have not been covered here would you wish to raise with the Cambridge Institute team at the next meeting?

2. When its 'new' programmes were established the Council expressed the aspiration that they would constitute a response to practitioner defined needs. The model was one of response to their concerns. Some Council officials I know felt this implied a certain strategy, that practitioner groups would secure the funding and then be directly responsible to the Council for the way the money was spent. The use of external personnel — from higher education, for example — would be up to practitioners to determine. Such personnel would not be directly responsible to the sponsor for the way the money was spent, and the strategy would ensure that they adopted a *facilitating* rather than a *controlling* role with respect to the professional development of teachers.

References

ARISTOTLE (1955) *Ethics*, Bk VI, Harmondsworth, Penguin.

DES (1979) *Aspects of Secondary Education*, London, HMSO.

EBBUTT, D. (1981) *Extracts from Recent Relevant Articles/Documents*, Working Paper No. 3, TIQL Project, mimeo, Cambridge Institute of Education.

ELLIOTT, J. (1981a) *Action Research: A Framework for Self-Evaluation in Schools*, Working Paper No. 1, TIQL Project, mimeo, Cambridge Institute of Education.

ELLIOTT, J. (1981b) *The Research Task for Teacher Groups in Project Schools*, Memo No. 3, TIQL Project, mimeo, Cambridge Institute of Education.

ELLIOTT, J. (1982) *What Do We Mean by 'Understanding'?* Working Paper No. 7, TIQL Project, mimeo, Cambridge Institute of Education.

ELLIOTT, J. et al. (1979) *Teacher Pupil Interaction and the Quality of Learning: A Proposal for Teacher-Based Action-Research*, TIQL Project, mimeo, Cambridge Institute of Education.

ELLIOTT, J. et al. (1981) *Teacher-Pupil Interaction and the Quality of Learning*, Memo No. 1, TIQL Project, mimeo, Cambridge Institute of Education.

GLASER, B. and STRAUSS, A.L. (1967) *Discovery of Grounded Theory: Strategies for Qualitative Research*, Chicago, Aldine.

LORTIE, D.C. (1975) *Schoolteacher: A Sociological Study*, Chicago, University of Chicago Press.

SCHATZMAN, L. and STRAUSS, A.L. (1973) *Field Research: Strategies for a Natural Sociology*, Englewood Cliffs, N.J., Prentice-Hall.

John Elliott

TIQL Project (1981) *Report of Conference Number One*, Working Paper
No. 4, mimeo, Cambridge Institute of Education.
Winter, R. (1982), 'Dilemma analysis: A contribution to methodology for
action research', *Cambridge Journal of Education*, 12, 3.

13   A Note on Case Study and Educational Practice[1]

Lawrence Stenhouse

Editor's Note: This paper was written two months before Lawrence Stenhouse's untimely death in September 1982. Accordingly, the version which is presented here is very much in keeping with the material presented in 1982. However, minor amendments, slight editorial revisions and the notes have been added by Jean Rudduck and myself. In a letter written to me in May 1982 Lawrence Stenhouse stated that this was a difficult area to come to terms with and he thought that when it came to rewriting the paper he needed 'to reread Aristotle, Habermas, and Polanyi as well as to check out on Kant and the American pragmatists.' However, he also had doubts about the extent to which he could extend his analysis as it was his view that the questions he had raised required further discussion backed up by a programme of research that would specifically investigate the relationship between case study and educational practice. In much of Lawrence Stenhouse's work a number of problems and puzzles were set out for himself and for the research community. Indeed, having set the problem, it was usual for him to begin to work towards addressing it. Sadly this is no longer possible but as always he has placed before us an important agenda that needs to be addressed by the research community in the coming years.

A strong tradition of educational research has equated practice with policy; and policy, defined by the *Oxford English Dictionary* as 'a course of action adopted and pursued by a government, party, ruler, statesman, etc.,' may be taken to be both deliberative and more or less general. It is formulated at the expense of some thought. It is taken to apply across cases. Indeed, it is partly because of a perception of a need for consistency in policy that thought is expended on it. If today's action holds precedent for tomorrow's, then we had better get it right.

My own view is that educational policy in this country is rather crude. For the most part it is concerned with the government of the state school system and the less well-endowed institutions of further and higher education by those whose children will be educated by other agencies or whose homes can confer advantage within the state system. It is thus more a matter of conscience than of effectiveness. And the expression of conscience is given its form more by the need to invite disparate interests to form a party than by deduction from principle or by evolving a strategy to achieve an aim.

Now it may well be that educational research may serve as a source of ideas for policy-makers by presenting them with alternatives they have not noticed, and there is a kind of fact-finding inquiry by survey that allows estimates of the size and scope and even the nature of problems that will confront action, but the main function of research in relation to decision-making about policy is persuasive or rhetorical. Having decided what the policy is to be, it is useful to find research to support it. As Bryan Dockrell (1980, p. 12) notes, there has been 'a fashion among administrators and politicians for referring to research findings as a justification for their actions.'

It is clear that since the actions of administrators and politicians will tend to have general effects, the kind of research likely to influence or to support their decisions will be that which offers general findings applicable across cases. I need not remind you of the familiar patterns of research that attempt to generalize about the state of the nation or about the effects likely to follow from courses of educational action; though it might be worth recording that there is some disillusion with such research.

Let me contrast the policy view of practice that I have just sketched with the practitioner view. I take the practitioners to be those who are engaged in educating or in the close-in management of education. Characteristically, they may be thought of as responsible, not for formulating policy across cases (though there is this element in their work), but for the conduct of their own cases familiar to them. Their need is to apply knowledge to specific and individual situations.

Now, there may be some general laws or predictions that hold for all cases and can thus be applied by practitioners. And there may be tendencies found to be statistically significant in large-scale experiments that it is worth keeping a weather eye on in one's own case. Further, it will be useful to have conceptual frameworks and perceptions that support critical evaluation of one's own case. But it is necessary also to cultivate prudence and shrewdness out of experience and through a consideration of wider experience provided by discussion with professional colleagues. Finally, one must learn to read situations rapidly in order to be effectively responsive.[2]

Before reviewing the relationship of case study research to educational practice, I want to make an observation about the relationship of research to practice in the classic disciplines. There is a sense in which the fruits of research as theory or as organized knowledge are relevant to the practice of research. Each research community organizes its area of knowledge — chemistry or history or sociology — in such a way as to help members of that community to locate problems or areas of inquiry likely to be significant or productive for the advancement of knowledge. Likewise, each research community has a perception of methodology and methods supportive of the practice of research. So it is that we are gathered in conference with — for this occasion at least — those with more interest in the practice of educational research than in the practice of education.[3]

Although research guided by disciplines is likely to extend knowledge and the extension of knowledge is likely to affect — even in due course to revolutionize — practical action, there is a distinction to be drawn between the priorities of substantive action and the priorities of the advancement of knowledge. And though it might be possible to devise in the form of a pedagogy an organization of educational knowledge marshalled to optimize the possibility of its systematic extension, we are not there yet. Nor do the conceptual frameworks of the so-called 'constituent disciplines' of educational research and study at present focus on educational action. That is to say, the hypotheses or conjectures to which they lead us are not by and large open to elaboration or testing by educational as opposed to research acts. It is of course possible to overstress the distinction I am making, but it is nevertheless a useful one.

Case study research is to be distinguished from research conducted in samples. Sample-based research is concerned to establish by calculation the relationship between a sample studied and a target population to which the findings in the sample are to be generalized. This enables variables in the sample to be abstracted from context. Context, seen as an impediment to generalization, is not required as a basis for judgments about the representativeness of the sample nor does generalization depend upon contextual analysis.[4]

In case study the relationship between a case, or a collection of cases that may superficially resemble a sample, and any population in which similar meanings or relationships may apply, is essentially a matter of judgment. Such judgment depends heavily upon assessments of multivariate complexes and of contexts, and it consequently demands a degree of descriptive verisimilitude or close interpretation of cases. Abstraction starves judgment of this kind.

Judgments of cases cumulate into prudence: 'the ability to discern the most suitable, politic, or profitable course of action; practical wisdom, discretion' *(Oxford English Dictionary)*. As Habermas remarks: 'On the road toward science, social philosophy has lost what politics formerly was capable of providing as prudence' (1974, p. 44). Case study reaches after the restoration of prudence, and also of perceptiveness, the capacity to interpret situations rapidly and at depth and to revise interpretations in the light of experience.

Indeed, the case study tradition may be seen as a systematization of experience within which interpretations are critically handled in the interests of preventing experience from becoming opinionated.

There are two major traditions of case study on which educational work may be seen to be drawing: the historical and the ethnographic. The relationship between the two is complex and I cannot even attempt to unravel it here.[5] However, some points are worth making as placing controversy on profitable lines.

First, history is essentially documentary, concerned with the discussion and interpretation of evidence accessible to scholars. Ethnography, though it draws on fieldnotes, seldom treats them as documents to be made available for critical discussion, depending for confirmatory responses upon the reader's experience of like situations, the cogency of the theory offered, and perhaps trust in the ethnographer.

Secondly, there is a sense in which history is the work of insiders, ethnography of outsiders. In its origins history has been how the ruling classes write about their own society; ethnography has been how they write about the societies of others. As these traditions have developed, history has been addressed to knowledgeable audiences — the history of trades unions to trades unionists, of horticulture to horticulturalists — and has relied on the knowingness of the reader. The historian, assuming a shared understanding of human behaviour, deals in the foreground of action. The ethnographer, by contrast, has used a degree of naiveté as a tool to call into question the commonplace. Originally concerned with exotic cultures, ethnography has become a means, first, of studying exotic elements within our own culture, later, of rendering the familiar exotic, a device whose capacity to illuminate was demonstrated fictionally by *Gulliver's Travels*. Ethnography calls the cultures it studies into question rather than building on their taken-for-grantedness. Lévi-Strauss (1968) expressed this by suggesting that historical explanation is in terms of the conscious, while the explanations of social anthropology are in terms of the unconscious.

What both history and anthropology have in common is that they deal with events and situations embedded in time: they are both concerned with the past and any timelessness they may achieve is a transcendence of this. Further, both offer thick descriptions: that is, representations whose virtue is verisimilitude as opposed to abstracted analyses.

How Do They Apply to Practice?

First, descriptive case studies of any kind provide documentary reference for the discussion of practice: workshop materials for practitioner groups. This is a simple, but an important function. When practitioners — or others — discuss problems of educational practice, they commonly each refer to a unique personal experience. It is as if each calls up private pictures of schools without realizing the extent to which this divergence of reference disables discussion. Personal experience needs to be referred to tabled cases in order to make it publicly available. Case studies are important as evidence.

Secondly, and only slightly less direct, is the relevance to practice of the comparison and contrast of other cases with one's own case: the case which above all one must come to understand if one's practice is to be effective. Whether the other cases be historical or ethnographic, such comparisons tend to open up new perspectives on one's own case, generating both a consciousness of one's knowingness and a sense of the accepted as problematic. One might see the most developed product of such comparison as an interpretation or a theory of one's own case.

Thirdly, crucial to practice is critique, that is to say, a systematic body of critical standards by which to interpret and evaluate practice. An excellent example of such critique in action is the informed discussion of such a sporting event as a cricket match in which the interpretation and evaluation of the play rests on the discussants' experience of many cases of such matches. The improvement of critique of classrooms and schools is central to the problem of quality in education, and it depends heavily upon practitioners extending vicariously their experience of schools and classrooms as cases.

Fourthly, the setting of such a critique within a broader social and political analysis (critical theory?) depends by definition on the development of the critique that is to be so disciplined by contextualization.

Finally, there is the question of theory that could be tested, or at least applied, at the level of rather general principles. Most social science and most history falters here in respect of education. Social science too often produces concepts (jargon) that seem stepping stones into a lake rather than across a river. History loses its grasp of the concrete (which is its strength) and falls back upon abstracted forces or trends which can too readily be preserved by ingenious interpretation. Case study seems to have been weak here, but then research which promises to produce stronger theory also seems to have failed. Perhaps general theory at the level of cause and effect is scarcely appropriate to educational study. Certainly, if it is appropriate, then it will have to stand the test of the study of cases: probabilistic theory exempted from the need to apply in every case is of little interest in such practical affairs as the practitioner is concerned with.

There will, of course, be some who think that I am demanding too rigorous a style of theory; to my mind, rigour is the sine qua non of theory. Where we cannot achieve it, then we are better to follow interpretative and humanistic traditions (fashionably dubbed 'hermeneutic') than to use scientific paradigms.

There are two final points. In an interpretative tradition, wise saws and aphorisms have their place! 'Schools that set out to change society will discover new ways of conserving it'; 'Open access to office holders and democracy are contradictory principles in schools: access makes sense only when it is access to power.' Secondly, a pedagogy may be an acceptable alternative to theory. Such a pedagogy would suggest patterns of classroom action that enable the pursuit of educational aims to be a means of capturing an understanding of educational process. In short, the possibility of studying one's case as one lives it may be built upon our case study tradition to the extent that the objectives of education and of the study of education can be fused in action.

Notes

1 When he took on this paper Lawrence Stenhouse made it clear that he was concerned 'with case study rather than ethnography'. We have tried to tease out what he may have meant by this. He was committed to writing a paper for the American Educational Research Association (AERA) Con-

ference which would have developed and justified the distinction made in this mischievously provocative statement. The title of the proposed paper was ' What's ethnic about ethnography?'. If we try to unpack the meaning of the title (taking some cues from statements in the paper reproduced here and in earlier papers which prefigure the argument he might have made in the AERA paper), we can identify several concerns about school studies in the *ethnographic* tradition: first, a concern that they tend to be *about* practitioners rather than *for* practitioners; secondly, concern that data tend not to be shared with or cleared by practitioners prior to public release of the study; thirdly, concern that a data base is not accessible so that the researcher's interpretations can be checked against data; fourthly, concern that the language of interpretation and explanation tends to be that of the sociologist and not that of the practitioner.

Some statements from an earlier paper (1981a) about Lawrence Stenhouse's view of case study are perhaps worth quoting:

> Case study research should be of benefit and interest to those people who are studied....

> Case study research should be directed to improving the capacity of those who are studied to do their job....

> In our present project (Library Access and Sixth Form Study) [interview] transcripts are returned to the interviewees and they are invited to strike out anything in their interviews which they wish to place off the record, or to correct any errors of fact that may have crept in.

2 In the paper on 'Using case study in library research', Lawrence Stenhouse outlined something of what he meant when he wrote:

> Experiments based on this logic have been powerful in improving the yield of crops and of animal proteins in agricultural research. The same logic lies behind surveys of attributes in populations and behind attitude and opinion polls. The results of such investigations are actuarial, describing trends or distributions in broad populations. We can readily calculate the distribution of heights of adult males in Britain, but that gives us little idea of how tall the man we're about to meet off a train will be. We can decide with a fair degree of probability on our side what strain of wheat, what fertilizers and what other treatments are likely to maximize the yield on an East Anglian farm, but we can say little about the fate of individual wheat plants in that field. When our need is to act or to devise a policy, such research techniques guide us only to the extent that the action, treatment or policy must be the same for every case we meet.
>
> In all social arts, such as education, administration or librarianship the practitioner aspires to modify action to meet the characteristics of particular cases. He or she diagnoses the case before treating it. In such situations practitioners need to know not only the broad trends which can be expected as responses to treatments but equally

importantly the pattern of variation across cases. Medical practitioners and researchers have long recognized this and have reported individual cases which illuminate the incidence and treatment of particular conditions. One may say that the reporting of cases improves the practitioner's judgement by extending his or her experience and by treating experience more reflectively and more analytically. (Stenhouse, 1981a)

He goes on to point out, however, that cases *may* be set side by side and generalizations may be made across a population of cases but the example he gives (Girouard's *The Victorian Country House*) is one where there is a known finite number of cases.

Lawrence Stenhouse helps the teacher-reader to see how to work from known statistical generalizations and case studies in an article 'Using research means doing research' (1979). The article reviews the outcomes of a project on the problems and effects of teaching about race relations (Stenhouse *et al.*, 1982). The measurement results indicate trends that are worth noting but which cannot reassure the teacher about which course of action to take in a particular classroom. Instead, the teacher has to use professional judgment, and judgment may be sharpened by reading the case study accounts of experiences of teaching about race relations in different classrooms.

3 The workshop at which this paper was originally delivered included sociologists and educational researchers with an interest in research methodology as well as those members of the research community interested in educational practice.

4 For further discussions of this topic see Stenhouse (1980; 1982).

5 Lawrence Stenhouse begins to unravel the differences in a paper called 'The verification of descriptive case studies' (1981b). Taking up Lévi-Strauss' point about the centrality of documents to historical study (1968) and the anthropologist's concern with things that differ from 'everything men ordinarily think of recording on stone and paper', Stenhouse comments:

> But the ethnographer does accumulate written records — his own notebooks — and would be thought vulnerable to criticism if he did not.... And the interpretation of field notes is clearly crucial for ethnography. Yet ethnographer's field notes are not published or placed in the public domain. The foundations of ethnography were laid by traditional European gentlemen in the nineteenth century. As has been wryly remarked: 'It's a good job they were gentlemen because we've only got their word for it.' This is not quite a fair comment but there is a grain of truth in it.

Stenhouse goes on to ask whether the ethnographer's fieldnote-book should be made publicly available — through microfiche, for instance — even as the historian's sources are in the public domain.

Another strand in the argument concerns the status and identity of what Stenhouse (borrowing from Hexter, 1972) calls the 'second record':

Verification in history depends upon a kind of replication in respect of the first record which in turn rests on a coherence of intersubjectivity in the second record (i.e. his total consciousness reflecting skills, knowledge, the set of the mind etc). . . . certainly the general second record, which is fed by experience of living in our culture, is called into question by ethnography. To the protest: 'People just don't behave that way', may come the response: 'Not in your culture, but in this culture they do'.

Of course, Stenhouse is here talking about 'classic ethnography' forged in the study of cultures other than our own and not about ethnographic-style studies of schools, although, as we saw earlier, some of the traditions of classic ethnography negatively — in his view — affect the conduct of such school studies.

References

DOCKRELL, B. (1980) 'The contribution of research to knowledge and practice', in DOCKRELL, W.B. and HAMILTON, D. (Eds) *Rethinking Educational Research*, London, Hodder and Stoughton.

HABERMAS, J. (1974) *Theory and Practice*, London, Heinemann.

HEXTER, J.H. (1972) *The History Primer*, London, Allen Lane.

LÉVI-STRAUSS, C. (1968) 'Introduction: History and anthropology', in LÉVI-STRAUSS, C., *Structural Anthropology*, Harmondsworth, Penguin.

STENHOUSE, L. (1979) 'Using research means doing research', in DAHL, J. *et al.* (Eds) *Pedagogikkens Søkelys*, Oslo. Universitetsforlaget.

STENHOUSE, L. (1980) 'The study of samples and the study of cases', *British Educational Research Journal*, 6, 1, pp. 1–6.

STENHOUSE, L. (1981a) 'Using case study in library research', *Social Science Information Studies*, 1, pp. 221–30.

STENHOUSE, L. (1981b) 'The verification of descriptive case studies', in KEMMIS, S., BARTLETT, L. and GILLARD, G. (Eds) *Perspectives in Case Study 2: The Quasi-Historical Approach-Case Study Methods*, Deakin University Press.

STENHOUSE, L. (1982) 'The conduct, analysis and reporting of case study in educational research and evaluation', in MCCORMICK, R. (Ed.) *Calling Education to Account*, London, Heinemann in association with the Open University.

STENHOUSE, L. *et al.* (1982) *Teaching about Race Relations*, London, Routledge and Kegan Paul.

14   Ethnography and Educational Policy-Making

Marten Shipman

The debate about the impact of social research on policy is usually conducted as if there were a small group of policy-makers who had clear objectives, who considered the available evidence on how to achieve them, who legislated without ambiguity and left the implementation to administrators and professionals who acted by the statute book. The role of the researcher in this process is to feed evidence to the politicians as the policy is formulated and on its success in action. The model is rational and linear.

In practice policy-making is neither rational nor linear (Weiss, 1980; Bulmer, 1982). Objectives are rarely clear and there is always a dearth of evidence on which to plan. This is why research continues to be funded, despite the disappointment of those who pay for it. There is always too much darkness, and any illumination is welcome even if it turns out to be more glimmer than glare. This is not to suggest that all research is welcome. Politicians, administrators and inspectors may oppose any investigation into sensitive areas. But they still want information and still hope researchers can provide it.

It is the way policies are remade as they are implemented that is even more important to researchers. In the education service, administrators, inspectors, advisors and teachers interpret, amend, supplement and excise the policies. This is why Educational Priority Area (EPA) and other intervention projects turn out to be different on the ground from their blueprints. The evaluations often turn out to be tales of woe (Barnes, 1975). That is usually due to lack of implementation or an unanticipated mode of operation in the programme or project that is being evaluated. These may bear little resemblance to the action intended because of the actions by those actually doing the job rather than those who made the policy.

This diffused, messy picture of policy-making and implementation presents opportunities to researchers that contrast starkly with the textbook model of research affecting decisions at one time, somewhere near the political apex of a hierarchy, among the great and good. In practice, the influence among thousands of teachers or hundreds of assistant education officers may be far more important than any influence on Sir Keith Joseph, the leader of the Inner London Education Authority (ILEA), or chief education officers. That opportunity is open to ethnographers as it is to empiricists.

The Motives of Educational Researchers

There seem to me to be three possible motives in the minds of researchers when they are investigating social situations. First, they may intentionally set out to influence policy, whether among teachers, in local education authorities (LEAs) or nationally. Secondly, they may be interested in developing substantive or formal theory. Thirdly, they may not be interested in anything beyond doing research. These three angles, policy-oriented, theory-oriented and autonomous may not be explicit when research is being planned. Most researchers have motives that mix all three. Each approach also contains expedient, selfish motives because of the importance of research in academic careers, as well as the urge to illuminate or influence.

However, the division between the instrumental and the autonomous approaches is crucial. Social research, and particularly ethnography, need have no relevance to policy or to theory, and I do not see why it should. There are two justifications for just doing research. First, good description is the common feature of all the activity based on these three approaches. Policy-makers always lack details of what is actually happening. They always make decisions without adequate information. But so do theoreticians. Illuminating, finding out for its own sake, describing may have low status, but they add to the basis for action. The second justification is that research is enjoyable as well as boosting your career and, providing you are fair to those you observe and question, can make often dull jobs such as teaching or administration more interesting. Research as an end in itself is not to be condemned, provided it is not sold to a funding agency as a panacea.

One further general point has to be made about social research in general and its relation to policy. The track record so far has been poor. Much of the justification for ethnographic or ethogenic approaches to research comes from the failures of empiricism to deliver evidence on which policy-makers, including teachers in their classrooms, could depend. The history of research into the nature of intelligence and its assessment is a warning that even a mainstream activity where there has been replication and an accumulation of evidence can not only turn out to be misleading, but can deny the validity of the commonsense opposition beyond the point where fraud as well as shaky evidence were being uncovered. Despite the authority of the psychologists involved, teachers and parents turned out to be right at the end. It is easy to document discrepancies, contradictions, deceptions and fraud in the human sciences used in studying education (Shipman, 1981). The customers have good reason to be sceptical of claims to validity.

Assuming that researchers have either an impact on policy, or an interest in theory-building in mind, what differences are there in the two approaches? There is a growing literature on the need for ethnographers to engage in theory-building (documented in Woods' paper in this book, Chapter 3). There is less on the contribution to policy. The two activities are clearly separable. The policy-oriented researcher has to meet a demand for a stable model that provides a dependable basis for prediction. Policy-makers spend other people's money. A one per cent error in estimating pupil numbers for the following year in the 1970s in the ILEA cost £4 million in teachers' salaries the following year. There has to be confidence that the researchers have it right. Secondly, the policy-oriented research that is welcomed is confirmatory. It adds to the confidence that a policy of positive discrimination or of encouraging in-service training is on the right lines. Thirdly, the quality and usefulness of the research is judged by outsiders to academia by reference to usefulness, feasibility and cost.

Contrast this with the lot of the theory-oriented researcher. First, the delight is in iconoclasm, breakthroughs, cracking the paradigm, not confirmation. The research that is hailed is that which demolishes current thinking. Secondly, this demolition is judged by academic peers as praiseworthy. Radicals still get promotion and referees still approve articles that attack them. Replication, even extensions of existing work, are shunned as unprofitable. The strength of the base for prediction takes second place to innovation. Mundane matters such as money are not factors that enter into this heady, exciting world. There is not a single evaluation of a Schools Council curriculum innovation that gives any sustained attention to costs. Yet that is the first concern of policy-makers whether considering new developments or reviewing existing practices.

This division is the result of the different careers and reference groups of those involved. This is easily illustrated from the common element that links the two, the production of descriptive data. Policy-making and theory-building both rest on description. Yet few researchers like to confess to describing events because there is no prestige in it. Even where there are chapters of description, they lead to the final analytical section where the writer gives his or her intellectual all. Once the book or article is published, academic mileage is extracted by papers on the methodology or the theoretical implications. In-house researchers also feel this itch. Description is a job for the artisan.

These differing interests among researchers do not divide them into those of interest to policy-makers and the rest. Consider the diffused, incremental model wherein policies are made and remade as they are implemented. Politicians who are over the novice stage appreciate that their influence is limited. They have to live with the unintended consequences of their decisions. They are on the look out for some understanding of the reasons why their policy for providing nursery education for the poor ends up with places taken by the children of wealthy commuters. The contribution of researchers in providing explanations, concepts and theories is often more influential than concrete evidence on events. This can be seen in the contributions of social scientists to various Presidential Commissions in the USA (Komarovsky, 1975). They provided ideas not facts. Indeed, the time available eliminated any chance of collecting evidence. But explanatory ideas were required to summarize and order the views presented to the Commissions.

The need for evidence and ideas suggests that research is welcomed by policy-makers. If it is clearly written, topical and relevant, policy-makers will take it as part of the package of evidence available from many sources within the service. Of course there is suspicion of researchers and a reluctance to accept the uncomfortable. But there is also a surprising reluctance among researchers to prepare their evidence so that it will be used.

A small part of the evidence from social research reaches politicians, administrators, inspectors, advisors, teachers directly through books, articles and papers at conferences or discussions with researchers. But few researchers press for such direct contact. The Research and Statistics group in the ILEA employed an administrator to chase researchers for reports to send on to senior officers and politicians, but only a minority fulfilled their contracts with the Authority and sent in such a report. Once the research was completed they did not seem to be interested in dissemination. The access had been gained by promising useful information, but it was rarely forthcoming despite reminders of the obligation. The few exceptions were old hands around government such as M. Rutter or J. Tizard who sent in papers, fed back information to teachers and were prepared to attend research seminars at County Hall.

The major part of research evidence reaches policy-makers second-hand through the media or through summaries produced by in-house researchers or advisors. This is unsatisfactory because it is diluted, even biased. It was a long, hard fight in the ILEA to persuade politicians that Hargreaves' *Social Relations in a Secondary School* (1967) was not conclusive evidence for the avoidance of labelling by getting rid of all pupil records. Journalists are skilled at this wholesaling of evidence and, unlike researchers, see it as their job. For ethnographers, as for all researchers, influence is usually exerted indirectly, at second-hand, often by interested parties. If researchers are interested in influencing policy, they have to keep with it beyond finishing the writing up.

The Special Problems of Ethnographers

Behind the special difficulties faced by ethnographers is the obvious point that policy-makers, like funding agencies, have an image of social research as empiricist. Researchers are not keen to disabuse them because much work is funded on this often false premise. In public we press our conventional scientific claims. In private we press the image of research as a social process (Burgess, 1984). But ethnographers face an additional difficulty. On the surface at least their activities appear very similar to those engaged in by advisors, inspectors and teachers. The methods used are not only kept open-ended and opportunistic, but are often reported autobiographically. The one distinguishing feature that researchers of all persuasions should have is being frank and full about the methods that were used to collect the data. That enables peers and lay persons to assess credibility. But a frank and full account of open-ended observations is likely to confirm to the outsider that ethnography is what inspectors do in a more detached way, teachers do in a more experienced way and journalists do in a more readable way.

This parody cannot be dismissed. Most of the methods in the studies described in this book are remarkably flexible. Indeed, many local inspectors and HMI are far more constrained in their observations than the more free-ranging researchers who use the title 'ethnographer'. Here is an example to highlight the problem. The Research and Statistics group in the ILEA carried out an ethnographic study of open-planned primary schools in the mid-1970s. Looking back, it was an insightful study well before its time (Bennett, 1980). But at the time it caused disagreement. Inspectors maintained that their observations of these schools led them to very different conclusions about their organization. Apparently straightforward aspects such as the time spent on mathematics or reading were seen in startlingly contrasting ways. The ILEA never tried to get a research report changed, but I agreed not to press this one to publication although it would be available to researchers on request. I made this decision after consulting the teachers in the schools involved, not over their views on publication, for they did not mind, but over factual accuracy. There was no way of sorting this out. Whether the time spent on mathematics was a few minutes or many hours a week depended on how you defined and observed the activities of the children. Inspectors saw a lot of mathematical work, the researchers saw less. To have published would have fed sensationally low figures for time on basic skills to the national press, just as the Black Papers were being published. I took the coward's way out. But the dispute taught me the problems of using ethnography to influence policy.

Recently HMI in particular have moved in an empiricist direction, just as social researchers have moved further way. The primary and secondary surveys contain more quantitative survey material than most contemporary educational research. HMI also show their reports to senior colleagues, they discuss observations among themselves, they show their comments to those observed, they triangulate their methods, they have to remain on good terms with those inspected and now they publish the results. But this confirmation and cross-checking is not confined to inspectors or advisors. Teachers who are the subjects of ethnography are often engaged in moderation of public examinations, self-assessment and evaluation working parties. They have far more experience of their classrooms than the ethnographer. They are often sophisticated in their detachment and perception, for blocked mobility has increased the expertise about research among teachers. It is no wonder that Nixon (1981) has pointed to the academic patronage that often typifies exchanges between academic and teacher. It is at least anomalous or arrogant when the teacher is given a lesson in what she is actually doing in her classroom by a researcher visiting for a few afternoons and apparently making up methods as he or she goes along. This is another parody, but the status of ethnographic evidence in a service that is run by professionals experienced in observing children and teachers cannot be assumed.

Looking at the papers in this book from a policy-maker's viewpoint, it is difficult to be confident that many would provide a dependable basis for action as distinct from insightful accounts. Yet the latter also come from journalists, inspectors, advisors and teachers. The ethnographic evidence is not necessarily superior, more reliable or more valid. It is just different, providing another perspective hopefully derived from an established theoretical framework. The credence placed on it will rest, for the policy-maker, on the apparent strength of the methods used and the way this is linked to theories that provide insights. That means that methodology and techniques should be reported in full in a language that can be understood by lay persons not versed in technical language.

The Uses of Ethnography

The reason for intentionally becoming an ethnographer or for choosing it as a label after drifting into this style of research would usually be an urge to describe and to understand. That is a sufficient motive for researching. If it influences policy it's a bonus. Yet that leaves quality control to chance. I do not grieve for the little impact of research on policy. I do worry about the indiscriminate way research has been influential. Because policy-makers are outside the academic community, are not alerted to look between the spaces for the shortcomings, and do not know the personal, professional and political leanings of researchers, they are badly placed to add that academic pinch of acerbic salt that enables social scientists to savour evidence in an objective, knowing way.

Ethnographic research is no different from the rest of social science in this chancy selection for influence. Indeed, the reluctance to spell out in detail how work was planned and implemented makes it more likely that the sensational yet shifty will carry more clout than the modest and honest. Policy-makers are busy people. They are likely to throw the good out with the bad and take in the bad with the good. Yet they are often knowledgeable about the contexts where ethnography flourishes. In LEAs, for example, politicians will often know the area, the schools, the people, from long experience. The context-free, swinging account of this school, that set of football supporters and those thugs will soon be put into the context of the conditions faced by those observed. The ridiculous contrasts in the evidence on the attitudes of school leavers, football hooligans and teachers were embarrassingly easy to document after listening to the derisory comments of administrators on research on these subjects (Shipman, 1981). Yet politicians and administrators were hungry for research evidence to lay alongside that from their inspectors, advisors and teachers. Similarly, politicians appreciate the detached researcher's view and the theoretical insights and concepts that help them interpret events.

Thus the conclusion has to be that ethnography starts with a disadvantage in looking similar to methods used by other professionals in the education service and among journalists. But it can be influential as one among many sources of different evidence — different, not superior or inferior, for the insight from theory and the control from genuinely ethnographic methods can be balanced by length of experience and knowledge of context among practitioners. Lastly, it is to control over methods and a full published account of how this was achieved that this paper points as the key, not only to influencing policy, but in avoiding deception in so doing. If control over methods employed is jettisoned, I cannot see why the ethnographer has any claim to insight beyond his or her knowledge from training, theory or reading. That claim can be countered by teachers and others who have other sources for their perceptions. Thus it is essential that the methods used are spelled out honestly and in sufficient detail for them to be assessed by a lay readership. If the intention of the researcher is to affect policy, then the policy-maker must be able to judge the reliability of the methods used. Very few accounts stand up to that condition.

References

BARNES, J. (Ed.) (1975) *Educational Priority*, Vol.3. London, HMSO.
BENNETT, N. (1980) *Open Plan Schools*, Windsor, National Foundation for Educational Research.
BULMER, M. (1982) *The Uses of Social Research*, London, Allen and Unwin.
BURGESS, R.G. (1984) 'Introduction', in BURGESS, R.G. (Ed.) *The Research Process in Educational Settings: Ten Case Studies*, Lewes, Falmer Press.
HARGREAVES, D.H. (1967) *Social Relations in a Secondary School*, London, Routledge and Kegan Paul.
KOMAROVSKY, M. (Ed.) (1975) *Sociology and Public Policy*, New York, Elsevier.
NIXON, J. (1981) *A Teachers' Guide to Action Research*, London, Grant McIntyre.

√ SHIPMAN, M.D. (1981) *The Limitations of Social Research* (2nd ed.) London, Longman.

WEISS, C.H. (1980) *Social Science Research and Decision-Making*, New York, Columbia University Press.

Notes on Contributors

Clem Adelman is presently Research Coordinator at Bulmershe College of Higher Education, Reading. He taught in secondary schools, a polytechnic and technical college, before doing research at the Centre for Science Education, London. He subsequently (1972 –76) engaged in research and evaluation at the Centre for Applied Research in Education, University of East Anglia. Between 1976 and 1979 he directed the DES Student Choice project from Bulmershe College. His main publications include (with Rob Walker) *A Guide to Classroom Observation* (1974); *Uttering, Muttering* (Ed.) (1981); (with R.J. Alexander) *The Self-Evaluating Institution* (1982); *Bread and Dreams — A Case Study of Bilingual Schooling in Boston, Mass.* (1982); *The Politics and Ethics of Evaluation* (Ed.) (1983).

Robert Burgess is a Senior Lecturer in Sociology at the University of Warwick. His teaching and research interests include the sociology of education and social research methodology, especially field research. He is particularly interested in ethnography and its use in educational settings. He is the author of *Experiencing Comprehensive Education: A Study of Bishop McGregor School* (1983); *In the Field: An Introduction to Field Research* (1984); and the editor of *Teaching Research Methodology to Postgraduates: A Survey of Courses in the U.K.* (1979); *Field Research: A Sourcebook and Field Manual* (1982); *Exploring Society* (1982); and *The Research Process in Educational Settings: Ten Case Studies* (1984). He was Honorary General Secretary of the British Sociological Association, 1982–4.

Lynn Davies is currently a Lecturer in Sociology of Education in the Commonwealth Unit of the Birmingham University Faculty of Education. She studied at Exeter University (BA Languages) and Birmingham University (MEd, PhD Sociology). She has taught in primary and secondary schools in Mauritius and Malaysia as well as in this country, and lectured in sociology of education for six years at Wolverhampton Polytechnic. She is an Executive Editor of the *British Journal of Sociology of Education*. Her main research and publications have been on deviance and sex roles in school; current interests are sociology of development and women in the Third World.

Sara Delamont graduated in Social Anthropology from Girton College, Cambridge in 1968, and went to Edinburgh to do a PhD. In 1973 she went to lecture in the School of Education at Leicester University, teaching with Gerry Bernbaum and Tom Whiteside. Since 1976 she has been in the Sociology Department at University College, Cardiff. Between 1976 and 1983 she was attached to the ORACLE project at Leicester University, and is the author of three chapters in M. Galton and J. Willcocks (Eds) (1983) *Moving from the Primary Classroom* and the joint author, with M. Galton, of *Inside the Secondary Classroom* (forthcoming). She was the first woman President of the British Educational Research Association (BERA) in 1983/84.

Tony Edwards is Professor and Head of the School of Education at Newcastle University. He taught history at several London secondary schools and then lectured in education at the Universities of Exeter and Manchester. Apart from the collaborative work with John Furlong on which they reflect in this volume, he has published books on *The Changing Sixth Form* (1970) and *Language in Culture and Class* (1976), and has written extensively on children's language, classroom language and (more recently) post-compulsory education and training. He is currently working (with Geoff Whitty) on a study of the Assisted Places Scheme.

John Elliott is a former head of humanities in a secondary school, where he has also taught some biology. From 1967 to 1972 he was a member of the central team of the Schools Council's Humanities Curriculum Project. From 1972 to 1976 he was a Lecturer in the Centre for Applied Research in Education at the University of East Anglia where he directed the Ford Teaching Project. In 1976 he was appointed Tutor in Curriculum Studies at the Cambridge Institute of Education. Together with teaching Advanced Diploma Students, he has coordinated of the part-time MA course in Applied Educational Research. John Elliott was the national evaluator of the Schools

Council 'Progress in Learning Science' Project and has directed two research projects: the SSRC Cambridge Accountability Project and the Schools Council's project on 'Teacher-Pupil Interaction and the Quality of Learning'. His major interest is in developing research and evaluation strategies which teachers and schools can use as a means of professional and institutional development.

V.J. Furlong is a Lecturer in Education at the University of Cambridge. He taught in a London comprehensive school for four years in order to carry out fieldwork for his PhD into pupils' perceptions of school. The research described in this book was undertaken while he was a Research Associate at the Department of Education at the University of Manchester. Since that time he has participated in a major project at Brunel University, studying disaffected pupils (Bird *et al.*, *Disaffected Pupils*, 1981) and is currently codirecting a DES funded project examining teacher training. He has published articles on pupils' classroom behaviour, their perceptions of school and the problems of classroom research.

Maurice Galton, recently promoted to a Chair in Education at the School of Education, University of Leicester, has co-directed the ORACLE project since its inception in 1975. He is co-author of *Inside the Primary Classroom* (1980); editor of *Progress and Performance in the Primary Classroom* (1980); co-editor of *Moving from the Primary Classroom* (1983); and a contributor to *Research and Practice in the Primary Classroom* (1981).

Christine Griffin completed her PhD in social psychology at Birmingham University in 1978. From 1979 to 1982 she worked at Birmingham University's Centre for Contemporary Cultural Studies, on the SSRC-funded 'Young Women and Work' project. Over the past year she has been writing a full account of this research for *Typical Girls?*, a book to be published by Routledge and Kegan Paul in 1984. Chris Griffin has also worked on a Girls' Night at a local authority youth club since 1980. She has recently started a two-year project at the Centre for Mass Communications Research, Leicester University, on unemployment amongst Asian, Afro-Carribean and white youth.

Andrew Pollard has been a Senior Lecturer in Education at Oxford Polytechnic since 1981, having taught in primary, middle and infant schools for the previous nine years. His main research interest is social processes in primary school classrooms. His ethnographic analysis, *The Social World of the Primary School*, will be published by Holt, Rinehart and Winston in 1985.

Sue Scott graduated in sociology from Newcastle-upon-Tyne Polytechnic in 1974. She then worked as a research officer for the Health Education Council. In 1977 she moved to Lancaster University to do postgraduate research, and from January 1979 to January 1982.she was a research associate there in the Sociology Department working on the 'Postgraduate Research Project'. After completing the academic year 1981–82 in Lancaster as an honorary research fellow she took up her present post as researcher on the Mansfield Community Health Project. She is a member of the British Sociological Association's Executive, and currently chairs the BSA's Sex Equality Committee. She has written several articles on women postgraduates and postgraduate education.

Marten Shipman worked in industry and served in the Royal Navy and the Police before taking a first in sociology at the London School of Economics. After professional training he taught in secondary modern schools before lecturing at Worcester College of Education from 1961 to 1969. He moved to the University of Keele as Senior Lecturer in Education in 1969, continuing research into school organization and curriculum. From 1972 to 1978 he was Director of Research and Statistics at the ILEA, then Professor of Education at the University of Warwick and is currently Dean of Education at the Rochampton Institute of Higher Education. He is the author of many books and articles on the sociology of education, social research methods and the curriculum.

Lawrence Stenhouse was Director of the Centre for Applied Research in Education (CARE) at the University of East Anglia from its inception in 1970 until he died in 1982. He was given a personal chair in Applied Research in Education in 1979. In 1967 he was appointed Director of the Schools Council/Nuffield Foundation Humanities Curriculum Project. He came to the Humanities Curriculum Project from Jordanhill College where he was Head of the Education Department. At CARE he directed two projects on teaching about race relations, undertook pioneering work in case study methods which influenced the design of his last project, a multi-site case programme looking at library access and sixth form study. His publications include *Culture and Education* (1967); *Discipline in Schools* (1967); *An Introduction to Curriculum Research and Development* (1975); *Curriculum Research and Development in Action* (1980); *Teaching about Race Relations: Problems and Effects* (1982); and *Authority, Education and Emancipation* (1983).

John Wakeford graduated from the University of Nottingham in 1959 having read sociology. He held academic posts at the Universities of Wales, Exeter and Brunel, before moving to the University of Lancaster in 1969. Much of his research has concerned education. His PhD thesis on public boarding schools was the basis of *The Cloistered Elite* (1969). He edited jointly with John Urry a reader, *Power in Britain* (1973), and has throughout his career been interested in teaching sociological research methods and practice. He was director of the research project on which Mary Porter and Sue Scott were the research associates.

Rob Walker is in the School of Education, Deakin University, Victoria. Before moving to Australia he was previously Acting Director of the Centre for Applied Research in Education at the University of East Anglia. His interest in classroom ethnography dates from the late sixties when he was a Research Fellow at the Centre for Science Education at Chelsea College where he worked with curriculum development specialists in trying to assess the impact of Nuffield Science on teacher-pupil relationships. Currently his interests are in school case study and in the work of inspectors and advisers. Publications include (with Clem Adelman) *A Guide to Classroom Observation* (1975); (with Barry MacDonald) *Changing the Curriculum*, (1976); and two case studies for the National Science Foundation (*Pine City* and *Greater Boston*). He is also a part author of a recent case study of bilingual education, *Bread and Dreams* (1982).

Janine Wiedel studied photography with Ansel Adams and at the University of California at Berkeley. She has published *Irish Tinkers, Looking at Iran* and *Vulcan's Forge* and had exhibitions at the Photographers' Gallery, the Half Moon Gallery, the Whitechapel Art Gallery and the Belfast Museum. In 1977–78 she carried out a major project in the West Midlands on an Arts Council Bursary and was the subject of an ATV documentary film, *A Camera in the Street*. She has considerable experience of working in schools for publishers, for the

Schools Council and for *The Times Educational Supplement*. A travelling exhibition of her work, *Classrooms*, has been made by the Half Moon Gallery, and she took the photographs for *A Guide to Classroom-Observation*.

Peter Woods is Reader in Education at the Open University. He took his first degree in history at London University, taught in schools in London, Norfolk and Yorkshire, and studied education and sociology at Sheffield, Leeds and Bradford Universities. He came to The Open University in 1972 and has contributed to courses E353 Society, Education and the State, E202 Schooling and Society, and E200 Contemporary Issues in Education. He is the author of *The Divided School* (1979), *Sociology and the School* (1983), and numerous articles for the educational and academic press.

Index

Index

Index